# LAXMI'S VEGETARIAN KITCHEN

SIMPLE
HEALTHFUL
RECIPES FROM
INDIA'S GREAT
VEGETARIAN
TRADITION

BY LAXMI HIREMATH
ILLUSTRATIONS BY BROOKE SCUDDER

HARLOW & RATNER
EMERYVILLE, CALIFORNIA

BOOK DESIGN: MCCLAIN DESIGN
TYPOGRAPHY: SCOTT HAMMOND

Library of Congress Cataloging-in-Publication Data

Hiremath, Laxmi.
    Laxmi's vegetarian kitchen: simple, healthful recipes from
India's great vegetarian tradition / by Laxmi Hiremath:
illustrations by Brooke Scudder.
        p. cm.
    Includes index.
    ISBN 0-9627345-9-4
    1. Vegetarian cookery. 2. Cookery, Indic. I. Title.
TX837.H57 1995
641.5'636'0954—dc20                                          95-9480
                                                                CIP

PRINTED IN SINGAPORE
10 9 8 7 6 5 4 3 2 1

HARLOW & RATNER, 5749 LANDREGAN ST., EMERYVILLE, CALIFORNIA 94608

TO MY MOTHER

FOR TEACHING THE ART OF COOKING

AND

TO MY FATHER

FOR GIVING THE PRECIOUS GIFT OF WISDOM

# ACKNOWLEDGEMENTS

When I first shared a recipe of Savory Cabbage Rolls with a local daily in Columbus, Ohio, little did I know I would venture into authoring a cookbook. What first started as a hobby soon turned into a passion and lifelong commitment.

This book wouldn't have evolved without the loving support and encouragement of my family. My "secret seasoning" who brought the best out of me and stood by every step of the way is my dear husband, Mahantesh. Thanks are due to my sons Kailash and Kedar for their ready smiles, seamless patience, and joyful enthusiasm during this endeavor. I wish to credit my parents for their inspiration and motivation. They surely know I have come a long way in cooking! I am deeply indebted to my father-in-law for his relentless letters espousing the use of grains, greens, and garlic in meals. My sincere thanks are due to my mother-in-law for several constructive suggestions.

I take this opportunity to express my love and affection to my sister Smita, who shared valuable culinary techniques and filled me in with developments in Indian cooking. I credit my brother, Sunil, for presenting me a special spice box that is a cynosure of all eyes during my classes. My sister-in-law Keertilata spent hours with me discussing cooking skills and sharing her prized recipes. My grandmothers kept me enthralled as a child and filled my life with pleasant memories that I have shared with the readers. Prema aunty and Kusum aunty passed on several helpful tips on southern Indian dishes. My sisters-in-law, Anjali and Uma, never hesitated to give me their time and cooking ideas during my visits to India. Again, thank you all. When I think of my family, I envision the marigold garland, it is as strong as the floral thread that runs around it.

When I first broached the idea of an Indian vegetarian cookbook to my editor Jay Harlow and publisher Elaine Ratner, I was delighted that they quickly agreed to it. The book has undergone a careful review under Jay's watchful eye, and many of the recipes received a final stamp of approval in Jay and Elaine's kitchen. The book has been further enhanced by Dan McClain's elegant design and Brooke Scudder's lively illustrations.

Thanks are also due to Sue Dawson, food editor of the *Columbus Dispatch,* and Arvind Kumar, editor of *India Currents,* for their encouragement and support. A special acknowledgment is extended to Michael Bauer, executive food editor of the *San Francisco Chronicle.* In addition to publishing my recipes and articles for a wider Bay Area audience, it was through the *Chronicle* that I came in contact with Jay and began my voyage to the world of cookbook authorship.

Finally, I want to thank my many American friends, both here and in Ohio, who have enjoyed the dishes I have served and encouraged me to compile them into a cookbook. And especially to the super-talented "tasting panel" of my sons' friends; nothing has made me happier than when they asked for seconds.

# CONTENTS

INTRODUCTION  8
NOTES TO THE COOK  11

THE ART OF SEASONING  12
A TOUR OF INDIAN SPICES  14
SPICE BLENDS  20
APPETIZERS  26
SOUPS  42
BREAKFAST AND BRUNCH  56
BREADS  76
VEGETABLE DISHES  92
PILAFS AND OTHER RICE DISHES  128
LEGUMES: LENTILS, PEAS, AND BEANS  146
PANEER CHEESE  162
SALADS: RAITAS, CHAATS, AND KACHUMBERS  172
CHUTNEYS AND PICKLES  190
DESSERTS  208
BEVERAGES  224

APPENDIX  234
MISCELLANEOUS INGREDIENTS AND RECIPES  235
KITCHEN EQUIPMENT  242
INDIAN TABLE MANNERS  244
MENU PLANNING  245

INDEX  249

# INTRODUCTION

My motivation in writing this book is simple: to provide the reader with an exquisite collection of Indian vegetarian recipes ideally suited to Western kitchens and cooks. For those who are already well versed in the art of Indian cuisine, there is a sizable offering of new dishes and innovative procedures. For beginners and skeptics, I want to open my heart and let out the secret that I was among you not very long ago. If I could make the transition from novice in Indian cooking to expert and finally author, you too can make this cuisine your own.

My campaign of conquest of Indian cooking began in the home of my well-to-do family in Belgaum, a city in southwestern India on the border of the states of Maharashtra and Karnataka. We had a very reliable maid who prepared fresh meals daily and kept the kitchen immaculately clean. She would make curry paste, chop vegetables, and fix breads, but the final responsibility of assembling and seasoning the vegetables, lentils, and other dishes went to my mother. I loved to watch the duo at work (and I still do — they are still working together nearly twenty years later). It was fascinating to see mounds of colorful spices, fresh herbs, garlic, and ginger transformed into the flavor base for so many dishes. A basketful of flatbreads always graced the dining table and the aroma of simmering basmati rice filled the kitchen.

Unfortunately, watching is all I did; only later did I realize that I could have learned much more by helping. Being the eldest child meant that my parents provided extra attention and I could get away with little indulgences. Painting and handicrafts kept me busy through vacations and holidays, and later, my college years were occupied with grueling chemistry lab work. When I graduated with a bachelor's degree in science, I was engaged to be married. Then my father insisted that it was time I learned to cook. I would make brief forays to the kitchen to keep him happy, but I quickly disappeared, pretending I had some other important things to do. After I got married, and my husband's work for the Indian Railways took us to Calcutta, I knew that my aversion to cooking had to end. However, I was fortunate once again to have very talented maids and cooks. Their cooking methods were different from my family's, as were the delicacies they prepared.

I had come this far without ever making any effort in the kitchen. But how long could my procrastination continue? Not very long! When we relocated to Columbus, Ohio, I knew my "freebie" was over. I started just as any beginner would — making endless mistakes, messing up recipes, and burning breads. It was then that I resolved to do something about it. I began with a conscious effort to be systematic, and things got better. The Indian flatbreads, so common back home, were the most challenging. I bought a food processor to bypass the elaborate process of preparing the dough by hand. It worked wonders. Now all I had to concentrate on was rolling and cooking. To my delight and my husband's relief, the first set of chewy and soft breads started to roll out. I had mastered the flatbreads!

Emboldened by my early successes, I responded to a query from a reader in the local daily and sent in a recipe. The next day I got a call from the editor, who had found the recipe interesting and said she would publish it the following week. My joy knew no bounds when I saw my name in the list of contributors. So began my journey of becoming a food writer. I continued to share recipes every week. My interest grew and I experimented with locally available items. Columbus had only one Indian market, so I turned to the regular grocery markets and learned to innovate. A few readers also called to check whether I had written a cookbook.

I was flattered, and I determined to generate a collection of recipes.

My first article sent to a national magazine in the United States was about vegetarian dishes. I had handwritten it and not paid much attention to editing. To my surprise, the editor called to report that my recipes were selected to be published in the magazine. About this time, we moved to California and I got an offer to write about Indian cooking in a San Francisco monthly publication for the Indian community. My articles generated considerable interest in the local communities and I began to contribute articles to local daily newspapers. When Jay Harlow and Elaine Ratner offered to publish a book of my recipes, my dream had come true.

## My Life as a Vegetarian

I have been a vegetarian all my life. For many other Indians, vegetarianism is a religious matter, but in our family it is simply a matter of tradition and preference. I come from a typical Indian family; religious, caring, and fun-loving. I recall my mother making hearty and nutritious meals, combining varied tastes, color, and textures to please both the eyes and the palate. Our meals consisted of bread and rice, a couple of vegetable dishes (made from fresh produce from our garden, or bought that morning from door-to-door vendors), and a dish of lentils, split peas, or other legumes. To accompany these main dishes, we would have a yogurt-based relish (raita) and a chutney or some pickles or both. As we enjoyed these freshly cooked meals together, we would discuss the events of the day, and my brother and sister and I would take turns talking about what we learned in school. We would end the meal with rice mixed with plain yogurt to soothe the hot and sour tastes.

On school days, our *dabbawallah* (lunch-box man) would deliver a home-cooked lunch to me. At the stroke of the recess bell, he would be there to greet me with a hearty smile. My parents did not think highly of restaurants or snack bars, but once I went away to college they reluctantly approved of my eating in the restaurant and cafeteria, as there was no other choice. At this time my breakfast usually consisted of flatbreads stuffed with vegetables, herbs, and spices, with soups or stews.

I spent many summer vacations visiting aunts who lived in southern, western, and northern parts of India. There I watched them create different variations on the same theme of grains, legumes, fruits, and vegetables. The same produce that my mother cooked into a quick stir-fry was put into a sauce, relish, or pickle; lentils and grains were turned into other forms like breads or crepes. When I got married, I moved to Calcutta on the east coast, and also spent some time in Jaipur and Baroda in the western part of India. In each of these places, I had the opportunity to see and taste different regional fare and to sample a plethora of cooking styles, each more delectable than the other.

Through all these different phases of my life, and different parts of India, my basic food habits remained the same. I had plenty of opportunity to try meat dishes, whether at a birthday party as a child or in the college cafeteria, but I never thought of changing my vegetarian ways.

Most challenging was the move to America. I had worried that I might not be able to obtain the familiar foods of my youth, but I was pleasantly surprised to find most all of them and more. Various lentils, beans, grains, and flours could be found in the supermarkets as well as specialty food stores. In addition to the fruits and vegetables I already knew, I was delighted to make new discoveries like Brussels sprouts, endive, kiwifruit, and avocado. The farmers' markets that were beginning to return to many American cities reminded me of the street vendors in India, and the unknown (to me) garden treasures they sold encouraged me to experiment and find new ways to prepare them. My American friends have loved and enjoyed the "light" (as they called the vegetarian dishes) and subtly seasoned fare when they visited our house.

Today, my diet is essentially the same as it has been all my life. My family's everyday meals reflect the southwestern region of India where I was raised, where wheat and rice are equally important staples. I typically serve both rice and flatbread, accompanied by one or two vegetable dishes, a dal, and a salad. There is no single main dish in large quantity, rather an assortment of foods rich in nutrients and low in fat and cholesterol. Together, these foods make up a nutritionally balanced, appetizing, and satisfying diet.

If this kind of eating sounds familiar, it is because health authorities in the West are now recommending a diet based primarily on vegetables, fruits, grains, and legumes, with less emphasis on meat and fats. A few years ago, the World Health Organization singled out the food of Maharashtra as the most healthful and nutritionally balanced among all cuisines of India, and nominated it as one of the recommended diets for the world at large.

I know that I enjoy good health on a vegetarian diet. (I also exercise regularly, and fast one evening each week to give a rest to my system and to keep the mind fresh.) When I first decided to see a dentist at age 35 after much procrastination, the dentist took a good look and said "What a healthy line of teeth — no stains or cavities. You seem to eat a nutritious diet."

Ours is not a strictly vegetarian household; my husband and children eat meat occasionally (the children love pepperoni pizza). I cook non-vegetarian dishes for them, but at no time have I felt like partaking of them myself.

Whatever your reasons for picking up a book on Indian vegetarian cooking, there is something in these pages for you. I assume many readers are already committed to vegetarianism; your choice may be based on religious, ethical, environmental, or health concerns, or other reasons of your own. Or you may be an omnivore who is gradually changing your diet to incorporate more vegetable, grain, and legume dishes. Or you may have a family member who is a vegetarian. Or perhaps you are simply fond of the flavors of Indian cuisine, and you want to expand your repertoire of Indian dishes. In any case, I invite you to try these recipes as a sampling of the rich and varied Indian vegetarian tradition.

The compilation presented here is designed to speed your journey toward becoming an expert. I have tried to be innovative, restructuring many traditional recipes to meet the demands on time and dietary concerns of the 90s. Indian cooking often uses oil liberally, but I have made a conscious effort to reduce the amount of oil wherever possible, while still preserving the essential flavors and textures of the food. Baking is not a traditional Indian cooking technique, but many of the recipes here make use of the convenience of a Western-style oven. Knowing that time is of the essence, I have selected a number of savory breakfast dishes that cook in fifteen minutes or less. The vegetable dishes reflect my thinking that vegetables need to be bright and crisp, not dull, limp, or overcooked.

Indian cooking is often characterized as spicy, hot, complex, and time-consuming. As you cook with this book, you will realize that it is a delectable combination of subtle flavors and tastes that can be a pleasure to create. Let practice, determination, and innovation be your bywords. The end results are for you, your family, and your guests to appreciate. I hope that as you turn these pages you will see the image of a friend willing to offer a helping hand.

LAXMI HIREMATH
*Martinez, California, April 1995*

# Notes to the Cook

**Preparation Times** at the top of each recipe are approximate; your actual working time may vary according to the heat of your stove and how fast you are at chopping, grating, and other basic tasks. I have separated out long stretches of time, such as soaking legumes, resting batters, and unattended baking.

**Microwave** instructions are given where appropriate. All the times are based on testing in a 1350-watt microwave oven, which produces fine results with reasonable speed. Times will need to be adjusted for ovens of higher or lower wattage.

For information on **ingredients,** see the Appendix, page 235. Spices are covered in The Art of Seasoning, page 12. Certain other categories of ingredients, like legumes and bread flours, are covered in their respective chapter introductions.

# The Art of Seasoning

GARAM MASALA

CHAAT MASALA

CURRY POWDER

MY MOTHER'S 25-INGREDIENT SPICE BLEND

SAMBAR POWDER

AROMATIC SPICE POWDER

MUGHAL READY MIX

Babur, founder of the Mughal empire in India, wrote in his memoir, "Had my countrymen had the knowledge of spices the Indians have, I would have conquered the world!" Indeed, the art of seasoning is an ancient one in the Indian subcontinent. Particles of cumin, coriander, mustard seeds, and cinnamon have been found in 4,500-year-old grinding stones from the prehistoric cities of Mohenjo Daro and Harrappa in the Indus Valley, in what is now Pakistan. In later centuries, spices were the exotic treasures that lured daring explorers from afar to India. The European advances led to warfare and colonization, and changed the course of history. In spite of all the geopolitical transformation that has eroded its wealth, India still remains the bastion of spices, and spices are a proud symbol of Indian culture and heritage. They serve three main functions in the subcontinent — as seasoning in cooking, preservatives in the tropical climate, and remedies in the ancient form of medicine, Ayurveda.

To this day, the Indian cook's most striking feature is her ability to bring out flavors through the meticulous use of spices. Different spices dominate in different regions of the country. Cinnamon, nutmeg, bay leaves, cloves, cumin, and coriander are prominently featured in the north, while mustard seeds, fenugreek seeds, turmeric, peppercorns, chile peppers, and kari leaves govern the south.

To master spices, one has to learn to mix them judiciously and in proper sequence. I firmly believe that food tastes best when its natural flavor is accented with the right amount of seasoning; the seasoning should never overpower the dish. My simple advice is season to satisfy your personal taste. Try recipes as I've written them first, then move on to create your own dishes. Start with a few spices and experiment.

## OIL SEASONING

One of the most important ways spices are used in Indian cooking, and a technique fundamental to many Indian dishes, is to flavor oil — either the oil in which the dish is cooked or as a final seasoning to be stirred into or drizzled on top of the finished dish. Seasoning oil with spices is an ancient skill, and I consider it my country's most significant and notable contribution to the art of seasoning.

To make seasoned oil, heat the oil over medium heat until it ripples when you tilt the pan slightly. Add whole mustard and cumin seeds and cook until they sizzle and splutter and release their distinctive bouquet (this generally takes less than a minute; any less and they will remain "raw"). Perfectly toasted mustard seeds look grayish, and cumin reddish-brown; do not cook too long or they will turn dark and taste bitter. A few seeds will pop like popcorn; if you are afraid that a seed might accidentally pop in your eyes or mess up the cooking range, you can hold a spatter screen or a lid over the pan, but do not cover it fully or the seeds will steam rather than frying. If a recipe calls for fresh kari leaves, they are added now and fried until crisp, which takes just a few seconds. At this point, the spice-infused oil is called *tarka* or *ogarne* and it is used as a topping on raitas, salads, soups, and curries.

If the recipe calls for moist ingredients like onion, garlic, ginger, or chiles, add them to the pan when the seeds begin popping. This is also the time to add turmeric and other ground spices, which might burn if added earlier. I prefer to sprinkle the turmeric over the onion. That way it does not burn and imparts a nice hue to the dish. If there are no onions but only ground spices, it is all right to toss them in the oil, but be ready to add other ingredients right away or remove the pan from the heat immediately to keep them from burning.

# A Tour of Indian Spices

Most of the spices mentioned in this book can be found in supermarkets and specialty food stores, but the best way to buy them is in bulk in Indian markets. The prices are lower, and due to faster turnover, the flavor is usually better. Look for fragrant, plump, unshriveled spices. For best results, they should be bought in small quantities (most are sold by the ounce) and stored whole rather than ground, since they keep better. Preground spices oxidize more rapidly, losing their vital volatile oils resulting in a flat taste. Store whole spices in tightly covered containers, away from direct light, for 4 to 6 months at cool room temperature, or in the refrigerator for up to 8 months; freeze for longer storage. Don't throw away any stale spices; you can mix them with dried rose petals and pine cones from a florist and display the mixture in bowls to make a potpourri for the bedroom or bathroom.

## ASAFETIDA (Hing)

Along with caraway, celery, fennel, parsley, and numerous other herbs and spices, asafetida belongs to the carrot family, or Umbelliferae. In this case, it is not the seeds or leaves that are used, but the secretions that flow out when the plants are cut. These are dried into a resin-like solid that is sold in solid pieces or in powdered form (the solid pieces are more fragrant). It is very pungent, with an unappealing sulfurous smell, but it gives off much of its strong odor as soon as it is heated, leaving behind a subtler flavor. Still, use it sparingly. A bit of minced garlic can be used as a substitute.

## BAY LEAVES (Tej Patta)

Indian cooks use two kinds of bay leaves — the lemony bay laurel familiar to Western cooks and the mellow tasting Indian bay (cassia). In Western cooking, bay leaves are usually added to simmering liquids, but in India the leaves are toasted in hot oil before being added to pilafs, vegetable dishes, and spice blends. The recipes will work with either type; discard them before serving. When I grow the leaves in my herb patch, I pick them a day ahead of time and dry them overnight on the kitchen table for the best flavor.

## CARDAMOM (Elaichi)

Cardamom, "the queen of spices," is the seed pods of a plant of the ginger family that grows profusely in the wet hills of southern India. It is used to flavor a host of entrees, desserts, and spice blends as well as beverages in Indian cookery. For a hint of sweet scent the whole pods are used in pilafs, and for a more redolent effect the seeds are crushed as in desserts and sweetmeats. It comes in three varieties. My favorite is the small green pods, which have a delicate flavor similar to eucalyptus. Nibbled after meals, green cardamom acts as a natural breath freshener (I always carry some in my purse). The large brown or black cardamom is almost twice the size of the green type, with a mellower flavor; it is used in savory and rice dishes. The large bleached white cardamom commonly sold in supermarkets is the least flavorful.

To determine freshness of cardamom, pull open the pod. The seeds should be black-brown, plump, and slightly sticky, not wilted and brownish gray. For the best quality, I suggest you purchase and store the whole pods, and that is how the recipes specify the amount to use. Loose seeds are convenient, but do not keep as well. A quarter teaspoon of seeds is roughly equal to 3 pods.

## CARUM SEEDS (Ajwain)

Another member of the umbellifer family, ajwain (Carum copticum) is also referred to as lovage (although it is not the same as the European herb of that name), omam (in southern India), or bishop's weed. The seeds are the size of celery seeds, light brown in color, with a sharp thymelike flavor. They are used whole to flavor fried snacks, appetizers, some vegetables, and crushed in pickles. I like to toss them in my paratha dough, and they will add an exotic touch to other breads. They are probably sold only in Indian markets, under the name ajwain.

## CHILES *(Mirch)*

Chiles are America's gift to the culinary world. The Portuguese introduced them to India some 500 years ago, dislodging black pepper from its number one spot as the hot spice of choice. Today chiles are cultivated around the globe, mainly in tropical countries. Dried or fresh, chiles range from mild to volcanic. They are rich in Vitamin A and C.

All the recipes that use chiles in this book are mildly flavored; feel free to adjust the taste by using more or less than called for.

### *Dried Red Chiles (Lal Mirch):*

These small orange-red peppers, about 2 inches long, are ripened on the plant and then sun-dried. Their heat is centered in the seeds. Sometimes they are soaked in water to soften the skin and tame the pungency. Used widely in Goan and south Indian cooking to give a hot-smoky flavor to dishes. Available in the produce and Mexican sections of supermarkets, and in Chinese and Southeast Asian markets, which are often the cheapest source.

### *Fresh Hot Green Chiles (Hara Mirch):*

Fresh chiles vary in shape and size. In general, chiles with a broad base and rounded tip are moderately hot. Chiles with a narrow base and tapered end are the most fiery. Fresh green chiles are available at supermarkets. Those most frequently called for in this book are Anaheim and serrano.

*Anaheim chiles* average about 6 to 8 inches in length and 1 to 2 inches wide at the base. They vary from mild to hot and are good for stuffings. Unfortunately, there is no way to tell how hot they are when you buy them, but you can always reduce the heat by removing the seeds and ribs.

*Serrano chiles* are 1½ to 2 inches long and slightly tapered at both ends. They are medium-hot. This is the small green chile I used in developing and testing the recipes in this book. I personally do not seed the chiles and find it unnecessary, but you can do so if you like. If you want to be able to spot the chiles easily in the finished dish, slit them in half or in fourths lengthwise rather than chopping.

Serrano chiles are available in supermarkets and Indian, Mexican, and Asian markets. If you can't find them, the larger, slightly milder and more widely available jalapeño will do as a substitute.

## CILANTRO (FRESH CORIANDER) *(Hara Dhania)*

Another member of the umbellifer family, the coriander plant provides both a spice (coriander seed) and an herb (the fresh leaves and stems). In other parts of the English-speaking world, the herb form is known as fresh coriander or Chinese parsley, but in this country it is most identified with Mexican cooking, so it is usually sold under its Spanish name, cilantro.

With its tender leaves and delicate aroma, cilantro is extensively used in Indian cooking, in chutneys, curries, and vegetables and as a garnish. When we first moved to Columbus, Ohio in 1983, my only source was my garden or the one and only Indian market that sold five sprigs for more than a dollar. You can imagine my delight a few years later when the supermarkets began to sell good-sized bunches of it in the produce section.

Cilantro keeps well in the refrigerator, but it will rot easily if too moist. To store, chop off the root ends and discard any wilted leaves. Do not wash. Wrap the cilantro loosely in paper towels (if it is very wet you might want to dry it first in a salad spinner) and place it in a plastic bag in the refrigerator.

A few recipes call for dried cilantro. The kind in the spice jars will do, but you can easily dry your own at home. Wash the fresh leaves, pat or spin

them dry, and lay them out on a plate or a cookie sheet. They should be crisp and crumbly after 2 to 3 days at room temperature. For faster drying, set the cookie sheet in a 350°F oven for 12 to 15 minutes.

## CINNAMON (Dalchini)

Cinnamon is obtained from the young bark of two different trees of the laurel family, cultivated in the Caribbean islands, Sri Lanka and eastern parts of India. False cinnamon is more intensely flavored and comes from the bark of the cassia tree; the sticks are thick, flat, and small. On the other hand, true cinnamon has a sweeter scent and the sticks are longer and more tightly rolled. Either variety can be used in Indian cooking. Sticks of cinnamon are used to flavor pilafs; powdered cinnamon is used in curries and spice blends. In olden times its sweet aromatic flavor was rumored to inspire love.

## CLOVE (Lavang)

The English name of this ancient spice comes from the Latin *clavus,* meaning "nail," which describes the shape of the spice. Cloves, the dried unopened flowers of a tree native to Southeast Asia, are considered a "hot" spice in India, with a powerful pungency and a warm aftertaste. They are used in pickles as a preservative and also in north Indian dishes. Cloves should be bought whole; look for those that are oily and plump.

## CORIANDER SEEDS (Dhania)

These are the spherical seeds of the cilantro plant. Ground into a fine powder, they provide both flavor and a bit of thickening to many Indian dishes. Two kinds of coriander seeds are available in America. I recommend the pale green Indian variety, which has a taste similar to lemony sage with a sweet touch and makes a pleasant and appealing sauce. The brown or Moroccan variety is less flavorful and makes sauces darker and duller. Lightly toast the seeds until crisp before grinding.

## CUMIN SEEDS (Jeera)

Another umbelliferous spice, cumin seeds resemble those of fennel and caraway. Along with mustard and turmeric, this is one of the indispensable ingredients in my spice box. Cumin seeds are used whole, crushed, or ground to flavor breads, vegetables, legumes, beverages, spice blends, and salads. They combine favorably with coriander and fennel as cooling spices. Two varieties are available in Indian markets. Ordinary white cumin seeds *(safed jeera)* are the same as those carried in supermarkets. More rare is the black, or royal, cumin *(shahi jeera* or *kala jeera)* a dark variety with a sharp ridged surface that looks a lot like caraway seeds. Native to Kashmir and Iran, this variety is used extensively in Mughal dishes for its sweet, mellow taste. I like to use it in pilafs and sprinkle it on rolled paratha (page 82).

## CURRY POWDER (Kari Pudi)

This spice blend is not an authentic part of Indian cooking, but a standard blend of typically Indian spices put together by British spice merchants to recreate the flavor of various Indian sauces. Still, it is convenient for certain uses. Numerous prepackaged varieties are sold in supermarkets, but most use too much turmeric for my taste. The Madras brands with a sun or a ship on the label are the best choices; still, I suggest you limit the use of store-bought variety to one dish per meal to avoid a monotonous taste. For a more aromatic version, try the homemade *kari pudi* recipe on page 22.

## FENNEL SEEDS (Saunf)

Another member of the umbellifer family, fennel has plump, yellowish-green, highly aromatic seeds that look like curled cumin and taste similar to anise. Whole fennel seeds are used in numerous vegetable dishes, desserts, spice blends, and fruit chutneys. Raw, toasted, or candy-coated fennel seeds are served after meals to aid digestion. They also act as a natural breath freshener; I have a little box of cardamom pods, cloves, and fennel seeds in my purse, and on long journeys in the car, I like to chew them in place of gum. I always keep a jar of dry-roasted fennel at home which I also offer to guests after meals. Toast the whole seeds in a skillet on medium heat until fragrant, crisp, and starting to darken, then sprinkle with salt and fresh lime juice for a captivating aroma. To make a candied version, add sugar, sweetened flaked coconut, and sesame seeds. Mix well, cool and store in a tightly covered container.

## FENUGREEK LEAVES (Hari Methi)

Fenugreek, found from India to Greece and Egypt, is another plant used both for its seeds and its leaves. Fragrant and slightly bitter, the fresh leaves are used as both an herb and a leafy vegetable, in breads, pilafs, raitas, salads, and my favorite Indian-style pasta, or simply cooked like spinach. In some parts of the country, fresh fenugreek greens can be found (mainly in the spring) at Indian and Middle Eastern markets and farmers' markets. It's also easy to grow your own in a kitchen window box or in the garden, using the whole seeds from the spice bin. Begin harvesting the tender sprouts at the two-leaf stage for refreshing salads and raitas, or let it grow further and use the mature greens like spinach. Dried leaves (known as *sukhi* or *kasoori methi*) can be crushed or powdered to flavor vegetable and legume dishes and some spice blends; discard the tough stems first. If using dried, use half the quantity of fresh leaves.

## FENUGREEK SEEDS (Methi Dana)

Used as a spice, the small, cylindrical, yellowish-brown seeds of fenugreek have a powerful burnt-caramel flavor that compliments *dal* dishes and pickles. To bring out their best flavor, toast the seeds lightly (see page 20).

## GINGER (Adrak)

Ginger is the yellowish-brown underground rhizome of a tropical plant. It is used both fresh and dried in Indian cooking, but the two are not interchangeable. Sliced or crushed, fresh ginger gives a flavor boost to curries, legume dishes, pickles, sauces, and chutneys. Look for tender, firm, and unwrinkled fresh ginger at supermarkets and Asian groceries. Stored in a brown paper or plastic bag in the refrigerator, it keeps fresh for up to 3 weeks. When ginger is young and the skin is tender, I don't bother to peel it.

Dried ginger (*sonth*) is available in small lumps or powdered form; the fresh rhizomes are dried in the sun, then ground and stored. It has a sharp, hot aftertaste. Dried ginger is mostly used in vegetables, spice blends, beverages, and desserts.

## KARI (CURRY) LEAVES (Kari Patta)

Even a small house in southern India will have a curry plant in the yard. Native to southwest Asia, this plant has sprigs of thin, shiny, dark green leaves used as an herb. When lightly fried in hot oil or toasted over a flame, they release a distinctive, enticing aroma which enhances lentils, vegetables, rice dishes, and raitas. Fresh or dried kari leaves are available at Indian markets. Fresh leaves keep well in the refrigerator for 2 weeks covered with plastic. Dried ones store well at room temperature for up to 6 months. If you visit Indian markets only infrequently, you can buy the fresh leaves in quantity and air-dry them yourself; arrange on a plate in a single layer and set out on your dining table until dry and crumbly, 2 to 3 days. Store in a plastic bag. If you are unable to find kari leaves, omit them from the recipe or replace with cilantro.

## MACE. SEE NUTMEG.

## MANGO POWDER (Amchur)

Mango powder is prepared by drying and then grinding small segments of unripe mango. Sour and astringent in flavor, it is used in curries, chaats, and spice blends. Lemon juice or tamarind makes an acceptable substitute. Mango powder is available in Indian markets, as are leathery, biscuit-colored dehydrated mango slices. The slices are simply stirred in the curry sauce for a tart flavor.

## MUSTARD SEEDS (Rai)

The tiny, round seeds of the mustard plant are taste and visual enhancers in scores of Indian dishes. Both black and brown mustard are popular in Indian cooking, and they differ only in color, not in flavor. (The yellow seeds sold in supermarket spice racks have a slightly sour flavor, but they can also be used in the recipes in this book.) Generally mustard seeds are used in small quantities, either whole or crushed. When they are added to hot oil, they sizzle and splutter and taste pleasantly nutty. Besides adding flavor, they act as a preservative.

## NUTMEG (Jaiphal)

Nutmeg is the seed of the fruit of an evergreen tree native to Indonesia. Delicate and naturally sweet with fruity overtones, it is usually grated straight into desserts and beverages (unlike most other spices, it does not need toasting). Since nutmeg rapidly loses flavor when grated, it is best to buy it whole in Indian markets or supermarkets and grate it just before using.

As a bonus, the nutmeg seed is covered with a bright-red fibrous layer which, when dried, is known as mace (javitri), a minor spice in Indian cooking. Mace, which is quite oily, is toasted until brittle and then ground with other spices to make spice blends. Mace blades are available in gourmet and Indian markets, and the ground version is also quite good.

## PAPRIKA (Deghi Mirch)

A mild to sweet pepper called deghi mirch from the valley of Kashmir is sun-dried and ground to make Indian paprika. It is valued for the extraordinary brilliant orange-red color and flavor it brings to vegetable curries, paneer cheese dishes, and lentils. Sold as paprika at Indian markets; the common sweet Hungarian paprika makes a fine replacement.

## PEPPERCORNS (Gol Mirch)

Peppercorns are the fruit of a plant of the vine pepper family, of Southeast Asian origin. Green, black, and white varieties are available, and all three are used in Indian cooking. Green peppercorns are berries that are picked while still unripe and pickled; they add a delicate herbal flavor to salads. Black peppercorns are unripe berries that have been sun-dried until their fleshy skin shrinks, turns dark brown, and becomes hard. Their flavor has universal appeal and readily enhances almost any food. White peppercorns are made from berries that have been allowed to ripen on the vine. After picking they are dried and their outer skin is removed. They are milder in flavor than black peppercorns, and are often used in spice blends and curry sauces that use yogurt. For best results, purchase whole peppercorns at gourmet markets or supermarkets.

## SAFFRON (Kesar, Zaffron)

Saffron, used in pilafs, beverages, and desserts, consists of dried stigmas from the purple flowers of the saffron crocus. It is grown in China, India, Spain, and Turkey, with Spain being the largest exporter. The whole cultivation process, from planting to harvesting, is manual. After being hand-picked, the delicate scarlet and yellow stigmas are spread on a sieve, cured for 30 minutes over heat, and carefully packaged. It takes about a quarter of million flowers to produce one pound of saffron, making it the most expensive spice in the world. But the very rich and captivating bouquet of saffron and the beautiful hue it imparts to dishes make it worth the price.

Saffron is available both as threads and ground at Indian, gourmet, and Middle Eastern markets. Personally I prefer to buy the threads, which I toast on low heat until brittle and crush with the back of a spoon or a rolling pin before adding to hot milk or water. The flavor is at its best when the saffron is under a year old, so buy from a store that has a good turnover.

## STAR ANISE *(Badaam Phool)*

Star anise is the eight-pointed, star-shaped fruit of a small evergreen tree of the magnolia family native to China, dried to a hard, almost woody texture. Whole pods are available in gourmet, Chinese, and Indian markets. A seed is embedded in each of the eight points of the star; Chinese cooks use the whole thing, but my mother thinks the seeds taste slightly bitter, so she has always discarded them, and I have continued to do so.

## TURMERIC *(Haldi)*

Turmeric is a Southeast Asian plant related to ginger, which yields a dried spice that bestows a characteristic yellow hue to all the regional cuisines of India. When fresh, the interior of the rhizome is a brilliant orange-yellow color, and it is used in this form in certain dishes. But most of the harvest is boiled in water and dried in the scorching sun until light and brittle, then sent to the mill to be ground into the familiar yellow powder. Turmeric is commonly added to legumes, beans, and vegetables, and has a preservative effect in pickles and other foods. The flavor is strongly bittersweet and the aroma slightly musty, so I always recommend using it in moderation. Ground turmeric is inexpensive and widely available in supermarkets.

# SPICE BLENDS

Spice blends are called for in some of the recipes in this book. Indians do occasionally use commercial spice powders for convenience, but homemade spice blends are so much fresher, more aromatic, and more flavorful that I recommend you make your own. It takes only a few minutes to toast and grind enough for two or three months, which is as long as they will stay fresh on your spice shelf. Here are recipes for a few of my favorite spice blends. Store them in tightly covered jars, as moisture can cause the blends to cake. Spice blends make nice gifts, in pretty jars with a few recipe tips attached with a neat bow.

The first step in making these spice blends is to toast the whole spices. Toasting, also known as dry-roasting, improves the flavor, eliminating the raw aftertaste, and makes them easier to digest, and makes grinding effortless. Preheat a heavy skillet (cast iron or nonstick), add the spices, and toast on medium heat, stirring or shaking the pan frequently, until they have a nice bouquet, and start to become reddish-brown and crisp, anywhere from 2 to 8 minutes depending upon the amount and kind of spices (for instance, cumin seeds take less time than fenugreek seeds). Don't cook for too long, or they will lose their volatile oils; blackened spices will give a bitter flavor. Use a spice mill, or a coffee grinder kept exclusively for this purpose, to grind the spices to a fine powder, working in several batches if necessary.

# GARAM MASALA

Makes a heaping ¼ cup
Preparation time:
    15 minutes

2 tablespoons coriander
    seeds
2 teaspoons cumin seeds
½ teaspoon fennel seeds
1 teaspoon peppercorns
½ teaspoon whole cloves
1-inch stick cinnamon,
    broken
2 whole pods star anise
    (remove the seeds if
    you like)
Seeds from 10 green
    cardamom pods
    (about ¾ teaspoon)
6 bay leaves, crushed
2 blades mace
¼ teaspoon freshly
    grated nutmeg

*Garam* translates as "warm" and *masala* means "spice blend." This aromatic blend of spices is commonly used in north Indian dishes, either sprinkled in at the end as a final seasoning or added earlier in the cooking for a more intense flavor. It's also good for perking up leftovers.

1. Preheat a large heavy skillet and add all the spices except the nutmeg. Toast the spices over medium heat until they are aromatic and the seeds turn reddish-brown, about 5 minutes. Add the nutmeg and toast another 2 minutes. Cool slightly.

2. Transfer the spices to a spice grinder and grind to a fine powder. Store in an airtight glass jar in a cool place for up to 3 months or refrigerate up to 6 months.

# CHAAT MASALA

Makes ½ cup
Preparation time:
    15 minutes

2 teaspoons carum seeds
1½ tablespoons cumin
    seeds
¼ teaspoon black
    peppercorns
2 tablespoons dried mint,
    crushed
⅛ teaspoon asafetida
¼ teaspoon nutmeg
2 tablespoons mango
    powder (amchur)
½ teaspoon hot or sweet
    paprika
1 tablespoon *kala namak*
    or Real Salt
¼ teaspoon salt

This special tangy mix of spices adds a wonderful flavor to salads and chaats. The blend is perked up by *kala namak,* the smoky-tasting "black salt" found in Indian markets (the color is actually a pinkish gray). Real Salt, a brand from Utah with a similar pinkish gray color from trace minerals, is an excellent substitute, obtainable at natural-food stores. If you are unable to get either one, simply omit it, but don't substitute additional table salt in the recipe. The Hi-Tech brand of chaat masala available at Indian markets is fairly good.

1. Preheat a large heavy skillet over medium heat. Add the carum, cumin, and peppercorns and toast, shaking the pan frequently, until fragrant, about 4 minutes. Reduce the heat to low and add the mint, asafetida, and nutmeg and continue toasting for another 2 minutes. Cool slightly.

2. Transfer the contents of the pan to a spice grinder and grind to a fine powder. Stir in the mango powder, paprika, *kala namak,* and salt. Mix well. Store the spice powder in an airtight glass jar for up to 2 months in a cool place or refrigerate up to 6 months.

# CURRY POWDER
## (Kari Pudi)

Makes ⅓ cup
Preparation time:
  15 minutes

½ tablespoon mustard
  seeds
1 tablespoon cumin seeds
1½ tablespoons
  coriander seeds
½ teaspoon fenugreek
  seeds
1 teaspoon cardamom
  seeds
1-inch stick cinnamon,
  broken
20 fresh kari leaves or
  1 teaspoon crushed
  dried kari leaves
½ teaspoon cayenne
¼ teaspoon turmeric

Indian cooks seldom use packaged "curry powder," preferring to use different spice mixtures for each dish. However, the familiar commercial spice does have an approximate counterpart in authentic Indian cooking: a deep yellow powdered mixture of lightly roasted kari leaves, spices, and lentils, used occasionally by southern Indian cooks. The name of this mix, *kari pudi,* translates as "curry [leaf] powder," and it shares some (but not all) of its ingredients with the curry powder popularized by British spice merchants. *Kari pudi* is a pleasing combination of spices, and I use it occasionally to flavor vegetable and legume dishes and salads. Here is a recipe for a homemade version that will be fresher than any you can buy in a can or jar, and that you can use in place of curry powder in Western dishes. A couple of small dried red chiles may be used in place of cayenne; toast them along with the other spices.

1. Preheat a large heavy skillet and add the seeds, the cinnamon, and the kari leaves. Toast the spices over medium heat, shaking the pan frequently, until aromatic and the seeds start to darken, about 6 minutes. Cool slightly.

2. Transfer the toasted spices to a grinder and grind to a fine powder. Stir in the cayenne and turmeric. Store the curry powder in an airtight glass jar for up to 3 months in a cool place or refrigerate up to 6 months.

# MY MOTHER'S 25-INGREDIENT SPICE BLEND

## (Kala Masala)

Makes scant 1 cup
Preparation time:
    25 minutes

2 whole pods star anise
2½ tablespoons
    coriander seeds
2 tablespoons cumin
    seeds
1½ tablespoons
    mustard seeds
½ teaspoon fenugreek
    seeds
¼ teaspoon black
    peppercorns
⅓ teaspoon white
    peppercorns
1 teaspoon whole cloves
Seeds from 12 cardamom
    pods (about 1 teaspoon)
2-inch stick cinnamon
2 dried red chiles
1 teaspoon black cumin
    seeds (shahi jeera)
4 teaspoons sesame seeds
4 bay leaves
2 blades mace
½ teaspoon white
    poppy seeds
1 tablespoon unsweet
    ened coconut flakes
2 teaspoons dried
    cilantro leaves, crushed
2 teaspoons dried kari
    leaves, crushed
½ teaspoon garlic
    powder
½ teaspoon ginger
    powder
¼ teaspoon nutmeg,
    freshly grated
¼ teaspoon asafetida
    (powdered)
⅛ teaspoon turmeric
½ teaspoon salt

In India, every household has its signature spice blends, and recipes are passed on from one generation to the next like family heirlooms. My mother, on a visit to California, showed me how to make my maternal grandmother's "stamp," which I am passing along to you. This mix has an alluring aroma which mellows down and permeates the dish with the gentle perfume of roasted spices. Although it calls for twenty-five ingredients, the recipe takes little more than half an hour to make from start to finish, and only five ingredients are exotic— and they can be purchased at gourmet and Indian markets. Use this blend in small amounts to flavor vegetables, lentil dishes, and pilafs. For something different, try it on croutons.

1. Crack open each point of the star anise pods and discard the shiny seed inside. Preheat a large skillet and add the star anise and all the remaining whole spices and coconut. Toast over medium heat, stirring constantly, until the mixture is aromatic, the mustard seeds begin to pop and the spices are crisp, about 8 minutes. Transfer to a plate; set aside.

2. Reduce the heat to low. Add the remaining ingredients to the pan. Toast, shaking the pan frequently, for 8 minutes. Add the contents of the pan to the spices toasted earlier. Mix well. Grind the entire mixture, in portions, to a fine powder. Store the powdered spice blend in an airtight glass jar for up to 4 months in a cool place or refrigerate up to a year.

# SAMBAR POWDER
## *(Sambar Pudi)*

Makes a heaping ⅓ cup
Preparation time:
  15 minutes

2 teaspoons yellow
  chick peas (chana dal)
1 teaspoon white gram
  beans (urad dal)
1 teaspoon dried yellow
  split peas
¼ teaspoon white or black
  peppercorns (optional)
2 tablespoons coriander
  seeds
½ tablespoon cumin
  seeds
1 teaspoon fenugreek
  seeds
1 tablespoon raw long-
  grain white rice
1-inch stick cinnamon,
  broken
20 fresh kari leaves
  *or* 1 teaspoon crushed
dried kari leaves
1 or 2 dried red chiles
  *or* ¼ teaspoon cayenne

Sambar powder is a classic mix of toasted and ground spices, herbs, and dried dals used to flavor and thicken southern Indian lentil and vegetable stews and rice dishes. Dexterous southern cooks use the dals as seasoning which gives a nutty flavor, velvety texture, and a pleasant yellow color to the sambar. My grandmother taught me to add raw rice grains to the spice mix in addition to the dal to help thicken sauces.

1. Preheat a large skillet and add all the ingredients (except cayenne, if using). Toast over medium heat, stirring constantly, until the mixture is aromatic and the rice grains are lightly browned, about 6 minutes.

2. Cool the mixture slightly, then grind it to a fine powder. If you are using cayenne, stir it in now. Store the sambar powder in an airtight glass jar for up to 3 months in a cool place or refrigerate up to 6 months.

# AROMATIC SPICE POWDER
## (Yellin Pudi)

Makes ½ cup
Preparation time:
   15 minutes

2 tablespoons raw long-
   grain rice
4 teaspoons sesame seeds
2 teaspoons fenugreek
   seeds
4 tablespoons unsweet-
   ened coconut flakes
1 teaspoon cayenne,
   or to taste

My sister-in-law Keertilata uses this *pudi* in many of her southern-style stews. I make it in large batches, 2 to 4 pounds at a time, and store it in the freezer, where it remains fresh up to a year. But the recipe here is for a more modest supply. This spice mixture works wonderfully in Mangalore Pineapple Curry (page 113). You may also fold it into other curried dishes to impart an exquisite nutty flavor. As in Sambar Powder, the raw rice in the spice blend helps thicken gravies to a velvety texture.

1. Preheat a large heavy skillet. Add the rice and seeds and toast over medium heat until the mixture is aromatic and the rice grains are lightly browned, about 6 minutes. Add the coconut and toast 2 minutes longer. Remove from the heat and cool slightly.

2. Grind the toasted ingredients to a fine powder. Stir in the cayenne. Store the spice powder in an airtight glass jar for up to 2 months in a cool place or refrigerate up to 6 months.

# MUGHAL READY MIX
## (Mughal Masala)

Makes about ⅔ cup
Preparation time:
   10 minutes

¼ cup raw almonds
¼ cup raw unsalted
   cashews
Seeds from 12 cardamom
   pods, ground (about 1
   teaspoon)
½ teaspoon saffron
   threads

During one of my visits to India, my sister Smita suggested this fragrant make-ahead mix. Mughal dishes often call for cashew and almond paste for both flavor and thickening. Instead of grinding nuts for each dish, I keep a jar of this mix in the refrigerator to use in dishes like the cashew *nan* on page 86. It also makes a lovely topping for ice cream, coffee cakes, and puddings.

1. Preheat a large heavy skillet over medium heat. Add the almonds and cashews and toast, stirring or shaking the pan frequently, until fragrant, about 5 minutes. Add the cardamom and saffron and continue toasting for another 2 minutes. Transfer the contents of the skillet to a blender, food processor, or spice grinder and grind to a fine powder. Cool completely. Store in an airtight glass jar up to 2 months in the refrigerator.

# APPETIZERS

Sweet-Spiced Royal Almonds

Roasted Honey Pistachios

Candied Whole Cashews

Hasty Lentil Wafer Platter

Toasted Lentil Wafers

Baked Cottage Cheese Pastries (Samosa)

Festive Spinach and Split Pea Spread

Green Tomato Spread with Peanuts

Baked Popcorn Croquettes

Tandoori Cheese

Paneer Cheese Walnut Kababs

Quick Spinach Bites

Tamarind-Apple Dipping Sauce

Garbanzo Bean Spiral Crunchies

Appetizers in the Western sense — small or light dishes served before the main courses to stimulate the appetite — are not a traditional Indian dining course. In India, the dishes described here would be served at the table along with the rest of the meal, or else offered as snacks or at tea time. When I entertain, I often follow the Western model, serving one or several of the dishes in this chapter as a separate appetizer course, to set the mood for the meal to follow.

Flavored toasted nuts are always a favorite appetizer. The three variations included here can all be made well in advance and are suitable for either formal or informal dining. Lentil wafers (*papad* or *pappadam*), especially the 1-inch size, make another convenient first course. I have recommended five different techniques for toasting the wafers and an assortment of simple toppings to serve as a Hasty Lentil Wafer Platter. As a dip for vegetables, breadsticks, or toast triangles, try the nutritious Festive Spinach and Split Pea Spread or one of several other dipping sauces made from apple, cilantro, and tamarind.

Choosing an appetizer also helps in selecting the courses that follow, and vice versa. Tandoori Cheese, grilled chunks of Indian paneer cheese in a spicy sauce, makes a tempting appetizer, but I wouldn't follow it with another dish containing cheese. Quick Spinach Bites make appealing morsels on toothpicks, but serving a main course of koftas (see page 95) would create a redundancy of textures.

Serve these appetizers at the table or as a separate course before coming to the table, as you like. They also make excellent party food, on a buffet or passed on trays. As a first course, they will certainly bring applause and requests for seconds, but don't let your guests consume a whole plate. After all, you do want them to leave room for the main course!

# SWEET-SPICED ROYAL ALMONDS
## (Sultani Badaam)

Makes 1 cup
Preparation time:
 15 minutes

¾ to 1 teaspoon cayenne
½ teaspoon crushed
 fennel seeds
½ teaspoon cinnamon
¼ teaspoon freshly
 ground black pepper
¼ teaspoon salt
1 cup whole raw
 (skin on) almonds
2 tablespoons granulated
 sugar
2 tablespoons powdered
 sugar
Light-tasting vegetable
 or avocado oil for
 deep frying

A north Indian favorite, these outstanding almonds are fragrantly spiced. As a topping they add a special touch to pilafs, chaats, ice creams, or a bowl of mixed sliced fruits. You can adjust the amount of cayenne up or down to taste.

1. Combine all the spices and salt in a medium mixing bowl and set aside.

2. Bring about 2 cups water to a boil in a medium saucepan. Add the almonds and boil uncovered for 4 minutes. Drain well. Transfer them to a pan (the same pan is fine) and add both the sugars. Toss well.

3. Fill a wok or deep fryer with oil to a depth of 1 inch and heat to 350°F. With a slotted spoon, transfer half the nuts to the hot oil, and fry until they are golden brown and covered with foam from the melted sugar, 2 to 3 minutes. Lift the nuts out of the oil, drain well, and spread on a cookie sheet or dinner plate. Repeat with the remaining nuts. Transfer the hot nuts immediately to the spice mixture (if any are clinging together, gently break them apart first) and toss well. Let cool to room temperature before serving; stored in an airtight container, they will keep up to 2 weeks in a cool place.

# ROASTED HONEY PISTACHIOS
## (Huzur Pasand Pista)

Makes 1 cup
Preparation time:
 25 minutes

2 tablespoons honey
¾ tablespoon mild
 peanut oil
½ teaspoon Mexican-
 style liquid chile sauce
 or Tabasco
½ teaspoon salt
1 cup shelled roasted
 pistachios

Mildly flavored roasted pistachios are delightful as the prelude to an elegant dinner. Those who prefer fiery flavors may want to double the hot sauce.

1. Place a rack in the center of the oven and preheat to 325°F.

2. Place the honey in a medium bowl and whisk in the oil. Add the hot pepper sauce and salt, and stir to blend. Add the pistachios and toss to coat. Spread in a single layer on a cookie sheet (preferably nonstick) and bake until golden brown, about 20 minutes. Transfer the nuts to a dinner plate, stir to separate, and cool to room temperature. Store leftovers in an airtight container for up to 2 weeks.

# CANDIED WHOLE CASHEWS
## (Masala Kaju)

Makes 1 cup
Preparation time:
    15 minutes

1 cup whole roasted and
    salted cashews
¼ cup sugar
¾ to 1 teaspoon cayenne
½ teaspoon ground
    cumin

Candied cashews are always a great hit on my hors d'oeuvre tray. Pack them in an airtight jar, tie a plaid ribbon around the neck, and you have a fabulous gift. These are fairly hot; for a milder flavor use the smaller amount of cayenne.

1. Place the cashews in a 10- to 12-inch frying pan over medium heat. Cook, shaking the pan frequently, until the cashews are hot and start to brown, about 3 minutes.

2. Sprinkle the sugar, cayenne, and cumin over the nuts; stir until the sugar melts and coats the nuts all over, 10 to 12 minutes.

3. Pour the nuts onto a cookie sheet or dinner plate. Immediately separate them with a fork. Cool and serve, or store in an airtight container up to 2 weeks in a cool place.

# HASTY LENTIL WAFER PLATTER
## (Papad Masala)

Serves 8
Preparation time:
    6 minutes

4 plain lentil wafers,
    toasted (see page 30)
¼ cup finely chopped
    onion
2 to 4 red and green
    fresh hot chiles,
    stemmed and chopped
2 tablespoons finely
    chopped fresh cilantro
½ teaspoon chaat
    masala, homemade
    (page 21) or bought
Sweet or hot paprika
2 teaspoons fresh lime
    or lemon juice

Lentil wafers offer endless possibilities to imaginative cooks. As an appetizer to dip in green chutneys, lentil wafers are quite popular at Indian restaurants, especially with Westerners used to the tortilla chips and salsa in Mexican restaurants. Dipped in water for a minute and drained briefly, they can be stuffed with a vegetable mixture, rolled into neat packets, and baked like enchiladas or deep-fried. They can even be cut into thin strips and boiled like noodles to serve with vegetables. But I like them best as a quick and simple yet elegant appetizer, with a colorful topping.

1. Place the wafers on a serving platter. Distribute the chopped onion, chiles, and cilantro on top. Drizzle with chaat masala, paprika, and lime or lemon juice. To serve, gently break into large pieces.

# TOASTED LENTIL WAFERS
## (Papad/Pappadam)

Crisp, thin wafers of lentil dough are a favorite in both northern and southern India, where they are known as *papad* and *pappadam* respectively. The sun-dried wafers can sit in the pantry for months, ready to be toasted in minutes to an appealingly crunchy texture as a snack or to add crunch to a meal.

Papads are made from a dough of white gram beans (urad dal) or yellow mung bean (mung dal), sometimes with added flavorings (spices, garlic, or chiles). As a child, I used to be part of the papad-making marathon during summer vacations, when the dry weather was perfect for making and drying the wafers. The terrace of our house would be cleaned and white sheets laid out. Friends and neighbors would bring their rolling pins and boards and help, chatting and laughing as they rolled out portions of dough into thin discs. My sister and I carried the rolled-out papads in trays and spread them on the sheets in a single layer to dry and covered them with plastic. After the wafers were completely dry, we packed them airtight and kept them in a cool place. On other days my mother would participate in similar gatherings at other homes, and by the end of summer every family would have nearly a year's supply of papads in an assortment of sizes and flavors.

As much as I enjoyed these papad-making sessions as a child, I am happy for the convenience of the packaged, ready-to-cook lentil wafers available at Indian and gourmet markets. They come in many sizes and varieties, with diameters from 1 inch to 8 inches, plain or with spices or garlic added, and either dry or "fresh" (the latter are thinner and softer, the former dry and rigid). I have tested all the recipes here with 4-inch fresh (flexible) wafers.

Deep-frying and toasting over a flame are the two traditional Indian cooking methods for crisp papads. Frying may be convenient for restaurants, but it's messy for the home cook, and adds unnecessary calories. Instead, I have devised five simpler techniques of toasting wafers either for two or for a large crowd. I prefer to use a conventional oven, because even if the wafers are thick, they get toasted perfectly on all sides, and it's a snap to prepare enough for a crowd. For a family dinner, the stovetop method will be a welcome choice if you don't want to turn on the oven.

Whichever toasting method you use, the wafers will stay crisp for 2 to 4 hours at room temperature. If they get limp due to humidity, stack the wafers together and reheat by any of the following methods until crisp, 1½ to 2 minutes. If not serving them immediately, let them cool, and as soon as they are cool (which is almost instantly), store them in a tightly covered container, where they will keep up to 1 week.

1. *Baking:* Position a rack in the center of the oven and preheat to 400°F. Place the wafers in a single layer on cookie sheets. Bake until they lighten to a pale cream color and are covered with little blisters, 2½ to 3 minutes.

2. *Broiling:* Position two broiler pans 6 inches away from the heat source and preheat the pans and the broiler about 2 minutes. Place the wafers in a single layer on the pans and broil on one side just until crisp and cream colored, 1 to 1½ minutes; watch closely so they do not burn.

3. *Stovetop:* Set your burner, gas or electric, on medium-high heat. Place a rack over it (if you have one). Hold one wafer with tongs on the rack or directly on the burner, and rotate it constantly until light in color and evenly flecked with light brown spots. Flip and cook on the other side until crisp, about one minute in all to toast both sides. Repeat with the remaining wafers.

4. *Outdoor Grill:* You will need moderate heat, so plan to start before the coals are intensely hot. Place the wafers directly on the grill and toast both sides until crisp, 30 to 60 seconds per side.

5. *Microwave Oven:* This works only with thin fresh (soft) wafers; thicker ones brown too unevenly. Place one wafer on a microwavable saucer or small plate. Place the plate off to one side, not in the center of the microwave, to avoid burnt spots. Toast at full power for 45 seconds. If the wafer is toasted unevenly, turn and toast for a few more seconds. Repeat with the remaining wafers.

# BAKED COTTAGE CHEESE PASTRIES
## (Samosa)

Makes 20 samosas
Preparation time:
   30 minutes, plus 1
   hour resting and 25
   minutes baking

1½ cups unbleached
   all-purpose flour, plus
   additional for dusting
½ teaspoon salt
4 tablespoons butter or
   margarine, melted
1 container (8 ounces)
   low-fat or nonfat
   cottage cheese
½ recipe Seasoned
   Potato with Peas and
   Raisins (page 97)
Cilantro Onion Chutney
   (page 192)

Here's a fresh look at a popular pastry. Baking samosas rather than frying makes them lower in calories but still rich-tasting. The potato stuffing is only one of a variety of savory fillings that can be used; try also Anaheim Chiles Smothered with Sesame Seeds (page 100), or crumbled flavored paneer cheese (page 163). Feel free to experiment with other fillings.

1. Mix the flour and salt in medium-size bowl. Make a well in the center. Add the butter and cottage cheese and mix until the flour is evenly moistened and the mixture holds together in a soft dough. Cover and let sit for 1 to 2 hours. (At this point the dough can be refrigerated up to 1 day; bring to room temperature before continuing.)

2. Position a rack in the center of the oven and preheat to 375°F. Divide the dough into 10 portions. Roll each portion into a ball. Place on a floured work surface and roll into a 5-inch circle, dusting with flour as necessary. Cut in half. Form each semicircle into a cone by folding half of the straight edge over the second half. Pinch the seam to seal. Hold the cone facing up and stuff with 1½ tablespoons of the potato filling. Pinch the open sides together to enclose the filling; if necessary, moisten the edges with a little water to help seal them.

3. Place the samosas 1 inch apart on a nonstick cookie sheet. Bake for 25 minutes until lightly browned. Serve hot with chutney.

**Note:** To reheat samosas, place in a cold oven and turn it to 300°F. Bake until hot, about 10 minutes. The samosas may be stuffed one day ahead. Place on a cookie sheet, cover loosely, and refrigerate. Bring to room temperature before baking.

# FESTIVE SPINACH AND SPLIT PEA SPREAD
## (Sindhi Sai Bhaji)

**Makes 1 cup**
**Preparation time:**
**35 minutes**

¼ cup dried yellow split
  peas, rinsed
1 cup packed chopped
  fresh or frozen
  spinach, thawed
1 small potato, peeled
  and diced
1 small carrot, sliced
  coarsely
½-inch piece fresh
  ginger, crushed
1 fresh hot green chile,
  stemmed and slit
  lengthwise
⅛ teaspoon turmeric
1 cup water
⅛ teaspoon tamarind
  concentrate soaked in
  1 tablespoon water
¼ teaspoon ground
  coriander
¼ teaspoon salt
Iceberg lettuce leaves,
  washed and crisped

Traditionally served as a side dish vegetable, this generous mix of vegetables intermingled with tamarind and seasonings makes a nutritious and easy spread. Crunchy breadsticks and toasted pumpernickel triangles make good scoopers.

1. Combine the peas, spinach, potato, carrot, ginger, chile, turmeric, and water in a medium saucepan. Bring to a boil. Reduce the heat, cover, and cook until the peas are soft, 20 to 25 minutes.

2. Stir in the tamarind, coriander, and salt. Cook 2 minutes longer and remove from the heat. Transfer to a food processor and process in pulses until semi-pureed. Let cool to room temperature, then mound onto a serving plate lined with lettuce leaves. Offer with crisp toasts or breadsticks.

Note: If not serving right away, spoon the spread into a crock, cover, and chill up to 4 days. Bring to room temperature before serving.

# GREEN TOMATO SPREAD WITH PEANUTS
## (Hara Tamatar Chatni)

**Makes 1¼ cups**
**Preparation time:**
**25 minutes**

From my childhood in India I remember the bountiful tomatoes in my mother's organic kitchen garden. She enjoyed taking a morning stroll in the garden and would pick a basketful of green tomatoes. Instead of ripening them she would prepare this delectable spread. All she did was to stir-fry tomatoes, garlic and chiles, toss in nuts and seasonings, and set aside. When our maid arrived she would grind it in a stone mortar. We would have the green toma-

1½ tablespoons mild
  vegetable oil
1 pound (4 medium)
  green tomatoes,
  coarsely chopped
2 to 4 cloves garlic, sliced
2 fresh hot green chiles,
  stemmed and chopped
¼ cup coarsely chopped
  cilantro with stems
⅓ cup roasted peanuts
1 teaspoon toasted
  ground cumin
1 tablespoon light brown
  sugar
½ teaspoon salt
Watercress sprigs, for
  garnish

to chutney waiting for us at the table to spread on toasts or chapat
emerald spread goes beautifully in sandwiches too.

1. Heat the oil in a wok or saucepan over medium heat. Add the tomatoes, garlic, and chiles. Stir and fry until the tomatoes are lightly browned, about 15
minutes.

2. Transfer the tomato mixture to a blender or food processor. Add the peanuts,
cumin, sugar, and salt and blend until smooth. Serve with an assortment of
crackers or warm toast rounds.

Note: The green tomato spread can be made ahead and kept, covered, in the
refrigerator for 1 month or frozen up to 6 months. Bring to room temperature
before serving.

# BAKED POPCORN CROQUETTES
## (Jhatpat Saandge)

Makes 12 croquettes
Preparation time:
  20 minutes, plus 10
  minutes soaking

2 cups popped corn
1 or 2 fresh hot green
  chiles, stemmed and
  minced
¼ cup packed finely
  chopped fresh cilantro
1 teaspoon cumin seeds
2 tablespoons rice flour
2 tablespoons finely
  chopped walnuts
½ teaspoon salt
2 large red cabbage
  leaves, washed and
  crisped
1 tablespoon lemon juice

Popcorn and spice contrast wonderfully in this hors d'oeuvre. Moist on the
inside and crisp on the outside, the healthful popcorn is formed into croquettes
and baked. Serve nestled elegantly in cabbage-leaf "bowls" with a splash of
lemon juice or any dipping sauce.

1. Soak the popcorn in water for 10 minutes. Drain, squeeze out all of the
water, and place the popcorn in a mixing bowl. Add the chiles, cilantro,
cumin, rice flour, walnuts, and salt and mix well.

2. Position a rack in the center of oven and preheat to 400°F. Make 1-inch balls
with the popcorn mixture and place on a nonstick cookie sheet. Bake until
lightly browned, about 15 minutes.

3. Lay the cabbage leaves cupped side up on a platter. Place the croquettes in
the leaves and sprinkle with lemon juice.

Note: The croquettes can be prepared 2 hours ahead. Cover loosely with foil
and store at room temperature. Rewarm in a 250°F oven for 12 minutes.

# TANDOORI CHEESE
## (Paneer Tikka Hariyali)

Serves 8 to 10
Preparation time:
   15 minutes, plus 1
   hour refrigerating
   time

1 pound (double recipe)
   paneer cheese (page
   165)
1 teaspoon ground cumin
1 teaspoon garam masala,
   homemade (page 21)
   or store-bought
2 teaspoons minced fresh
   ginger
½ teaspoon cayenne
1 teaspoon salt
¼ cup plain nonfat or
   low-fat yogurt
¼ cup half-and-half
1 tablespoon chick-pea
   flour
1 medium red onion,
   peeled and sliced
1 lemon, cut into wedges

Unlike some other cheeses, the homemade unripened cheese called paneer (page 165) has enough body to be roasted or grilled without disintegrating. The following recipe is a vegetarian version of the popular tandoori chicken. Large chunks of paneer are gently rubbed with aromatic spices and fresh ginger, then bathed in yogurt and cream to mellow the spices, and finally roasted to create a sublime taste. For a spectacular presentation, serve surrounded by onion rings, with a mist of lemon juice.

1. Cut the cheese into 1 x 1½ x 1-inch chunks; you should have about 16 pieces. Prick all sides gently with a fork. Combine the cumin, garam masala, ginger, cayenne, and salt in a small bowl and mix well. Rub the spice mixture onto the cheese. Cover and set aside for 10 minutes at room temperature.

2. In a 2½-quart bowl, combine the yogurt, half-and-half, and flour. Whisk until smooth. Add the cheese and turn to coat the pieces evenly. Cover and refrigerate for 1 hour, turning several times.

3. Place the cheese pieces ½ inch apart on a greased broiler pan. Place the pan 4 inches from the heat and broil, turning to heat all sides, until lightly browned all over. Alternatively, prepare a charcoal grill, and thread the cheese chunks on lightly greased skewers about ½ inch apart. Turning occasionally, cook until lightly browned.

4. Arrange on a heated platter and serve surrounded with sliced onions and lemon wedges.


# PANEER CHEESE WALNUT KABABS
## (Reshmi Kabab)

Serves 4 to 6
Preparation time:
   10 minutes

In this lighter version of grilled paneer cheese, a glaze of tomato and chile sauces seals in the moisture, making the cheese silky soft. Impress your special guests with these sophisticated kababs that are quick to fix, when you have a batch of paneer cheese in the refrigerator.

½ pound (1 recipe) paneer cheese (page 165), crumbled
⅓ cup finely chopped raw walnuts
1 teaspoon garam masala, homemade (page 21) or store-bought
2 tablespoons tomato ketchup
1 teaspoon hot chile sauce
2 tablespoons rice flour
½ teaspoon salt
Butter lettuce leaves, washed and crisped
2 small onions, preferably white, peeled and sliced
1 lemon, cut into wedges

1. Combine the first 7 ingredients in a medium mixing bowl. Mix well. With your fingers, shape the paneer mixture into long cylindrical logs around 3 thick skewers.

2. Prepare a medium fire in a charcoal grill, with the grill 2 inches above the heat. Grill the skewers, turning carefully until the cheese mixture is lightly browned in places, 3 to 4 minutes. Alternatively, cook the kababs under a broiler, with the pan 4 inches away from the heat; or grill directly over a gas flame on the stove top (see page 95).

3. Loosen the cheese mixture gently from the skewers and slide onto a plate. Cut into 1-inch pieces. Pierce each piece with toothpick if desired. To serve, arrange the lettuce leaves on a serving platter, spread the kababs on top, and surround with onion slices and wedges of lemon. Serve immediately.

# QUICK SPINACH BITES
## (Palak Pakora)

Makes 24 (6 to 8
  servings)
Preparation time:
  25 minutes

Leaves and tender stems
  from 1 pound fresh
  spinach, chopped (3
  cups, firmly packed)
½ cup finely chopped
  onion
2 fresh hot green chiles,
  stemmed and chopped
3 large cloves garlic,
  finely chopped
1½ teaspoons cumin
  seeds
1 teaspoon salt
3 slices bread, preferably
  soft white or wheat
3 tablespoons
  unbleached all-pur-
  pose flour
3 tablespoons chick-pea
  flour or corn flour
Mild vegetable or
  avocado oil for frying
1 recipe Tamarind-Apple
  Dipping Sauce (oppo-
  site)

I used to make spinach *pakoras* (fritters) with a binder of potatoes. But once when I did not have cooked potatoes ready, I tried substituting soaked bread, sprinkled with plenty of garlic and onion. The pakoras turned out to be delicious, and they have been one of my specialties ever since. When I presented them at the World Vegetarian Day celebration at Stanford University, they got rave reviews from the food professionals and visiting guests. Either plain or with a tart-sweet dipping sauce, they will make a splendid addition to your repertoire of appetizers. Use only fresh spinach leaves for a crisp texture.

1. Combine the spinach, onion, chiles, garlic, cumin, and salt in a large bowl. Set aside.

2. Place 2 cups of water in a container. Add the bread slices and let them soak for a minute. Remove one by one and squeeze dry as much liquid as possible by pressing between your hands. Add to the bowl, separating the bread if it is lumpy. Sprinkle in both the flours and mix well to form a firm (dough-like) mixture.

3. Fill a wok, fryer, or skillet with oil to a depth of 2 inches and heat to 365°F. Make 1-inch balls of the spinach mixture and fry a few at a time, without crowding, until golden brown on all sides, about 3 to 4 minutes. Adjust the heat as needed to maintain the oil temperature between 350° and 365°F. Drain on paper towels. Serve the spinach bites hot, with cocktail sticks for spearing and dipping in the sauce.

**Note:** The spinach bites can be made 2 hours ahead. Tent loosely with foil and set aside. Just before serving, warm in a 250°F oven for 10 to 12 minutes.

# TAMARIND-APPLE DIPPING SAUCE
## (Seb Aur Imli Chatni)

Makes ⅔ cup
Preparation time:
    20 minutes plus 1
    hour soaking time

½ cup lightly packed
    peeled and pitted
    tamarind pulp *or* 8
    whole tamarind pods
    (see Note)
1½ cups hot water
½-inch piece fresh
    ginger, crushed
½ teaspoon salt
½ teaspoon cayenne
1 small Gala or red apple
Fresh lemon leaves for
    garnish

I like to serve this light and nourishing tart-sweet dipping sauce with lentil wafers, pakoras, onion rings, and fried zucchini. Naturally sweet Gala apples provide just the right amount of sweetness to balance the tart and hot flavors without any additional sugar. If using other apple varieties, you may have to add sugar to achieve the same balance.

1. Place the tamarind in a small glass bowl (if using whole tamarind pods, crack open the shell-like skin first) and add the hot water. Set aside for 1 hour. With your fingers, rub the tamarind to separate the soft pulp from the skins, seeds, fibers, and any other roughage. Force the mixture through a large strainer, pressing to extract as much liquid as possible; discard what remains in the strainer.

2. Combine the tamarind pulp, ginger, salt, and cayenne in a small saucepan. Cover and simmer on medium heat for 8 to 10 minutes.

3. Discard the ginger and transfer the tamarind mixture to a blender or food processor. Core and cut the apple into large chunks and add to the blender. Cover and process until smooth, about 2½ to 3 minutes.

4. Transfer to a serving bowl and garnish with fresh lemon leaves. Arrange the sauce in the center of a serving platter and surround with asparagus spears, young sugar snap peas, or vegetable fritters.

**Microwave:** Place the step 2 ingredients into a microwavable bowl. Cook uncovered at full power for 5 minutes. Let stand, covered, for a few minutes, then continue with step 3.

**Note:** The sauce will keep in the refrigerator for 1 week, or in the freezer up to 3 months. Bring to room temperature before serving.

If whole tamarind pods are not available, use the peeled form sold in blocks in Indian, Middle Eastern, and Southeast Asian markets; soak and strain as directed in step 1. The tamarind concentrate sold in jars from India is convenient, but it will not give the right thickness in this recipe.

# GARBANZO BEAN SPIRAL CRUNCHIES
## (*Chakli*)

Makes 20 chaklis
Preparation time:
   30 minutes

1 cup cooked garbanzo
   beans, drained and
   rinsed thoroughly
½ teaspoon ground
   cumin
½ teaspoon ground
   coriander
¾ to 1 teaspoon cayenne
½ tablespoon sesame
   seeds
½ teaspoon carum seeds
1 teaspoon salt
2 tablespoons butter
   or margarine
2 cups rice flour
Scant ¾ cup water
Mild vegetable or
   avocado oil, for frying

In India this is a very popular snack like the pretzel is in America. Every time my sons visit India, they ask for and thoroughly enjoy them. They often pester me to make them. In the traditional way of making chakli, putting together the flour is itself a tedious process. Rice, chana, urad, and mung dals are washed, dried, roasted separately and then mixed. The mixture is then taken to the flour mill by the housemaid. For the pace of today's lifestyle, I have developed an easy method of making the snack with commercially available garbanzo beans. When I made them the first time, my little son asked, "Mom, did Grandma send these chaklis from India?" It was a sure winner.

1. Combine the garbanzo beans, cumin, coriander, cayenne, sesame seeds, carum seeds, and salt in a food processor and process until the beans are completely mashed, about 2 minutes. Cut the butter in chunks and add it to the processor; add 1 cup rice flour and process until the mixture is crumbly, 1 more minute. Add the remaining flour and ½ cup water. Process on low speed until the dough begins to pull from the sides of the bowl. Gradually add the remaining water in a thin stream while the machine is running. Process until the dough begins to clean the sides of the bowl.

2. Lightly coat your hands with oil, remove the dough from the processor, and knead briefly, about 2 minutes. (The dough should resemble cold mashed potato in texture.) Fill a wok or skillet with oil to a depth of about 3 inches and heat to 350°F. Put the dough in portions in a cookie press fitted with a star-shaped metal disk, or a pastry bag with a star tip. Press the dough out into the oil in a spiral shape about 2 inches in diameter. Make 3 to 4 at a time, adding dough to the cookie press as necessary. Do not crowd. Fry, turning once, until crisp and light golden, about 2 minutes per side. Remove with a slotted spoon and drain on paper towels or a brown paper bag. Repeat with the remaining dough. Serve at room temperature. Cool and store in an airtight container for up to 4 weeks.

**Note:** Alternately, you can purchase a wooden or brass chakli mold at an Indian market, which works more or less the same as a cookie press.

**Variation:** COCONUT-GARBANZO CRUNCHIES
Add ¼ cup grated fresh or unsweetened dry coconut to the food processor along with the garbanzos.

# DEEP-FRYING TIPS

Although I have adapted many traditional Indian fried dishes to other cooking methods, there are a few that simply need to be deep-fried. Eaten in moderation, they are a delicious addition to your diet. Here are some tips for frying foods with a minimum of trouble and a minimum of oil absorption.

❀ The deep, bowl-shaped Indian *kadai,* very similar in shape to a Chinese wok, is an ideal pan for deep-frying. Both pans provide a large frying area with a relatively small amount of oil. A deep skillet will work if you have neither, but it uses a lot more oil. Avoid using long-handled pans, which might tilt.

❀ For frying small batches, start with 1½ to 2 inches of oil; you can always add more later if required.

❀ The oil must be hot enough so that small pieces of food form a crust immediately and absorb less oil. An oil thermometer is best for watching the temperature. Lacking a thermometer, drop in a morsel of food to be fried; if the oil is at the right temperature, it will come to the surface immediately, bubbling and sizzling. If the food browns instantly, the oil is too hot. Regulate the heat accordingly.

❀ Place very small items like nuts, split peas, etc. in a fryer basket or in a large wire strainer preheated in the oil to prevent sticking. Fry in batches, and do not crowd.

❀ Drain fried foods in a single layer on a cookie sheet lined with brown paper bag and crumpled paper towels on top to remove excess oil.

❀ If you are making several batches, most fried foods can be kept warm in a 150°F oven up to half an hour. Of course, for the best flavor serve as soon as possible.

❀ I recommend using avocado oil for frying because it is monounsaturated and has a high smoking point of 520°F. Another of my favorites is canola oil, which has the least saturated fat of all vegetable oils and is well suited for Indian cooking. Peanut oil can also be used. The leftover oil can be reused by straining it through a fine strainer once it cools. Store used oil in a tightly sealed container.

# SOUPS

VEGETARIAN GUMBO WITH ROASTED KARI LEAVES

HEARTY VEGETABLE SOUP

AROMATIC LENTIL SOUP

YELLOW CHICK-PEA SOUP WITH DILL OIL SEASONING

FRAGRANT YELLOW LENTIL SOUP

VEGETABLE MULLIGATAWNY WITH PINK LENTILS

CLASSIC MIXED GREENS SOUP

SOOTHING SPICY TAMARIND AND YELLOW CHICK-PEA BROTH

ZIPPY CUCUMBER AND MINT SOUP

CREAMY CORN AND YELLOW MUNG BEAN SOUP

MELON-MANGO MIST

HOT YOGURT SOUP WITH ROASTED KARI LEAVES

Although Indian cookery offers a spectacular range of soups — hot or cold, sweet or sour, mild or fiery, light or hearty — soups do not have a special position in a meal; they can be used as starters, or as main and side dishes. It is this versatility of Indian soups that, I believe, makes them so attractive and adaptable to the Western kitchen.

The soups in this chapter represent four basic styles, typical of the four main geographic regions of India. The *shorbas* of the north are robust and chunky. With a main course that prominently features bulky flat breads, this style furnishes excellent balance. My Hearty Vegetable Soup features a melange of vegetables topped with angel hair pasta strands.

The *rasams* of the south, on the other hand, are pureed smooth soups made from dals and flavored with fiery spices that are native to the region. Legumes and vegetables combine with fragrant herbs, tamarind, and coconut milk to lend an extraordinary texture that provides the perfect counterpoint to the rice dishes that dominate southern Indian meals. Aromatic Lentil Soup and Vegetable Mulligatawny with Pink Lentils are two examples that make a delightful first course for entertaining.

The eastern *dalnas* are velvety and creamy soups of dal and leafy vegetables with lively seasonings. They are generously spooned over the main rice course. You must try the superb Creamy Corn and Yellow Mung Bean Soup for a novel family dinner.

The *saars* of western India are herbal and elegantly spiced broths or stocks, well balanced for a meal comprising both flatbreads and rice. On a cold windy evening, there is nothing quite like the comforting aroma of Hot Yogurt Broth ladled from a steaming pot.

None of the soups require time-consuming techniques. They can be made several days ahead and stored in the refrigerator, to be reheated just before serving. Further, not all soups have to be hot. As the mercury rises, you can rely on several cool classics for comfort. Smoothly pureed raw vegetables and fruits make refreshing low-calorie delights. Serve the Melon-Mango Mist after morning workouts, or Zippy Cucumber and Mint Soup with pilaf for a quick light lunch.

# Vegetarian Gumbo with Roasted Kari Leaves

## (Tamatar Shorba)

Serves 2 to 4
Preparation time:
   25 minutes

2 cups chopped peeled
   tomatoes (fresh or
   canned), with juices
1½ tablespoons light-
   tasting vegetable oil
¼ teaspoon mustard
   seeds
¼ teaspoon cumin seeds
2 tablespoons chick-pea
   flour
½ teaspoon ground
   coriander
½ cup green beans, cut
   into ½-inch lengths
½ cup carrots, cut in
   1-inch cubes
2 cups water
3 or 4 sprigs fresh kari
   leaves
¼ cup cooked rice
1 teaspoon salt
½ teaspoon sugar
Cherry tomatoes, for
   garnish

I loved to watch my mother roast kari leaves. She made it look so simple! Even before the soup came to a simmer, she would go in the kitchen garden, pluck 4 or 5 sprigs of kari leaves, wash and pat them dry. She would then roast the sprigs until almost charred and slip them in the soup. The ardent lemon vibrancy of kari gives the soup its distinct character.

When I first came to America almost a decade back, cilantro was rarely available, but today it is offered in almost every grocery store. I am hopeful that kari leaves also will find a niche in Western markets. Since the soup is so satisfying, pair it with Whole Wheat Flatbread (page 79) and serve plain basmati rice with Stewed Blackeyed Peas with Cherry Tomatoes (page 153) as the main course.

1. Puree the tomatoes in a blender and set aside.

2. Heat the oil in a medium saucepan over moderate heat. Add the mustard and cumin seeds. When the seeds begin to sizzle and splutter, stir in the chick-pea flour and coriander. Cook, stirring constantly, until the flour is lightly browned and aromatic, about 4 minutes. Add the vegetables; stir and cook 4 minutes longer. Gradually add the water and mix well.

3. Hold the sprigs of kari leaves 1 inch above an electric or gas burner set on medium heat. Constantly move the sprigs until the edges of the leaves are slightly charred, a matter of seconds. Slip the kari sprigs into the soup.

4. Stir in the pureed tomatoes, rice, salt, and sugar. Increase the heat and bring to a boil. Reduce the heat, cover, and simmer for 15 minutes. Give the soup a good stir, then spoon into soup bowls, discarding the kari stems and leaves. Garnish with the cherry tomatoes and okra croutons and serve hot.

**Note:** The gumbo can be made 4 days ahead and set aside in the refrigerator. Since the storage tones down the herbal fragrance, enliven the soup with fresh roasted kari sprigs just before serving. Reheat on moderate flame.

# HEARTY VEGETABLE SOUP
## (Sabji-Sevia Shorba)

Serves 4 to 6
Preparation time:
    35 minutes

1 tablespoon mild
    vegetable oil
3 large cloves garlic,
    sliced thinly
½ cup sliced onion
½ cup sliced carrot
1 small (2 ounces) turnip,
    diced
½ cup shredded green
    cabbage
½ cup diced celery
½ cup cauliflower, cut
    into 1-inch florets
½ cup peeled diced
    potato
¼ cup peas, fresh or
    thawed
5 cups water
1 cup chopped tomato
    (fresh or canned), with
    juices
1 teaspoon salt
Freshly ground black or
    white pepper to taste
2 teaspoons desi ghee or
    butter
2 ounces angel hair pasta,
    broken into pieces
⅓ cup grated Swiss
    cheese

This is one of my family's favorite cold-weather meals-in-a-bowl. If you dine out for two days in a row and have farm-fresh vegetables in the crisper section of your refrigerator, here is a nice way to make use of all of them. Delicate thin angel hair pasta strands stirred in just prior to serving look dainty against the chunky vegetables. Partner the soup with Peasant Cucumber Flatbread (page 81) and follow it with Jahangir Pilaf with Mung Beans (page 144) for a complete meal.

Browning uncooked vermicelli in ghee before adding water is a typical Indian technique that makes the dish very flavorful and aromatic. The same technique is also used to make a delicious sweet pudding; the pasta is first browned in ghee and then simmered with milk and sugar. Use the thinnest vermicelli you can find, or the even thinner angel hair pasta.

1. Heat the oil in a soup kettle over medium-high heat. Saute the garlic and onion until light brown, about 4 minutes. Add the vegetables except the tomato and 4 cups water. Bring to a boil, reduce the heat, cover, and simmer until the vegetables are just tender, about 10 minutes.

2. With a slotted spoon, remove 2 cups of vegetables and reserve. Add the tomato to the soup, cover, and cook another 10 to 12 minutes. Pass the soup through a strainer, pressing on the solids to extract as much puree as possible. Season with salt and pepper and set aside.

3. Melt the desi ghee in a small skillet over medium heat. Lightly brown the pasta, add 1 cup water, and cook until al dente, 6 to 8 minutes. Drain and set aside.

4. To serve, ladle the soup into soup bowls. Spoon ¼ cup of the reserved cooked vegetables and 2 to 3 tablespoons of pasta in each soup bowl. Garnish with Swiss cheese and serve piping hot.

**Note:** The soup puree can be made 2 days ahead and kept, covered, in the refrigerator. Reheat the soup and reserved vegetables on a medium flame, and cook the angel hair just before serving.

# AROMATIC LENTIL SOUP
## (Rasam)

Serves 4
Preparation time:
   40 minutes

4 medium tomatoes
   (1 pound)
3 cups water
1 cup cooked yellow split
   peas or yellow lentils
   (toovar dal)
¾ cup grated onion
2 teaspoons crushed
   garlic
1½ tablespoons sambar
   powder, homemade
   (page 24) or bought
½ teaspoon cinnamon
5 whole cloves, ground
½ teaspoon freshly
   ground black pepper
¼ teaspoon cayenne
1½ teaspoons salt
Chopped fresh cilantro
   or parsley
Desi ghee or unsalted
   butter

A smooth, gratifying soup. If you already have cooked yellow split peas or lentils in the refrigerator, this dish will take only minutes to assemble. Grated onion, crushed garlic, and spices are tied together into an herb-spice bundle and simmered with tomato-lentil puree to allow only a hint of their flavors. In southern India, rasam traditionally accompanies a rice dish such as Quick Savory Rice with Peas and Peanuts (page 135). Since the soup is light, I also love to pair it with buttered Mung Bean-Spinach Wholesome Flatbread (page 83), a salad, and a rice dish.

1. Blanch the tomatoes in boiling water for 2 minutes, then plunge in cold water. Peel and chop. Combine with 1½ cups of the water in a medium saucepan and cook on medium-high heat for 10 minutes. Transfer to a blender container and process until pureed. Whisk the peas or lentils until smooth and add to the tomato puree.

2. Combine the onion, garlic, sambar powder, cinnamon, cloves, black pepper and cayenne in a small bowl. Mix well. Wrap these seasonings in a small piece of cheesecloth and tie into a secure bundle. Return the tomato puree to the saucepan, add the spice bundle and the remaining 1½ cups water, and simmer 20 minutes on medium heat. Discard the spice bundle. Just before serving, season the soup to taste with salt. To serve, spoon into individual soup bowls, garnish with cilantro, and pass melted desi ghee at the table.

**Microwave:** Combine the blanched, chopped tomatoes with water in a 2½-quart microwaveable dish. Cook at full power for 10 minutes. Puree the mixture and whisk in the peas. Add the spice bundle and cook at full power for 15 minutes longer. Serve as suggested above.

**Note:** The soup can be made 5 days ahead and kept covered in the refrigerator. Reheat on a moderate flame.

**Variation:** For an exotic taste, accent the soup with the typical Indian oil seasoning. Heat 1½ tablespoons desi ghee or oil in a small skillet over medium heat. Add ½ teaspoon mustard seeds, a pinch of asafetida, and 10 to 12 fresh kari leaves. When the seeds begin to sizzle and splutter, remove the pan from the heat and pour the oil over the rasam.

# YELLOW CHICK-PEA SOUP WITH DILL OIL SEASONING
## (Kadale Bele Rasam)

Servings: 6 to 8
Preparation time:
    25 minutes

½ cup cooked yellow
    chick peas (chana dal)
    or yellow split peas
2 cups peeled and
    chopped tomatoes
    (fresh or canned), with
    juices
½ teaspoon tamarind
    concentrate dissolved
    in 1 tablespoon water
2 cups water
1½ teaspoons light
    brown sugar
⅓ teaspoon cayenne
    pepper
1 teaspoon salt
½ tablespoon desi ghee
    or unsalted butter
½ tablespoon light-
    tasting vegetable oil
½ teaspoon mustard
    seeds
2 tablespoons chopped
    fresh dill or cilantro

A swirl of dill-infused oil mingles with mellow flavor in this sweetish-sour, soul-soothing soup. Creamy pureed chana dal lends rich body and a unique taste. You can also make this soup with split peas, in which case the taste will differ. Accompany with Yogurt Balloon Bread (page 90), Sweet Onion Salad in Tomato Baskets (page 182), and a rice dish such as Lemon-Sesame Rice Crowned with Vegetables (page 136).

1. Combine the chana dal, tomatoes, and tamarind in a blender and process until finely pureed. Transfer the mixture to a soup kettle and stir in the water, sugar, cayenne, and salt. Bring to a boil, reduce the heat, cover, and simmer until the tomato loses its raw aroma, about 18 to 20 minutes.

2. Meanwhile, heat the desi ghee and oil in a small skillet over medium heat. Add the mustard seeds. When the seeds begin to sizzle and splutter, add the fresh dill. Cook, stirring constantly, until the dill exudes its herbal aroma, about 2 minutes. Set aside.

3. Spoon the soup into a large tureen. Pour the dill oil seasoning on the soup, using a rubber spatula to scrape it all out of the skillet. Just before serving, stir once or twice to form swirls from the oil.

Note: The soup will keep up to 7 days in the refrigerator. Make the dill oil seasoning while the soup reheats.

# FRAGRANT YELLOW LENTIL SOUP
## (Tadka Dal)

Serves 4
Preparation time:
    20 minutes

1 tablespoon desi ghee
    or mild peanut oil
½ teaspoon mustard
    seeds
¼ teaspoon cumin seeds
1 fresh hot green chile,
    stemmed and slit
    lengthwise
⅛ teaspoon turmeric
1½ cups cooked yellow
    split peas or yellow
    lentils (toovar dal),
    whisked
1 cup water
¾ teaspoon salt
1 tablespoon lemon juice
Chopped fresh cilantro

My husband enjoys all the wonderful cuisines of the world but finds the dal-and-chapati combination of India to be the most comforting. The "secret" to this dish is the fundamental Indian technique of flavoring the oil with mustard and cumin seeds. Take care when frying the seeds; they need to sizzle and splutter to exude their nutty aroma, but if they are allowed to burn they will spoil the flavor.

The soup partners well with all the flatbreads. Follow it with Warm Cabbage Salad with Cracked Pepper (page 178) and Malabar Coconut Rice (page 138) for a substantial meal. Or simply spoon the soup over plain basmati rice for a quick light lunch.

1. Heat the desi ghee in a medium saucepan over moderate heat. Add the mustard and cumin seeds. When the seeds begin to sizzle and splutter and turn light brown, add the chile and turmeric. Stir and cook for 2 minutes.

2. Add the lentil puree and water. Bring to a boil, reduce the heat, cover, and simmer until thick, about 15 minutes. Just before serving, season to taste with salt. Add the lemon juice, give the soup a good stir, then ladle into bowls. Garnish with cilantro and serve.

**Note:** The dal soup can be made 4 days ahead and kept, covered, in the refrigerator. Reheat on moderate flame.

**Variation:** In step 1, add 2 large cloves garlic, crushed, or ⅓ cup chopped onion (or both) to the oil along with the chile and turmeric.

# VEGETABLE MULLIGATAWNY WITH PINK LENTILS
## (Milaguthunny)

Serves 4 to 6
Preparation time:
    40 minutes

1½ tablespoons light-
    tasting vegetable oil
3 cloves garlic, crushed
1-inch piece fresh ginger,
    crushed
½ cup finely chopped
    onion
1 cup chopped tomatoes
1 cup sliced fennel bulb
1 cup chopped green
    peppers
½ cup thinly sliced
    carrots
1 rib celery, sliced
½ cup dried pink
    lentils, picked clean
2-inch stick cinnamon,
    broken
1 teaspoon ground
    coriander
½ teaspoon ground
    cumin
⅓ teaspoon ground
    fennel
¼ teaspoon ground
    fenugreek
8 to 10 whole black
    peppercorns
2 tablespoons chick-
    pea flour
4 cups water
1 teaspoon salt
1½ teaspoons sugar
1 tablespoon fresh lemon
    juice
¼ cup whipping cream
    or coconut milk
Freshly cooked basmati rice
Fresh mint sprigs

The popular mulligatawny soup was derived by the British from a fiery lentil consomme or literally "pepper water" (from the Tamil *milagu,* pepper, and *thunny,* water). I have made this classic with favorite soup spices and a home-style combination of pink lentils and plentiful vegetables. Fresh mint sprigs stirred in minutes before serving lend an appealing aroma and color to the soup. For a classic soup and bread supper, pair it with Whole Wheat Puffy Bread (page 87).

1. Heat the oil in a soup kettle over medium-high heat. Add the garlic, ginger, and onion and cook until the onion is soft, about 3 minutes. Stir in the vegetables, lentils, spices, and flour.

2. Gradually add the water and mix well. Increase the heat and bring to a boil. Reduce the heat, cover, and simmer until the lentils are fully cooked but still hold their shape, 18 to 20 minutes. Uncover, and using a slotted spoon, remove 1 cup of the vegetables and lentils, and set aside. Pass the remaining soup through a strainer, pressing on the solids to extract as much puree as possible.

3. Add the salt, sugar, and lemon juice to the puree. Stir in the cream and cook on gentle heat until piping hot. Ladle into bowls and top each serving with basmati rice and the reserved vegetables and lentils. Garnish with mint sprigs and serve hot.

Note: The soup puree (steps 1 and 2) can be made 4 days ahead and refrigerated; wait until reheating time to add the seasonings, cream, and reserved vegetables.

# CLASSIC MIXED GREENS SOUP
## (Saag)

Serves 4
Preparation time:
    30 minutes

½ cup lightly packed
    chopped mustard
    greens
½ cup lightly packed
    kale
1 cup lightly packed
    chopped Swiss chard
2 cups lightly packed
    chopped spinach
1 fresh hot green chile,
    stemmed and chopped
4 cups water
3 tablespoons desi ghee
    or unsalted butter or
    mild olive oil
2 tablespoons whole
    wheat or rice flour
½ teaspoon salt
½ teaspoon freshly
    ground white pepper
Zesty Croutons or Garlic
    Croutons

The state of Bengal produces nearly half India's mustard crop, and mustard greens, oil, and seeds are used in many preparations. In the north and east of India, the greens are often used in the form of *saag,* a vegetable side dish. I have taken advantage of the bountiful variety of greens available in California to create this light soup version. To add crunch to the velvety texture, pass Zesty Croutons (below) at the table or float them in the soup. For a dieter's lunch, accompany with Light Yogurt Rice (page 133) and a dessert of Creamy Saffron Yogurt with Almonds (page 215).

1. Combine the greens, chile, and water in a large heavy pot. Bring to a boil, reduce the heat, cover, and simmer until the greens are tender, about 20 minutes. Remove from the heat and puree in a food processor or blender.

2. Heat the desi ghee in a medium saucepan over moderate heat. Add the flour and cook, stirring, until lightly browned, 5 to 6 minutes. Return the pureed mixture to the pan and cook until piping hot. Just before serving, season with salt and pepper. To serve, ladle into shallow soup bowls and offer with croutons.

### Zesty Croutons
    1 tablespoon mild olive or peanut oil
    1½ tablespoons salted or unsalted butter, melted
    6 slices French baguette
    ½ teaspoon ground cumin
    ¼ teaspoon cayenne
    ¼ teaspoon ground fennel

Place a rack in the center of the oven and preheat to 350°F. Combine the oil and butter. Lightly brush one side of each bread slice with the mixture. Combine the spices in a small bowl and sprinkle over the top. Place on a cookie sheet and bake until golden and crisp, 5 to 7 minutes. Serve hot.

### Garlic Croutons
Omit the spices in the Zesty Croutons and combine 2 minced or pressed cloves of garlic with the oil and butter. Brush and bake as above.

# Soothing Spicy Tamarind and Yellow Chick-Pea Broth
## (Kataachi Aamti)

Serves 4 to 6
Preparation time:
   40 minutes

1 tablespoon light-tasting
   vegetable oil
¼ cup coarsely chopped
   onion
2 large cloves garlic,
   crushed
1 bay leaf
4 whole cloves
Seeds from 2 cardamom
   pods
1 inch cinnamon stick
½ teaspoon cumin seeds
1½ teaspoons coriander
   seeds
1 tablespoon grated fresh
   or sweetened dry
   coconut
2¼ cups water
½ cup cooked yellow
   chick-peas (chana dal)
   or yellow split peas,
   whisked into a
   smooth puree
½ teaspoon tamarind
   concentrate, dissolved
   in 1 tablespoon water
¼ teaspoon cayenne
   pepper
½ tablespoon light
   brown sugar
1¼ teaspoons salt
Desi ghee or unsalted
   butter
Chopped fresh cilantro

This old-fashioned broth, made with a pinch of this and that from the spice rack, adds sizzle and will delight the palate. The broth is very popular in the southwestern region of India, and varies from household to household. It is usually prepared for special occasions where its spicy flavor counterbalances the sweetmeats. Split peas make a good substitute, but I suggest that you explore the soothing flavors of the broth with chana dal. Pair it with Tomato-Spinach Flatbread (page 81), a cool yogurt raita and any side-dish vegetable. Or simply serve topped with plain hot basmati rice.

1. Heat the oil in a medium saucepan over moderate heat. Add the onion and garlic and cook until the onion is soft, about 6 minutes. Add the whole spices and coconut. Cook, stirring, until the spices are aromatic and the coconut starts to brown, about 6 minutes.

2. Transfer the mixture to a blender container. Add ¼ cup water and blend until smooth. Return the puree to the saucepan and stir in the cooked chana dal, remaining water, tamarind, cayenne, sugar, and salt. Bring to a boil, cover, and simmer, stirring occasionally, until piping hot and slightly thick, 20 to 25 minutes.

3. Uncover, give the soup a good stir, and serve in cups. Garnish each serving with a trickle of desi ghee and a sprinkle of cilantro.

Note: The *aamti* can be made 10 days ahead and kept, covered, in the refrigerator. Reheat on moderate flame.

Variation: For an optional oil seasoning, heat 1 tablespoon oil, ⅓ teaspoon mustard seeds, a pinch each of turmeric and asafetida, and 2 dried chiles until the mustard seeds sizzle and splutter. Pour over the broth before serving.

# ZIPPY CUCUMBER AND MINT SOUP
## (Pudina Shorba)

Serves 2 to 4
Preparation time:
   30 minutes

1 tablespoon light sesame
   or light-tasting veg-
   etable oil
½ cup chopped onion
½ teaspoon grated fresh
   ginger
1 small (½ pound)
   cucumber, peeled and
   diced
1 small potato, peeled
   and diced
2 cups water
¼ cup chopped fresh
   mint *or* 2 tablespoons
   dried mint
¼ cup plain nonfat or
   low-fat yogurt or half-
   and-half
1 fresh hot green chile,
   minced (optional)
¼ teaspoon salt
¼ teaspoon ground
   toasted fennel
Garlic Croutons
   (page 51)

On a summer day, sipping a cool soup from a mug is pure pleasure. Make the soup ahead of time, chill it completely, then pack it in a cooler for picnics.

1. Heat the oil in a medium saucepan over medium-high heat. Add the onion and ginger and cook until the onion is soft, about 3 minutes. Add the cucumber and potato and cook, stirring, another 3 to 4 minutes.

2. Add the water and bring to a boil. Cover and simmer until the potato is tender, about 20 minutes. Remove from the heat and transfer to a food processor. Add the mint and process until smooth.

3. Turn into a serving bowl, and whisk in the yogurt. Add the chile, if desired. Cover and chill for 2 to 3 hours. Just before serving, season to taste with salt and fennel. Top with croutons and serve.

# CREAMY CORN AND YELLOW MUNG BEAN SOUP
## (Makkai-Mung Dal Dalna)

Serves 6 to 8
Preparation time:
    25 minutes

½ cup dried yellow mung
    beans (mung dal)
1 cup fresh corn kernels
    (from 3 medium ears)
    *or* 1 cup frozen cut
    corn, thawed
4 cups water
2 tablespoons desi ghee
    or unsalted butter
½ cup finely chopped onion
1½ teaspoons ground
    fennel
1 teaspoon salt
¼ teaspoon freshly
ground white pepper
1½ tablespoons lemon
    juice
Watercress sprigs, for
    garnish
Sour cream

Fabulous flavors from the creamy corn and yellow mung bean give richness, and caramelized onion lends sweetness and visual appeal. Sour cream swirled into the soup makes for a pretty presentation. For a charming soup and bread dinner, serve with Indore Spinach Puffy Bread (page 89), a sweet chutney, and any of the cool yogurt raitas.

1. Sort the mung beans to remove any debris and rinse thoroughly in water. Place the beans, corn, and 2 cups water in a medium saucepan. Bring to a boil. Reduce heat to medium, cover and cook until the mung beans are fully cooked, about 15 minutes.

2. Meanwhile, heat the desi ghee or butter in a small skillet on medium heat. Fry the onion until lightly browned, 12 to 15 minutes. Add the fennel, stir, and cook for 1 minute. Pour over the corn-bean mixture. Add the remaining 2 cups water and the salt. Cover and cook on medium heat until piping hot. Just before serving, season to taste with salt, pepper, and lemon juice. Ladle into deep soup plates, garnish with watercress, and serve with a swirl of sour cream.

**Note:** The corn soup can be made 2 days ahead and kept, covered, in the refrigerator. Reheat on moderate flame.

# MELON-MANGO MIST
## (Aam Ras)

Serves 6 to 8
Preparation time:
    5 minutes, plus
    chilling time

4 cups chopped honey-
    dew melon
2 cups canned mango
    pulp *or* 3 cups
    chopped ripe mango
¼ cup lime juice
3 tablespoons sugar
½ cup water
Freshly grated nutmeg

Deliciously light, this fruity soup may be served chilled or at room temperature. It is an ideal companion for savory brunch dishes such as Cream of Wheat with Veggies and Nuts (page 58), spongy cakes, or crepes. Use your choice of fresh mangoes or the excellent canned Alphonso variety (see page 238).

1. Combine the melon, mango, lime juice, sugar, and water in a blender or food processor. Process until smoothly pureed. For the best flavor, cover and chill 4 hours to overnight. Serve in goblets, with a pinch of nutmeg on each serving.

# HOT YOGURT SOUP WITH ROASTED KARI LEAVES
## (*Kadhi*)

Serves 4 to 6
Preparation time:
    20 minutes

2 tablespoons chick-pea
    flour
1 cup water
2 cups plain nonfat or
    low-fat yogurt, stirred
    to blend
¼ teaspoon ground
    cumin
¾ teaspoon salt
1 teaspoon sugar
½-inch piece fresh
    ginger, minced
2 cloves garlic, minced
1 fresh hot green chile,
    minced
2 teaspoons minced fresh
    cilantro
2 or 3 sprigs fresh kari
    leaves

This soothing soup is popular throughout India, with every region and every family adding its own distinctive touches. Yogurt or buttermilk (usually homemade, obtained from the butter-making process) is thickened slightly with chick-pea flour and cooked gently to a smooth and silky texture, like a cream soup but without the cream. After trying it you may be inspired to create your own variations by floating dumplings, koftas, sauteed greens, okra croutons, or cooked green papaya in the soup. Use homemade or store-bought yogurt, or use all buttermilk to replace both water and yogurt. Pair this low-calorie soup with Onion-Sesame Puffy Bread (page 91); follow it with Fragrant Baby Dill with Garlic and Mung Beans (page 152), Hyderabad Stuffed Zucchini (page 107), and Fresh Cilantro Pilaf (page 134) for a complete meal.

1. Combine the chick-pea flour and ½ cup of the water in a medium nonstick saucepan. Blend well with the back of a spoon. Add the remaining water and yogurt and whisk until smooth. Stir in the remaining ingredients except the kari leaves.

2. Hold the kari leaf sprigs 1 inch above an electric or gas burner set on medium heat. Constantly move the sprigs until the edges of the leaves are slightly charred (this takes only a few seconds). Slip into the yogurt mixture.

3. Bring the kadhi to a boil on medium-high heat, stirring constantly. Reduce the heat to low, cover, and simmer gently for 12 minutes.

**Note:** Kadhi can be made 6 days ahead and kept, covered, in the refrigerator. Since storage tones down the herbal aroma, just before serving enliven the broth with fresh roasted kari sprigs. Reheat on moderate flame.

**Variation:** For an added zesty flavor, make seasoned oil by heating 1 tablespoon oil or desi ghee with ⅓ teaspoon cumin seeds, 2 dried red chiles, and a pinch of asafetida. Pour on the kadhi before serving.

# BREAKFAST AND BRUNCH

CREAM OF WHEAT WITH VEGGIES AND NUTS

WARM CREAM OF WHEAT PILAF

BRAISED BREAD MORNING SPECIAL

SAVORY BREAKFAST BEATEN RICE WITH POTATOES

PEARL TAPIOCA PILAF

MADRAS SPONGY CAKES (IDLIS)

SPONGY CAKE CASSEROLE DRENCHED IN CREAM SAUCE

CREAM OF WHEAT CAKES WITH PETITE PEAS

BANGALORE SPONGY CAKE PLATTER

KANCHEEPUR CREAM OF RICE CAKES

SPONGY CAKE PIZZA, INDIAN STYLE

PAPER-THIN RICE CREPES UDUPI STYLE (DOSAS)

BANGALORE PANCAKES WITH GREEN PEPPER AND CABBAGE

MYSORE LACE CREPES WITH CRACKED PEPPER

In India, many of the recipes in this chapter are served as breakfast dishes, or for the light mid-morning or midafternoon meals called "tiffin." In a less traditional role, I find they make good entrees for a light lunch, supper, or potluck, and have brought favorable comments from my American friends. Of course, I can also recommend them as a change of pace from your usual breakfast.

For many Europeans, breakfast is a quick meal of porridge, toast, or rolls and coffee. To set the pace for the day, Americans typically turn to sweet flavors (packaged cereals, milk, juice, toast, pancakes or waffles with maple syrup) or high-protein, high-fat foods like bacon and eggs. Most Indians prefer to awaken the appetite with a combination of sweet and savory flavors. In the north, the choice might be a sweet or spicy cracked wheat porridge and rich flatbread (paratha). Southern breakfasts are more typically based on grain dishes, such as the savory cream of wheat known as *uppama* or the delicate, lacy rice crepes *(dosas).* Most of these are relatively bland by themselves, but they are enlivened with spices and chiles. Nuts and vegetables add nutritional value as well as flavor.

All the breakfast dishes selected here cook in fifteen minutes or less, although they may require soaking ingredients or mixing and resting batters overnight. The long list of ingredients should not discourage you; they are simply added one after another to a simple basic preparation. Only one of the ingredients, beaten rice *(poha,* page 61) is at all exotic, and it can be found in local Indian markets or from the mail-order sources listed at the back.

Also in this chapter are several dishes I call "light entrees." Most of them are made from rice or other grains, typically in combination with white gram beans *(urad dal).* Like the breakfast dishes, they are combined with vegetables and spices to create an array of classic flavors — sweet, bitter, salty, sour, pungent, and astringent. A few of these, like crisp rice crepes *(dosas)* and spongy steamed cakes *(idlis),* are familiar to many Westerners through Indian restaurant menus. But you may be surprised how easy the preparations are and what a wide variety of dishes can be made from the same basic ingredients. The only time-consuming parts of the recipes are the soaking, grinding, and resting periods, and in many cases I have reduced these steps by the use of quick-cooking ingredients like cream of rice cereal, instant rice, or cream of wheat.

# CREAM OF WHEAT WITH VEGGIES AND NUTS
## (*Uppama*)

Serves 4 to 6
Preparation time:
   15 minutes

3 tablespoons mild
   vegetable or peanut oil
1 cup quick-cooking
   cream of wheat or
   semolina
¼ teaspoon mustard
   seeds
¼ teaspoon cumin seeds
½ cup chopped onion
1 teaspoon grated fresh
   ginger
1 fresh hot green chile,
   stemmed and chopped
¼ cup carrot cut into
   ½-inch sticks
1 tablespoon roasted
   peanuts, salted or
   unsalted
1 tablespoon fresh or
   thawed petite peas
2¼ cups water
1 teaspoon salt
1 teaspoon sugar
1 tablespoon fresh lime
   or lemon juice
Grated fresh coconut
Fresh chopped cilantro
Melted desi ghee
   (optional)

One of the best-known south Indian specialties, *uppama* is a savory breakfast dish somewhere between couscous and polenta. Here pre-toasted (quick-cooking) cream of wheat is slowly steamed in water and allowed to swell to plump tenderness with home-style seasonings. Cream of wheat and peanuts not only make a flavorful alliance, but also form a light balanced meal complete with proteins that rival those from animal sources.

1. Heat 1 tablespoon of the oil in a large skillet or wok over medium heat. Add the cream of wheat and cook, stirring constantly, until fragrant but not browned, about 5 minutes. Transfer to a plate and set aside.

2. Add the remaining oil to the same skillet and increase the heat to medium-high. Add the mustard and cumin seeds. When the seeds begin to sizzle and splutter, add the onion, ginger, and chile. Cook until the onion is soft but not brown, 2 to 3 minutes. Add the carrots, peanuts, and fresh peas (if using frozen peas, reserve them until step 3). Stir and cook 3 to 4 minutes.

3. Add the water and bring to a boil. Cover and cook until the carrots are tender, about 2 minutes. Meanwhile, combine the cream of wheat, salt, and sugar and mix well. Set the heat on medium-high, uncover the skillet, and add the cream of wheat mixture in a thin stream, stirring constantly until all the water is absorbed. Reduce the heat to low. Sprinkle in the lime juice, add the peas now if using frozen, and mix gently. Cover and cook until heated through.

4. Turn off the heat and let the uppama rest, covered, until all the excess moisture is absorbed and the grains are plump, about 5 minutes. Just before serving, fluff gently, garnish with a sprinkling of coconut and cilantro. Serve on warmed plates. For a richer taste, drizzle with melted ghee.

**Note:** The uppama can be prepared 5 hours ahead and set aside at room temperature, or may be refrigerated up to 4 days. Reheat on moderate heat or in the microwave oven.

**Variation:** For a lovely presentation, pack the uppama in a decorative mold (or individual servings in custard cups) and invert onto a serving plate. Garnish with coconut and serve hot. My sister-in-law Anjali Hiremath adds turmeric along with the onions for additional flavor and a warm yellow color.

# WARM CREAM OF WHEAT PILAF
## (Garam Rava Biryani)

Serves 4 to 6
Preparation time:
    15 minutes

3 tablespoons mild olive
    or peanut oil
1 cup quick-cooking
    cream of wheat or
    semolina
5 whole cloves
1-inch stick cinnamon
1 bay leaf
½ teaspoon cumin seeds
1 fresh hot green chile,
    stemmed and chopped
½ cup chopped tomato
2¼ cups water
1 teaspoon salt
½ teaspoon sugar
½ tablespoon lime juice
1 tablespoon chopped
    cashews
Chopped fresh dill or
    cilantro

This dish is similar to the preceding, but with a different assortment of "warm" spices and tomato. The whole spices are not meant to be eaten; remove them just before serving. Serve warm or at room temperature for an afternoon snack or feature it at a buffet party.

1. Heat 1 tablespoon of the oil in a heavy large skillet or wok over medium heat. Add the cream of wheat and cook, stirring constantly, until fragrant but not browned, about 5 minutes. Transfer to a plate and set aside.

2. Add the remaining oil to the same skillet and increase the heat to medium-high. Add the spices and chile. Stir and cook until aromatic and the spices darken one or two shades, 1 to 2 minutes. Add the tomato and cook until barely soft, 3 to 4 minutes.

3. Add the water and bring to a boil. Meanwhile, combine the cream of wheat, salt, and sugar and mix well. Set the heat on medium-high. Gradually add the cream of wheat mixture in a thin stream, stirring constantly until all the water is absorbed. Turn the heat to low. Sprinkle the lime juice and cashews. Mix gently. Cover and cook until heated through.

4. Turn off the heat and let the pilaf rest covered for 5 minutes, or until the excess moisture is absorbed and the grains are plump. Just before serving, fluff gently and transfer to a serving dish. Serve with a sprinkling of fresh herbs.

**Note:** The pilaf can be prepared 5 hours ahead and set aside at room temperature or may be refrigerated up to 4 days. Reheat on moderate heat or in the microwave oven.

**Variation:** In place of the whole spices, use ½ teaspoon garam masala (page 21).

# BRAISED BREAD MORNING SPECIAL
## (Bread Uppama)

Serves 2 to 4
Preparation time:
    15 minutes

3 tablespoons mild
    vegetable oil
⅓ teaspoon mustard
    seeds
¼ teaspoon cumin seeds
½ cup finely chopped
    onion
2 fresh hot green chiles,
    stemmed and chopped
¼ teaspoon turmeric
1 tablespoon roasted
    peanuts, salted or
    unsalted
¾ cup chopped, peeled
    tomato
8 bread slices, preferably
    white bread, cut into
    ½-inch cubes
1 teaspoon salt
½ teaspoon sugar
½ tablespoon fresh lime
    or lemon juice
1 tablespoon fresh
    chopped cilantro or
    parsley
2 tablespoons grated
    fresh or sweetened dry
    coconut

Simple yet elegant, this dish is perfect for breakfast or brunch with sliced strawberries or peaches. Almost any variety of bread—white, wheat, or French—will work well. If you find the dish dry, sprinkle in some water toward the end of cooking.

1. Heat the oil in a large skillet over medium-high heat. Add the mustard and cumin seeds. When the seeds begin to sizzle and splutter, add the onion, chiles, and turmeric. Cook until the onion is soft, 2 to 3 minutes. Toss in the peanuts and tomato and cook, stirring, until the tomato is soft, about 4 minutes.

2. Add the bread cubes to the skillet and sprinkle with salt and sugar. Reduce the heat to low and mix thoroughly. Cover and cook until heated through. Add the lime juice and cilantro and mix well. Garnish each serving with coconut and serve immediately.

# SAVORY BREAKFAST BEATEN RICE WITH POTATOES

## *(Pohe)*

Serves 6 to 8
Preparation time:
    15 minutes

2 cups beaten rice
    (thick-type poha)
3½ tablespoons mild
    corn or vegetable oil
½ teaspoon mustard
    seeds
¼ teaspoon cumin seeds
1 small onion, finely
    chopped
2 or 3 fresh hot green
    chiles, stemmed and
    chopped
Scant ¼ teaspoon
    turmeric
1 small potato, boiled,
    peeled, and cut into ¼-
    inch dice
1½ tablespoons roasted
    peanuts, salted or
    unsalted
1 teaspoon grated fresh
    ginger
1 small tomato, finely
    chopped
2 tablespoons fresh or
    thawed peas
½ teaspoon sugar
1 teaspoon salt
1 tablespoon fresh lime
    or lemon juice
Chopped fresh cilantro
Grated fresh or sweet-
    ened dry coconut

This is an old-fashioned savory breakfast dish from southwestern India. The secret here is entirely in the preparation of the basic ingredient, the beaten rice. Known as *poha,* it consists of flat, creamy-gray flakes of rice, sold in Indian markets. Note that Indian markets sell two varieties, thick and thin; select the thick type for this recipe because it holds its shape during rinsing (the thin type disintegrates and gets mushy). Timing is critical, so be sure to have all the ingredients ready and follow the recipe sequence exactly.

Peeled raw or cooked potato can be added. If you plan to double or triple the recipe for potluck or tailgate picnics, sprinkle in a little water toward the end of cooking. This will keep the dish soft for a longer period of time.

1. Sort through the poha grains and remove any foreign matter. Place it in a colander, but don't wash it yet (see step 3).

2. Heat the oil in a large, heavy nonstick skillet over medium-high heat. Add the mustard and cumin seeds. When the seeds begin to sizzle and splutter, add the onion, chiles, turmeric, potato, nuts, and ginger. Cook, stirring occasionally, until the onion is soft, about 3 minutes.

3. While the onion cooks, wash the beaten rice in the colander under cold running water, swishing it to make sure every grain is soaked. Set aside to drain. Test a grain by pressing it between your fingers; it should be firm but not hard, like *al dente* pasta (if it is still hard, let stand a few minutes longer and test again). Fluff gently with your fingers to separate the grains.

4. Add the tomato and peas to the skillet and cook 2 minutes longer. Sprinkle the beaten rice with salt, sugar, and lime juice and mix well with your fingers. Add to the skillet. Reduce the heat to low and mix thoroughly. Cover and cook until the grains are heated through, about 5 minutes. Serve hot, warm, or at room temperature; garnish with a sprinkling of cilantro and coconut.

**Note:** The pohe can be prepared 3 hours ahead and set aside at room temperature. Reheat on medium heat, stirring occasionally. Do not use the microwave oven because the grains will get hard.

**Variation:** Bulgur wheat or couscous can be used in place of poha; cook according to package directions.

# PEARL TAPIOCA PILAF
## *(Saboodana Khichdi)*

Serves 6
Preparation time:
   15 minutes, plus 4
   hours soaking

1½ cups medium pearl
   tapioca, cleaned
2 tablespoons mild
   vegetable oil
2 tablespoons desi ghee
   or unsalted butter
½ teaspoon mustard
   seeds
½ teaspoon cumin seeds
1 large potato, boiled,
   peeled, and diced
2 fresh hot green chiles,
   stemmed and chopped
½ cup finely chopped
   onion (optional)
½ cup crushed roasted
   peanuts (page 239)
1 teaspoon salt
1 teaspoon sugar
2 tablespoons buttermilk
   or plain yogurt, stirred
1 tablespoon lime or
   lemon juice
1 tablespoon chopped
   fresh cilantro
Grated fresh coconut
   (optional)

Once a week I fast in order to give rest to the stomach and stimulate the mind. At the end of the day, I eat this light dish alongside fruits and buttermilk or yogurt. The secret of the pilaf lies in soaking the tapioca in very little water. If too much water is used, it tends to get mushy. Indian and other Asian markets sell three sizes of pearl tapioca: this recipe uses the medium variety, with grains about ⅟₁₆ inch in diameter. It is also available in the "oriental" section of many supermarkets.

1. Rinse the tapioca in several changes of water; drain. Place in a bowl with ¾ cup water, cover the bowl, and let soak for 4 hours.

2. Heat the oil and desi ghee in a large, heavy nonstick skillet on medium-high heat. Add the mustard and cumin seeds; when the seeds begin to sizzle and splutter, stir in the potato, chiles, and onion. Cook until the onion is soft, stirring occasionally, about 2 to 3 minutes.

3. Sprinkle the tapioca with peanuts, salt, and sugar. Mix well and add to the skillet. Stir in the buttermilk and cook, stirring constantly, until thoroughly mixed, about 5 minutes. Reduce the heat to low, cover, and cook until very hot. Sprinkle with the lime juice, mix gently, and remove from the heat. Serve hot, on warmed plates, with a sprinkling of cilantro and coconut.

Note: The tapioca can be soaked ahead and refrigerated up to one day. Bring to room temperature and continue with step 2.

# IDLIS AND DOSAS

Throughout India, millions of vegetarians get most of their daily protein from a combination of grains and legumes (see page 147). In the south, one of the most important grain and legume combinations is rice and *urad dal.* The rice provides bulk and most of the calories, and the dal contributes protein to a vegetarian diet.

Very often when I was growing up my mother would make large quantities of batter with these two humble ingredients, soaking the rice and dal until soft, then grinding them and letting the mixture ferment into a batter. Out of these seemingly repetitious basic ingredients, she made an assortment of breakfast entrees, each with a distinct taste, appearance, and texture. Steamed in a special tray, the batter would become spongy cakes *(idli),* to be served with *sambar* (a thick, spicy lentil and vegetable soup) and coconut chutney. Thinned with little more water, the same batter was cooked on a griddle to make various kinds of pancakes known as *dosa* and *appam,* or flavored with coconut and chile and fried into dumplings called *wada.*

Just as a Western chef is judged by his repertoire of pastries, so a southern Indian cook is distinguished for exercising skills in the consistency and flavor of these batters. Although the same basic batter can be used interchangeably, I have made some modifications for specific dishes. For example, I have found that a little instant rice added to the batter makes lighter and fluffier idlis. To make crisp, paper-thin crepes I add mung dal and fenugreek seeds; in addition to helping the fermentation, the fenugreek aids in reducing flatulence from the dal.

In a traditional south Indian kitchen, the cook would always have some fermented urad dal batter on hand, ready to add other grains. Otherwise, starting a batch of idlis or dosas from scratch is a 24-hour process, so it takes some advance planning. However, there are ways to make many of these treats on shorter notice. A few of the recipes in this chapter use cream of rice or cream of wheat cereal (which are similar in texture to the ground soaked rice of the traditional batter) plus baking soda for leavening.

In India, the grains for these batters are traditionally ground at home in a massive stone grinder called *rubbo kal* or *atta kal.* It consists of two parts — a large, heavy stone with a deep hole in the center and a 6-inch rim, and a smaller oval grinding stone that fits in the hole. The housewife proudly displays it in the pantry or backyard, gracing its place like sculpture. It is believed that stone grinding adds necessary dietary minerals to the food. These days the *rubbo kal* is often electrically operated, with the top half of the oval stone made of stainless steel and with an attachment for grating coconut. I doubt that many readers of this book will have one of these traditional grinders, so the recipes here have been developed with a blender.

The texture of the batter is crucial to making fluffy idlis and crisp dosas; if the grains are not ground finely enough, the finished dish can be grainy, sticky, or tough. There is nothing difficult about the process, it just requires patience and close attention. I prefer to use a blender, which is faster than a food processor. Grind in small batches, about one cup at a time, for 4 to 5 minutes. Properly ground rice has a soft texture, similar to cream of wheat cereal soaked in water. The urad dal paste must be smooth and silky. As for the dosa batter, it looks and feels like farina or semolina soaked in milk for a long period of time.

Do not stir batters while they ferment; stirring disturbs the growth of the fermentation bacteria, and can slow down or stop the fermentation. When properly fermented, the batter will look and feel as delicate and airy as mousse; see the individual recipes for how much each batter should increase in volume.

# MADRAS SPONGY CAKES
## (Idlis)

Makes 30
Preparation time:
  30 minutes, plus 8
  hours soaking, plus 12
  hours fermenting

2 cups raw long-grain
  white rice
¾ cup white gram beans
  (urad dal), picked
  clean
½ cup instant rice, such
  as Minute Rice
1¼ cups water
2 teaspoons salt
Mild vegetable oil, for
  brushing, or cooking
  spray

Light and fluffy idlis are gaining worldwide popularity because of their healthful ingredients, unique taste, ease of digestion, and appearance. White gram beans (urad dal) supplement the nutritional value of the rice. In addition, the urad dal helps the process of fermentation which yields a large amount of B-vitamins.

Preparing idli is simple and straightforward, but you'll need to know a few tricks in order to make them light and porous. First, the urad dal should be ground into a very soft creamy paste. It should not stick to your fingers; if it does, it needs to be blended further. To test, put a teaspoon of the urad dal paste into a cup of water; it should float. If it settles, blend it further. Second, use a long-grain rice such as the California variety; basmati or jasmine rice is too expensive, and it adds fragrance that is not needed. In summer, the batter will ferment within 12 to 15 hours. Stir and refrigerate if not using. Try to find a warm place (at least 75°F) for your batter to ferment; if the temperature is cold and the humidity high, it may have to rest longer, but not more than 32 hours. The hotter the temperature, the quicker is the fermentation; in India, where summer temperatures are often over 100°F, it can take as little as 4 hours.

Idlis are steamed in a special mold, or "idli stand." Looking like a multistory building, the stand consists of anywhere from 3 to 8 levels spaced apart on a central shaft. Each level has four compartments or molds, usually round but sometimes square, about 3 inches in diameter, 1 inch deep in the center and tapered at the edges. The molds have tiny holes that allow the batter to "breathe" freely, but not so large that the batter drips through (although this can happen if the batter is too thin, so I have been very specific about the amount of liquid in the batter). The molds are traditionally lined with damp linen or banana leaves or coated with oil before the batter is spooned into each compartment. The entire stand goes inside a large steamer containing 1 inch of water. It is then covered, and steamed. Depending on the size of the pot and the stand, anywhere from 12 to 32 idlis can be steamed at once.

Various sizes of idli stands are available in Indian markets here, to make everything from 1-inch bite-size rounds to large idlis 4 to 6 inches in diameter. If a tiered stand is unavailable, you can improvise with equipment from your own kitchen. Small metal cups set in Chinese steamer baskets work perfectly fine, as do the inserts from special egg-poaching pans. Muffin pans are another option, if you have a large enough steaming pot to accommodate them; they can be stacked by placing one or two small metal cup or other cylindrical containers about 1½ inches tall on the first pan, then setting the second on top.

Round cake pans can be used to make large idlis to be cut into pieces. A 6- to 8-quart pressure cooker without the weight will work as a steamer.

For a tropical presentation, serve idlis on a platter lined with banana leaves. Idlis traditionally accompany the Classic Madras Lentil Stew (page 154) and Flaked Coconut Chutney (page 194).

1. Put the rice and urad dal in separate medium-size bowls and rinse in several changes of water. Add enough water to cover by at least 2 inches. Soak separately 6 to 8 hours or overnight. Before you plan to blend the rice and urad dal, soak the instant rice in water for 30 minutes to 1 hour.

2. Drain the rice, urad dal, and instant rice. Place about a third of the rice and instant rice in a blender with a little water and blend to a thick, smooth to slightly grainy paste. (Use the water sparingly; you should use only the 1¾ cups water to blend all three ingredients.) Transfer the paste into a 4- to 5-quart glass bowl, scraping the sides of the blender well with a rubber spatula. Repeat the process with the rest of the rice, then with the urad dal, but be sure to blend the urad dal until silky smooth. Add to the bowl with the rice mixture.

3. Add the salt to the batter and mix thoroughly. (The ground rice, being heavier, tends to settle to the bottom — don't worry about it.) Cover and set aside in a warm place (70° to 90°F) for 12 hours. In cold and humid conditions, 24 to 32 hours will be needed for the batter to ferment. When the batter has expanded in volume and bubbles and cracks appear on the surface, it is ready. Stir gently but thoroughly in one direction. The batter should be thick and light as mousse, with a pleasantly fermented, slightly sour smell.

4. Set up a steaming pot and idli stand or substitute. Fill the pot with water to within ½ inch of the steaming rack or bottom tier of the stand. Bring to a boil. Spoon the batter into the molds, filling them half full. Cover securely and steam until puffed, and a toothpick inserted in the center comes out clean, 10 to 12 minutes.

5. Turn off the heat, replace the cover loosely, and let the idlis rest for 5 minutes. Just before serving, remove the stand and ease out the idlis with a butter knife dipped in hot water. Keep warm into a napkin-lined basket. Repeat with the remaining batter. Serve warm.

**Note:** Idlis are best freshly steamed, but they can be made ahead and set aside for 5 hours at room temperature or up to 2 days in the refrigerator. To rewarm, steam in batches in a steamer basket until hot, 6 to 8 minutes.

**Variation:** SPICED MADRAS CAKES *(Masala Idli)*

Fold ¼ cup chopped cashews, 1 teaspoon roasted cumin seeds, and 1 teaspoon whole black peppercorns into the batter just before steaming. Steam as described above.

**Variation:** IDLI UPPAMA

Leftover idlis can be crumbled and seasoned with mustard-cumin infused oil. Serve with a sprinkling of chopped fresh cilantro and cayenne.

# SPONGY CAKE CASSEROLE DRENCHED IN CREAM SAUCE
## *(Karnataka Special)*

Serves 4 to 6
Preparation time:
   35 minutes

8 to 10 Madras Spongy
   Cakes (page 64)
1 tablespoon mild
   vegetable oil
2 medium tomatoes,
   quartered
1-inch piece fresh ginger
¼ teaspoon cayenne
½ teaspoon paprika
¾ teaspoon salt
1½ teaspoons sambar
   powder, homemade
   (page 24) or bought
1 cup half-and-half or
   coconut milk
1½ teapoons sesame
   seeds
Chopped fresh cilantro

This dish of grilled idlis cloaked in a rich sauce is so delicious it will disappear from the dining table in a moment. I always try to save a few idlis to make this special casserole. Sesame seeds sprinkled on the top add a delicate crunch. The dish is wonderful with Kashmir Mixed Fruit Chaat (page 186). For a more elaborate meal, precede with Fragrant Yellow Lentil Soup (page 49).

1. Cut each spongy cake in half (to make two semicircles). Place on a broiler pan and brush lightly with oil. Broil 4 inches from the heat until the top is lightly browned, 2 to 3 minutes. Set aside under a foil tent to keep warm.

2. Combine the tomatoes and ginger in a blender and process to a smooth puree. Transfer to a small saucepan and add the cayenne, paprika, salt, sambar powder, and half-and-half. Stir to mix and bring to a boil. Reduce the heat, cover, and simmer until the tomato loses its raw aroma, about 15 minutes.

3. Meanwhile, place a rack in the middle of the oven and preheat to 400°F. Arrange the grilled idli halves slightly overlapping in an 8-inch square baking dish. Pour the sauce on top, sprinkle with sesame seeds, and bake, uncovered, until very hot, 12 to 15 minutes. Serve with a sprinkling of cilantro.

**Note:** Substituting coconut milk for the half-and-half in the sauce makes a delicious variation.

**Microwave:** In step 2, combine the sauce ingredients in a 2-quart microwavable bowl. Cook uncovered at full power for 12 minutes. Remove from the oven and continue with step 3.

# CREAM OF WHEAT CAKES WITH PETITE PEAS
## *(Rava Idli)*

Serves 4 to 6
Preparation time:
    20 minutes, plus 1 to
    2 hours soaking

1 cup quick-cooking
    cream of wheat
1 cup plus 2 tablespoons
    cultured low-fat but-
    termilk
¼ cup finely chopped
    onion
2 tablespoons thawed
    petite peas
1½ fresh hot green
    chiles, stemmed and
    chopped
1 tablespoon mild
    vegetable or peanut oil
¼ teaspoon cumin seeds
½ teaspoon mustard
    seeds
½ teaspoon salt
¼ teaspoon baking soda
Lettuce leaves, washed
    and crisped

A whisper of mustard- and cumin-scented oil and calcium-rich buttermilk lend a beautifully balanced undertone to the cake. Serve with Warm Cabbage Salad with Cracked Pepper (page 178) for a light meal.

1. Combine the cream of wheat and 1 cup buttermilk in a medium bowl. Mix well, cover, and set aside for 1 to 2 hours.

2. Stir the onion, peas, and chiles into the batter. Heat ½ tablespoon oil in a small frying pan over medium-high heat and add the cumin and mustard. When the seeds begin to sizzle and splutter, remove from the heat. Cool slightly and fold into the batter. Stir in the remaining buttermilk, salt, and baking soda and mix well.

3. Fill a steaming pan (see page 64) with water to within ½ inch of the steaming rack and bring to a boil. Lightly coat an 8-inch square cake pan with oil and pour in the batter. Place the cake pan on the rack, cover, and steam until a knife inserted in the center comes out clean, 8 to 10 minutes.

4. Turn off the heat and let the idli rest 5 minutes. Cut it into diamonds and ease out with a metal spatula. To serve, line a basket with lettuce leaves and arrange the idli pieces on top. Serve hot or warm.

**Note:** This batter can also be steamed in muffin pans or an idli stand (see page 64). You can also double the recipe and make a second idli in the same pan; just rub it with a little more oil. The idli may be steamed ahead of time and set aside up to 4 hours at room temperature or refrigerated up to 2 days. Reheat in a steamer basket until warm.

# BANGALORE SPONGY CAKE PLATTER
## (*Tatte Idli*)

Makes 2 cakes (6 to 8
   servings)
Preparation time:
   20 minutes, plus 8 to
   10 hours soaking

½ cup white gram
   beans (urad dal),
   picked clean
½ cup water
1¼ cups cream of
   rice cereal
1 cup cultured low-fat
   buttermilk
1 teaspoon mild
   vegetable oil, plus
   more for brushing
1 teaspoon fresh grated
   ginger
2 fresh hot green chiles,
   stemmed and chopped
½ teaspoon turmeric
   (optional)
1 teaspoon salt
½ teaspoon baking soda

In Bangalore in southern India, these idlis are steamed in large 8- to 12-inch-diameter tiered stainless steel plate-like molds, or in flat wicker baskets lined with two or three layers of cheesecloth; either shape produces a platter-sized cake. Flecked with wisps of ginger and chile, the cake is mild and delicate. Top the idli wedges with one of the dry chutneys on page 201.

1. Put the urad dal in a medium-size bowl and rinse in several changes of water. Add enough water to cover by at least 2 inches and soak for 4 to 6 hours.

2. Drain the urad dal and place it in a blender container. Add ½ cup water and process until silky smooth. Turn into a large glass bowl, scraping the sides of the blender. Add the cream of rice and buttermilk. Mix well, cover, and set aside for 4 hours.

3. Heat the oil in a small frying pan until it ripples when the pan is tilted. Pour the hot oil into the batter. Add the ginger, chiles, turmeric, and salt and mix well. Set aside. Lightly oil an 8-inch round or square cake pan. Fill a steaming pan (see page 64) with water to within ½ inch of the steaming rack and bring to a boil.

4. Stir the baking soda into the batter. Mix well and allow it to foam undisturbed for 2 to 3 minutes. Pour half the batter into the greased pan. Place the pan on the rack, cover, and steam until the idli is puffed and a toothpick inserted in the center comes out clean, 8 to 10 minutes.

5. Turn off the heat and let the idli rest 5 minutes. Remove the pan from the rack and ease out the idli with a metal spatula dipped in hot water. Transfer to a decorative serving platter. Cover with a clean kitchen towel or foil to keep the idli warm. Re-oil the pan and repeat with the remaining batter to make a second cake. Cut the idlis into wedges and serve warm or at room temperature.

**Note:** This dish can be prepared ahead and stored up to 6 hours at room temperature or 1 week in the refrigerator, or it can be frozen. Reheat in a steamer until warm.

# KANCHEEPUR CREAM OF RICE CAKES
## (Kancheepuram Idli)

Makes 10-12 medium-size idlis

Preparation time: 20 minutes, plus 4 to 6 hours soaking

½ cup white gram beans (urad dal), picked clean

1 cup water

½ cup cream of rice cereal

½ teaspoon cumin seeds

¼ teaspoon whole black peppercorns

1 tablespoon unsweetened dry coconut

½ teaspoon salt

¼ teaspoon baking soda dissolved in 1 teaspoon water

Oil or cooking spray (if not using banana leaves)

Banana leaves, washed and cut into 4-inch squares (optional)

In the temple of Kancheepur in south India, special idlis weighing approximately 3 pounds each are prepared daily. They are first offered to the deity, then sliced into 1-inch pieces and distributed among the devotees. As Westerners use foil for grilling or steaming, in India these spongy cakes are steamed in turmeric, jackfruit, or banana leaves for aromatic flavors. Frozen banana leaves are available at Asian markets, or you can order fresh ones from your local florist. (Be sure to let the florist know you are using them for cooking purposes.) Another advantage of steaming in leaves is you don't have to grease them. This idli is excellent served with Quick Tomato-Cinnamon Chutney (page 19).

1. Put the urad dal in a medium-size bowl and rinse in several changes of water. Add water to cover by at least 2 inches. Soak 4 to 6 hours.

2. Drain the urad dal and place in a blender container with ½ cup water and process until silky smooth. (This may have to be done in portions; use no more than ½ cup water in all.) Turn into a large glass bowl, scraping the sides of the blender. Add the remaining water and cream of rice to the bowl, mix thoroughly, cover, and set aside for 4 hours.

3. Stir the cumin, peppercorns, coconut, salt, and baking soda into the batter. Allow the batter to foam, undisturbed, for 2 to 3 minutes. The batter should be thick; if it is too thin, stir in 1 to 2 tablespoons of cream of rice cereal or self-rising flour.

4. Set up a steaming pot and idli stand or substitute (see page 64). Fill the pot with water to within ½ inch of the steaming rack or bottom tier of the stand. Lightly coat the molds with oil or cooking spray, or line the depressions with banana-leaf squares, pleating the corners and securing the pleats with toothpicks. (Softening the leaves in hot water for a few seconds makes them easier to fold without tearing.) Bring the water to a boil. Spoon batter into the molds, filling the cups half full. Set the tray in the pot, cover securely, and steam until the idlis are puffed, and a toothpick inserted in the center comes out clean, 8 to 10 minutes.

5. Turn off the heat and let the idlis rest for 5 minutes. Just before serving, remove the stand and ease out the idlis with butter knife dipped in hot water (they should slip easily out of the banana leaves). Repeat with the remaining batter. Serve warm on a serving platter lined with banana leaves.

**Note:** The idlis can be prepared ahead and stored at room temperature for 5 hours or for 1 week in the refrigerator, or they can be frozen. Reheat in a steamer basket until hot.

**Variation:** A miniature muffin pan, the kind with 1½-inch-diameter cups about ¾ inch deep, can be used to make bite-size idlis. Coat the cups with oil or cooking spray, fill with batter about three-fourths full, and steam as described above. To serve, place 8 to 10 cakes into a serving bowl and add a ladleful of Classic Madras Lentil Stew (page 154). Miniature idlis can also be served as appetizers with Tamarind-Apple Dipping Sauce (page 39).

# SPONGY CAKE PIZZA, INDIAN STYLE
## (Idli Pizza)

Serves 2 to 4
Preparation time:
    20 minutes

1 tablespoon mild
    vegetable or peanut oil
½ teaspoon mustard
    seeds
½ teaspoon cumin seeds
½ teaspoon sesame seeds
1 Bangalore Spongy Cake
    Platter (page 69)
½ cup tomato sauce
½ cup finely chopped
    onion
1 tablespoon chopped
    fresh cilantro
1 tablespoon grated
    Monterey jack cheese

Crunchy and aromatic from roasted seeds, idli pizza is simply ravishing on the palate. Visually attractive, this dish only takes minutes to assemble if you already have some prepared idlis. Serve at tea time or for snacks.

1. Heat the oil in a large heavy skillet over medium-high heat and add the mustard, cumin, and sesame seeds. When the seeds begin to sizzle and splutter, reduce the heat to medium. Place the spongy cake over the seeds. Cover and cook for 6 to 8 minutes until the bottom of the cake is crisp and lightly browned in places. Turn and cook the other side for 5 to 6 minutes.

2. Transfer the cake to a plate, seed side up. Spread the sauce evenly on top, then sprinkle with onion, cilantro, and cheese. Place under a preheated broiler for a minute or two until the cheese melts. Cut into wedges and serve immediately on an attractive platter.

# PAPER-THIN RICE CREPES UDUPI STYLE
## *(Paper Dosa)*

Makes 18 crepes
(6 to 8 servings)
Preparation time:
40 minutes (see Note),
plus 6 hours soaking
and 15 hours
fermenting

3 cups long-grain
white rice
¾ cup white gram
beans (urad dal),
picked clean
¼ cup yellow mung
beans (mung dal),
picked clean
1 tablespoon fenugreek
seeds
1¼ cups plus 2
tablespoons water
½ tablespoon salt
Mild vegetable oil,
for brushing

A specialty of Udupi, a small town in my home state of Karnataka, paper dosa are very popular in India and they are gaining popularity all over the world. Restaurants in India serves dosas as large as two feet in diameter, but these are a more manageable size for home cooks. The batter may be unfamiliar to Western cooks, but there is nothing difficult about making the crepes, and with a little practice you will master the art of making thin dosas with a crumbly, melt-in-your-mouth tender texture.

A well-seasoned cast iron griddle is ideal for yielding a crisp crust and feathery light interior. A nonstick skillet also works well, though it yields a slightly softer crust. Indian cooks use a special technique to oil the griddle: pierce half an onion or potato with a knife, dip the cut surface in vegetable oil, and rub it on the griddle, then wipe off the excess with a soft kitchen towel. Cooking spray works equally well.

I like to use my artistic talents while I am cooking; when these crepes are presented in the shape of hats, they look attractive on the table and are especially fun for the children. Serve them with Flaked Coconut Chutney (page 194) and Seasoned Potatoes with Peas and Raisins (page 97) for a light meal.

1. Combine the rice, dals, and fenugreek in a large bowl. Wash in several changes of water. Cover by at least 2 inches of water and soak for 6 hours or overnight. Drain.

2. Place the rice mixture in a blender and process in portions, dividing the water among the batches (but do not use any more water than the amount called for). Blend each batch until smooth and transfer it to a 4-quart glass bowl, scraping the sides of the blender. When all the mixture is ground, add the salt and mix well. Cover and keep in a warm place for at least 15 hours or until the batter has slightly risen in volume and smells slightly sour and pleasantly fermented.

3. Preheat a 12-inch or larger griddle or heavy skillet on medium-high heat for 3 minutes. (To test for the right temperature, sprinkle in a few drops of water; it will splutter and disappear immediately when the griddle is ready.) Brush a little oil on the griddle and wipe off the excess with a paper towel. Stir the batter thoroughly and pour ½ cup in the center of the griddle. Using the bottom of a large spoon or a metal cup, immediately spread the batter outward in a

continuous spiral motion, thinning the edge, to a circle about 8 inches in diameter. Drizzle ½ to 1 teaspoon of oil around the edge of the circle. To make the "hats," make a cut from the center to the edge. Cook uncovered until the bottom is lightly golden, 2 to 3 minutes. Ease the edges up with a metal spatula. Turn it into a cone shape from the cut side. Place onto a heated serving plate. Repeat with the remaining batter.

**Variation:** For stuffed dosa, do not cut the crepes. Place 2 tablespoons of Seasoned Potatoes with Peas and Raisins on one half of the crepe when the crepe is ready and starts to curl at the edges. Flip the other half over the filling. Transfer to a heated plate and serve immediately.

**Note:** The sharp-eyed reader may have noticed that while the rice and dals are soaked and ground separately in the recipes for idlis and other dishes, here they are all soaked and ground together. In years of trying to make crisp dosas, I realized that the batter does not need to be as light and airy as it does for idlis. After trying several different ways I have perfected this method, which is not only simpler but works better.

The batter can be fermented and kept covered in the refrigerator for up to 1 week. Bring to room temperature before use. With two griddles or skillets or a rectangular double-burner griddle, you can cook two dosas at once, reducing the cooking time.

# Bangalore Pancakes with Green Pepper and Cabbage
## (Uttappam)

Makes 12 pancakes
Preparation time:
    50 minutes (see Note),
    plus 6 hours soaking
    and 12 to 24 hours
    fermenting

3 cups long-grain white
    rice
1 cup white gram beans
    (urad dal), picked
    clean
1 tablespoon fenugreek
    seeds, picked clean
2¼ cups water
½ tablespoon salt
½ cup finely chopped
    onion
4 fresh hot green chiles,
    finely chopped
½ cup finely chopped
    tomatoes
½ cup green pepper
    cut in ½-inch pieces
½ cup finely shredded
    cabbage
¼ cup freshly grated
    coconut (optional)
Mild vegetable oil, for
    brushing

This especially easy version of the famous paper-thin rice crepes comes from Bangalore, the "garden city" of India. Scattered with tomato, bell pepper, and cabbage, this dish demonstrates how fresh, colorful and nutritive vegetables can transform a simple pancake into a masterpiece. Since it is filling, serve this pancake all by itself topped with melted butter. Pass Flaked Coconut Chutney (page 194) at the table if desired.

1. Wash the rice in several changes of water and place it in a bowl with water to cover. Wash the urad dal separately and combine it with the fenugreek seeds in another bowl. Add water to cover. Soak for 6 hours or overnight.

2. Drain the rice and urad dal. Place the rice in a blender and process until smooth, adding as little of the water as possible. (You should use only the 2-1/4 cups of water to blend both rice and urad dal.) Transfer into a 4-quart glass bowl, scraping the sides of the blender. Blend the urad dal separately in batches with the remaining water and add to the rice mixture.

3. Add the salt and mix the batter thoroughly. (Ground rice, being heavier, tends to settle; don't worry about it.) Cover and set aside in a warm place (70° to 90°F) for 12 to 15 hours. If the humidity is high and temperature cold, it takes from 24 to 32 hours for the batter to ferment. When the batter is covered with bubbles in places and expanded slightly in volume, it is ready. Stir gently but thoroughly in one direction.

4. Combine the onion, chiles, vegetables, and coconut in a bowl. Preheat a 12-inch or larger griddle or nonstick frying pan on medium-high heat for 3 minutes. (To test for the right temperature, sprinkle in a few drops of water; it will splutter and disappear immediately when the griddle is ready.) Brush a little oil on the griddle and wipe off the excess with a paper towel. Reduce the heat to medium. Stir the batter and pour ⅓ cup in the center of the griddle; immediately spread the batter with the back of a large spoon into a 6-inch circle ¼ inch thick. Sprinkle 2 tablespoons of the vegetable mixture on top, cover with a lid, and cook until the bottom is browned, 4 to 5 minutes. Flip on the other side if you want the vegetables slightly browned, and cook 2 minutes; otherwise, transfer to a serving plate, with the vegetable side on top. Repeat with the remaining batter and vegetable mixture. Cut in neat wedges and serve hot.

**Note:** The batter can be fermented and kept covered in the refrigerator up to 1 week. Bring to room temperature before use. Again, a double griddle or two single griddles or skillets will cut the cooking time in half.

# MYSORE LACE CREPES WITH CRACKED PEPPER
## *(Rava Dosa, Neer Dosa)*

Makes 6 crepes
  (3 servings)
Preparation time:
  30 minutes, plus 30
  minutes resting

1 cup rice flour
¼ cup quick-cooking
  cream of wheat
¼ cup unbleached
  all-purpose flour
⅛ teaspoon hot pepper
  flakes
¼ teaspoon coarsely
  crushed cumin seeds
½ teaspoon sugar
1 teaspoon salt
2 tablespoons finely
  chopped fresh cilantro
2 teaspoons lime juice
2¼ cups water
Mild vegetable oil, for
  brushing

This cousin to the Udupi-style dosas comes from Mysore, the "city of palaces, silks, and sandalwood." The name *neer dosa* means "water crepes," and refers to the very thin consistency of the batter. When poured from 3 inches above the pan, the thin batter splashes into a lacy motif. In this instance, rice is replaced by rice flour, and urad dal by quick-cooking cream of wheat, with a little all-purpose flour to bind the two. Once the batter is ready, the crepes require very little work. For contrast, pair them with Spicy-Sweet Pickled Dates (page 206), or stuff them with wild rice or couscous.

1. Combine all the ingredients except the water and oil in a large bowl. Whisk in the water until smooth. Cover and set aside for 30 minutes.

2. Preheat a 12-inch or larger heavy skillet on medium-high heat for 3 minutes. (To test for the right temperature, sprinkle in a few drops of water. It will splutter and disappear immediately when the pan is ready.) Brush a little oil on the griddle and wipe off the excess with paper towel. Stir the batter and from 3 inches above the pan, pour ½ cup in the center spreading outward in a continuous spiral motion. Do not try to spread the batter with a spoon. Drizzle 1 teaspoon of oil around the edge of the crepe. Cook uncovered until the bottom is lightly brown and the edges begin to curl up, 1½ to 2 minutes. Ease the crepe off the pan with a metal spatula and slip it into a serving plate. Repeat with the remaining batter. Serve immediately.

**Note:** The batter can be made 4 days ahead and kept in the refrigerator, but once the crepes are made they should be served immediately.

# BREADS

Whole Wheat Flatbread (Chapati)

Spicy Sesame Flatbread

Tomato-Spinach Flatbread

Peasant Cucumber Flatbread

Green Mango Flatbread

Rustic Kidney Bean Flatbread

Shredded Green Cabbage Flatbread

Calcutta Plain Flaky Bread (Bengali Paratha)

Mung Bean-Spinach Wholesome Flatbread

Grandmother's Village-Style Corn-Potato Flatbread

Rose-Cashew Skillet Nan

Whole Wheat Puffy Bread (Poori)

Indore Spinach Puffy Bread

Yogurt Balloon Bread

Onion-Sesame Puffy Bread

Many of my earliest food recollections have to do with breads — Grandmother roasting potatoes in the ashes of the fire and mixing them with sweet corn and spices to stuff a fragrant flatbread; my mother's maid rolling out thin rounds of an onion dough and frying them into crisp pooris she called "gypsy bread"; and the countless variations on everyday chapatis. Every day that I make bread these recipes bring back those happy memories.

From the clay oven to the iron griddle, breads have a significant status in Indian folklore. *Roti,* the famed primary food, is a generic term for all breads. Although made from the same basic ingredients, stoneground grains and water, Indian breads vary tremendously from tissue-thin and crackly to soft, moist, and chewy. Numerous flour mixtures, shaping techniques, and cooking methods yield an astounding range of flavors and textures.

In the decade I have resided in America, I have learned to streamline many of the old-fashioned bread recipes. My motivation has been to recreate the subtle, complex flavors of India while using modern conveniences to cut down on preparation time. The savory flavors aren't lost in this streamlining; instead they bring back the childhood memories for me. It has been simpler than I could ever imagine. In this chapter is a collection of Indian breads that will work well in a modern American kitchen and will guarantee success to the most inexperienced cooks.

The most basic form of Indian bread is pan-toasted flatbreads, of which the most common is *chapati* (see Whole Wheat Flatbread, page 79). Low in fat, made from whole wheat flour and water, chapatis are a daily staple for millions. Spicy Sesame Flatbread (page 81) is a quick variation of the simple chapati. Other variations include flours from other grains such as rice, barley, corn, millet, and *jawar.* (The last is a round yellow grain that grows abundantly in India, and is available in Indian markets; like millet flour, jawar flour is inexpensive but nutritious. Jawar dough is normally made with boiling water.) They are all unleavened, and require a minimum of preparation because there is no rising time required. They are all true dieter's delights.

Other, richer flatbreads include *paratha* and *nan.* Parathas are slightly thick, rich with butter and sometimes eggs, and rolled out into flaky layers. Nan is familiar to anyone who has eaten in *tandoori*-style restaurants, a rich, tender flatbread baked right on the walls of the clay oven. I have included my own versions of both of these breads, adapted to home cooking equipment.

Stuffed breads are another major category, with variations as diverse as the subcontinent itself. Traditionally, stuffed bread entails a long cooking process. The filling and dough are made separately. After the dough is filled, it is rolled again into a larger circle — a process that invariably leads to torn dough and spilled filling. I have remedied this by using a food processor and incorporating the "stuffing" into the dough itself. I simply toss in cooked potato, legumes (or shredded raw vegetables), chiles, cilantro, and flour, and then process into a smooth dough. It's now far easier to roll and bake on a griddle. Further, the raw vegetables retain their valuable nutrients.

Deep-fried breads are made occasionally for festivals and family get-togethers. The easiest and simplest of them is *poori.* Certainly, this is one of the two most popular Indian breads in the West, *nan* being the other. The dough is similar to chapati dough, but made with hot oil and a touch of cream of wheat added. Little balls of dough are rolled into small thick circles, and when slipped into hot oil they fill with steam and balloon instantly. Creative versions for more exotic menus include Yogurt Balloon Bread and Puffy Spinach Bread.

# Tips for Successful Bread Making

❀ None of the doughs is that difficult or time-consuming to mix by hand, but feel free to use a heavy-duty tabletop mixer or food processor if you are more comfortable that way. I find the food processor a great help for breads, as well as snacks and desserts that involve dough-like preparations. I make a large batch of the dough ahead and refrigerate it; when my children return from school in the afternoon, rolling and cooking chapatis is a breeze. Whenever I have some leftover vegetable dishes or curries, I toss them in the food processor along with assorted flours and turn them into delicious parathas. The only time I do not use the food processor is in making Mung Bean-Spinach Wholesome Flatbread or Spinach Puffy Bread; I prefer the discrete green flecks of spinach chopped by hand to the evenly green dough produced by the machine.

❀ Start by adding half the amount of water called for in a recipe. Flours vary in amount of liquid they can absorb. Add the remaining water in dribbles until the dough is the right consistency (usually medium-soft and slightly sticky). Less water will be needed in warm and humid weather, the full amount in cooler, drier weather.

❀ Adapting bread recipes from one country to another often means dealing with different kinds of flour, with different starch and gluten (protein) levels. Many of the bread recipes use a blend of all-purpose (white) flour and whole wheat flour, in an attempt to match the texture of Indian flour. However, if you have access to an Indian grocery, you might try Indian chapati flour instead. The latter is a finely ground whole wheat flour that produces just the right texture for chapatis and other flatbreads — the dough is easy to roll, and the breads come out soft and pliable. Chapati flour looks a lot like American whole wheat pastry flour, but it is made from a harder wheat (with a higher ratio of gluten to starch). If you cannot find chapati flour, a blend of American all-purpose and whole wheat flour gives about the same balance of starch and gluten content. A 1:1 ratio will make softer breads, but I prefer 3 parts whole wheat to 1 part all-purpose for a fuller flavor and higher protein content (I find chapatis made entirely with American whole wheat flour are too heavy). Another option is to substitute cake flour for all-purpose in the preceding ratios; it gives a more tender result. There is also a subtle difference in color between the American and Indian flours; the reddish-brown grains of American wheat make darker flatbreads than the cream color of chapati flour.

❀ Bread dough may be prepared ahead, then covered and refrigerated for three days, or freezer-wrapped and frozen up to 1 month. Bring the dough to room temperature before continuing.

❀ When forming the breads, always roll the dough with gentle pressure. The edges of the breads should be thin and the center a little thicker. This helps the breads to puff as they cook. Use a small amount of flour as necessary to keep the dough from sticking to the work surface and rolling pin; again, the amount needed is affected by heat and humidity. After rolling, slap the bread back and forth on your palms to dust off excess flour.

❀ At first, it's probably easier to roll out three or four breads at a time, then concentrate on cooking them. Lay the rolled-out breads on individual plates or waxed paper (do not stack them, or they will stick together) and keep the the uncooked breads covered with a clean cloth. Don't roll them out too far ahead of cooking, or they will not puff up on the griddle. With practice, you should be able to develop your own rhythm, toasting one while rolling out the next.

❀ The griddle for toasting the breads must be hot, 350 to 360.°F. To check the temperature of the griddle, sprinkle a few drops of water across the top. If they bounce and splutter, the griddle is ready. If the griddle is not hot enough, the breads will take longer to cook and will become dry and tough. To save time, you can work with two griddles or the large rectangular type that fits over two burners. A large, heavy skillet, preferably cast iron, also works fine if you don't have a griddle. An electric skillet is another option, and gives you precise control of the temperature.

❀ While toasting flatbread, do not flip often, or it will get dry and tough. Allow it to puff for at least 30 seconds. To help the breads puff while they cook, press them gently around the edges with a spatula. A folded, clean kitchen towel makes a good substitute.

❀ If you are not able to serve the breads immediately after cooking, wrap them in clean kitchen towels or several layers of paper towels (to absorb moisture), and store several hours in a bread box. Stacked between sheets of waxed paper, they can be freezer-wrapped and frozen up to 2 months. An optional brushing with ghee or butter when they come off the griddle prevents flatbreads from becoming tough in storage.

❀ To reheat the cooked breads, bring to room temperature, uncover, wrap in foil, and bake in a 250° to 300°F oven for 12 to 15 minutes. Breads are at their best hot from the griddle. Do not attempt to reheat in a microwave oven or they will toughen.

# WHOLE WHEAT FLATBREAD
## (Chapati)

Makes 8
Preparation time:
   20 minutes, plus 10
   minutes resting

1½ cups whole wheat
   flour
½ cup unbleached
   all-purpose flour
¼ cup water

When I pack chapatis spread with desi ghee and Powdered Peanut Chutney (page 201) for my son's school lunch, his American friends are eager to trade their turkey sandwiches with him. So I make it a point to have some extra chapatis in the lunchbox. When they visit our house, the American youngsters are quite content to spread the peanut butter on hot chapatis.

A little patience will go a long way in mastering chapatis. The first few chapatis may be uneven and not puff. Don't be discouraged, they will get better with practice. No matter what their shape, they are delicious. Serve chapatis with vegetable, legume, and curry preparations. Accompany with cool raitas or salads, and follow with plain basmati rice.

1. *To make the dough in a food processor:* Add the flours to the work bowl. Pour in ¼ cup water and process on low speed until the dough begins to pull from sides of the bowl. If the motor slows, stop the machine and redistribute the partially formed dough. With the machine running, gradually add the remaining water in a steady stream. Process until the dough pulls together into a ball and begins to clean the sides of the bowl. *With a heavy-duty mixer:* Add the flours to the work bowl. Pour in ¼ cup water and beat with the dough hook on medium speed. Add the remaining water and beat until the dough is medium-soft and pulls cleanly from sides of the bowl. *By hand:* Combine the flours in a large mixing bowl. Make a well in the center and add the water. Mix with your hands until the dough holds together.

79

2. The dough should be medium-soft and slightly sticky at
hold an impression of your fingertips when pressed. Form tl
smooth ball. Cover and let rest for 10 minutes. Lightly oil yc
the dough onto a work surface and knead for a few minutes un
smooth. Divide the dough into 8 equal portions; roll each p
your palms into a smooth ball, flatten slightly, put on a plate a

3. Place a piece of dough on a floured surface and roll to a 3-inch round.
lightly with oil, fold into a semicircle, and fold again to form a triangle. Repeat
with the remaining balls of dough. Meanwhile, preheat a griddle or skillet over
high heat for 2 minutes, then reduce to medium heat. If using an electric skillet, preheat to 375°F, then reduce to 350°F.

4. For each chapati, roll a triangle of dough from the center outward to about
twice its size; the finished shape will be somewhere between a triangle and a
ragged circle. Transfer the chapati to the hot griddle and cook until it starts to
puff, about 1 minute. Using a wide metal spatula, flip the chapati and continue to cook until it puffs again and the bottom is speckled lightly, 30 to 40 seconds. Press on the edges with the back of a spoon so that the bread puffs and
cooks evenly. Transfer to a plate, cover with foil or a kitchen towel, and keep
warm. While one chapati is cooking, shape another. Stack the chapatis and
keep covered. To serve, tear into fourths, place in a petal fashion in a napkin-
lined bread basket, and serve warm.

# FLATBREAD VARIATIONS

Indian flatbreads lend themselves to endless nutritious variations, each with its own color, flavor, and texture. Whenever I have some leftover vegetable dishes or curries, I toss them in the food processor along with assorted flours and turn them into delicious bread doughs. Some of the following are traditional, others are my own inventions. Process the dough as in the basic chapati recipe, but instead of the oiling and folding in step 3, simply divide the dough into 8 to 10 pieces and roll each one out to a 5-inch round. The cooking procedure is the same. Note that the water content of each variation depends on the moisture of the added ingredients.

## SPICY SESAME FLATBREAD (Dashmi)

Add ½ tablespoon sesame seeds, ½ tablespoon ground cumin, ½ to 1 teaspoon cayenne to the basic dough ingredients, and replace ¼ cup of the water with mild vegetable oil. The oil makes the dough especially tender and helps the bread stay fresh for several days.

## TOMATO-SPINACH FLATBREAD (Palak Roti)

Add 2 medium tomatoes, chopped, with their juices, ½ cup lightly packed chopped spinach (fresh or thawed), 2 tablespoons softened cream cheese or Channa (page 164), 2 tablespoons rice flour, and ½ teaspoon each red pepper flakes and freshly ground black pepper to the basic dough ingredients; no water is needed.

## PEASANT CUCUMBER FLATBREAD (Kaakdi Bhakri)

Add 2 cups peeled and grated cucumber (about 1 medium), 3 fresh chiles, stemmed and chopped, 3 tablespoons chopped fresh cilantro, ½ cup rice flour, and ½ teaspoon each ground cumin and turmeric to the basic dough ingredients (no water is needed). This can take a higher proportion of whole wheat flour, 1¾ cups to ¼ cup all-purpose.

## GREEN MANGO FLATBREAD (Kacha Aam Paratha)

Wash and wipe 1 medium green mango (about 10 ounces) and grate, skin and all, enough to measure 1 cup, loosely packed. Add to the processor with the basic dough ingredients plus a 1-inch piece fresh ginger, 2 or 3 stemmed fresh green chiles, 2 tablespoons chopped cilantro, 2 tablespoons shredded Monterey jack cheese, and reduce the water to ¼ cup. You might also experiment with green papaya, either fresh (see page 114) or the frozen shredded form sold in Southeast Asian markets.

## RUSTIC KIDNEY BEAN FLATBREAD (Rajma Roti)

Mince 4 cloves garlic, 2 stemmed fresh green chiles, and about 20 sprigs cilantro in the processor. Add the basic dough ingredients plus 1 cup cooked red kidney beans (homemade or canned), drained and rinsed, 1 teaspoon ground cumin, and 4 teaspoons oil, and process with ½ cup water. Garbanzo beans work just as well and give a lighter color.

## SHREDDED GREEN CABBAGE FLATBREAD (Kobichi Poli)

Mince 3 stemmed fresh green chiles and 2 tablespoons chopped cilantro in the processor. Add the basic dough ingredients plus an additional ½ cup whole wheat flour, 2 cups shredded green cabbage, ½ teaspoon each ground cumin and coriander, ½ tablespoon lime or lemon juice, and 1 tablespoon mild peanut or olive oil. Add a little more than the ½ cup water if necessary to moisten the dough.

# CALCUTTA PLAIN FLAKYBREAD
## *(Bengali Paratha)*

Makes 8
Preparation time:
   20 minutes, plus 2 to
   4 hours resting

2 cups self-rising flour
   (or 2 cups all-purpose
   flour plus ½ teaspoon
   baking powder)
½ teaspoon salt
¾ cup water
Desi ghee or butter for
   brushing
1 tablespoon rice flour
Pinch of freshly ground
   black pepper
1 to 2 tablespoons finely
   chopped cilantro
4 teaspoons (approxi-
   mately) mild vegetable
   oil

A decade ago when my husband and I lived in Calcutta, we had a maid who used to make excellent parathas. She enriched her doughs with liberal amounts of butter or desi ghee, and occasionally eggs, folded and rolled them out carefully to produce many tissue-thin layers, and shallow-fried the thick breads. They were tasty, but not very healthful. Modifying her basic approach, and testing various ingredients and methods of rolling out the dough, I have developed my own technique that makes tender, flaky parathas with far less oil. Serve with any of the paneer cheese dishes (pages 166-171), Crisp Okra Raita (page 176), and a rice pilaf. End the meal with a platter of sliced fresh fruits.

1. *To make the dough in a food processor:* Combine the flour and salt in the work bowl. With the machine running, gradually add water through the feed tube in a steady stream. Process until the dough comes together into a ball and begins to clean the sides of the bowl. *By hand:* Combine the flour and salt in a large mixing bowl. Make a well in the center and add the water. Mix until the dough holds together.

2. Shape the dough into a smooth ball, cover, and set aside to rest for 2 to 4 hours. Place the dough on a work surface and knead briefly. Divide into 8 equal portions and roll each portion between your hands to form a smooth ball. Put on a plate and cover.

3. Preheat a griddle or skillet over high heat for 2 minutes. Reduce the heat to medium. Place a piece of dough on a floured work surface and roll to a 5-inch round. Brush lightly with desi ghee, sprinkle a little rice flour, pepper and cilantro all over the round. Cut into five 1-inch strips. Place the strips one on top of another with the center one on the bottom and roll up the whole thing jelly roll fashion. Lay the roll on its side (with the spiral pattern facing up) on a floured surface. Roll into a 4- to 4½-inch circle, dusting with flour as necessary to keep it from sticking.

4. Transfer the paratha to the hot griddle and cook until it starts to puff in places, about 1 minute. Using a wide metal spatula, flip the bread and continue to cook until the bottom is lightly browned. Drizzle with ½ teaspoon oil. Press gently with the back of a spoon so the bread will cook evenly. Transfer to a plate and cover with foil or a towel. Repeat with the remaining dough. To serve, cut the paratha into quarters and pile into a towel-lined basket.

# MUNG BEAN-SPINACH WHOLESOME FLATBREAD
## (Mung Dal Paratha Anarkali)

Makes 6
Preparation time:
40 minutes

¼ cup dried yellow
    mung beans (mung
    dal), picked clean
1 cup water
1 cup packed chopped
    fresh spinach
1½ fresh hot chiles,
    stemmed and minced
1 teaspoon minced garlic
¼ teaspoon salt
¼ cup unbleached
    all-purpose flour
¼ cup whole wheat
    flour

I make flatbreads every day for my family, and for that reason alone I have to be innovative. Rich in protein and iron, this version is especially nutritious, yet simple to make. All you have to do is stir flour into a quickly cooked mixture of yellow mung beans and spinach, then roll it out and toast it like other flatbreads. Brushed with melted desi ghee or slathered with your choice of cheese spreads, it makes a perfect brunch or lunchbox favorite.

1. Place the mung dal in a medium saucepan and rinse. Drain well and add the 1 cup water. Bring to a boil on medium-high heat. Reduce the heat to medium, partially cover the pan, and cook until just tender, about 15 minutes. Add the spinach and cook uncovered until the beans are fully cooked and soft, the spinach is tender, and the liquid is all absorbed, another 6 minutes. Stir in the chiles, garlic, and salt and cook for 2 minutes. Remove from the heat and let cool completely.

2. Gradually add the flours to the spinach-dal mixture, mixing with a wooden spoon. Turn the dough out onto a floured surface and knead with lightly oiled hands into a medium-soft, slightly sticky texture. Divide the dough into 6 portions and roll each portion between your hands to form a smooth ball; flatten slightly and put on a plate.

3. Preheat a griddle or skillet over high heat for 2 minutes; reduce the heat to medium. Meanwhile, roll out a ball of dough into a 5-inch oval, dusting with flour as necessary. Transfer the flatbread to the hot griddle and cook until it starts to puff in places, about 1 minute. Using a metal spatula, flip the bread and continue to cook until the bottom is speckled lightly. Press with the back of a spoon gently so the bread will cook evenly. Transfer to a plate. Repeat with the remaining dough. Cut into wedges and serve on a heated platter.

**Note:** Do not use the food processor to make this dough; the breads should be bright creamy yellow with green streaks of spinach. If the dough is made in the food processor, the beans and spinach will become a green puree and you will have yellowish-green flatbreads with the same flavor throughout.

# GRANDMOTHER'S VILLAGE-STYLE CORN-POTATO FLATBREAD
## (Alu-Makkai Paratha)

Makes 6
Preparation time:
   20 minutes (after
   baking the potato)

1 fresh hot green chile,
   stemmed
1½ tablespoons coarsely
   chopped fresh mint
   leaves
¼ cup corn kernels,
   steamed until tender
1 large (½ pound) russet
   potato, baked, peeled,
   and mashed
1½ teaspoons grated
   fresh ginger
½ teaspoon ground
   coriander
½ teaspoon ground
   cumin
½ teaspoon salt
1 cup whole wheat flour,
   plus additional for
   dusting
¼ cup unbleached all-
   purpose flour
¼ cup rice flour
Melted desi ghee or
   butter, for brushing

I am reminded of my childhood visits to my grandmother's village when I make these hand-shaped, smoky-flavored breads. First she'd roast a large potato in the slow embers of her clay oven until butter-soft inside. Then she steamed kernels of tender corn, mashed them in a stone mortar, and combined them with the potato, spices, and herbs to stuff into a bread dough. As I watched, she would stretch and slap the dough back and forth into a perfect round, then half-roast the bread on a griddle, completing the cooking by holding the bread directly over the open fire. Hot off the fire, brushed with homemade butter, Grandma's breads just melted in my mouth. Today, I can use all the modern conveniences to recreate her magical flavors, except perhaps the smoky flavor of the open fire.

1. *To make the dough in a food processor:* Drop the chile and mint through the feed tube and mince. Add the corn and process until finely pureed. Add the remaining ingredients except the ghee and process until the dough begins to clean the sides of the bowl (see Note). *By hand:* Finely mince the chile, mint, and corn. Combine with the potato, ginger, spices, salt, and flours in a large mixing bowl. Knead to make a medium-stiff dough.

2. Lightly coat your hands with oil and shape the dough into a smooth ball. Divide into 6 portions and roll each portion between your hands to form a smooth ball; put on a plate. Preheat a griddle or skillet over high heat for 2 minutes. Reduce the heat to medium.

3. Place a piece of the dough onto a floured work surface and roll to a 4- to 5-inch circle, dusting with flour as necessary. Transfer the bread to the griddle and cook until it starts to puff in places, about 1 minute. Flip the bread and continue to cook until the bottom is speckled lightly. Press with the back of a spoon to ensure even cooking. Transfer to a plate and brush with desi ghee. Cut into neat wedges. Repeat with the remaining dough. Serve the breads warm or at room temperature.

**Note:** For the right results, both the potato and the corn must be warm when you make the dough. You might want to have another medium-size baked potato handy to adjust the consistency of the dough; if it is too stiff, mash the other potato and add some to the dough in step 1. If it is soggy and sticky add a little more flour.

# ROSE-CASHEW SKILLET NAN
## (Nawabi Nan)

Makes 10 nans
Preparation time: 25
    minutes, plus 2 hours
    resting time

⅓ cup whole toasted
    cashews *or* ¼ cup
    Mughal Ready Mix
    (page 25)
½ teaspoon ground
    cardamom (omit if
    using Mughal Ready
    Mix)
¼ teaspoon baking soda
1 tablespoon sugar
¾ teaspoon salt
2 cups unbleached
    all-purpose flour
1 teaspoon rose water
    (omit if using Mughal
    Ready Mix)
¾ cup half-and-half
Flour for dusting
Softened butter,
    for brushing
5 4-inch squares silver
    leaf (*varak,* optional)

*Nawab* means prince, and these fragrant flatbreads are fit for royalty, even if they are not made in the traditional manner. In India, nan is made with flour, eggs, and yeast and the bread is slapped right on the inner walls of the smoky clay oven (tandoor) where it bakes at a very high heat. The heated clay is part of the authentic flavor and texture of the nan, distributing a mellow perfume that permeates the nans. I have tried various recipes for baking nans in a Western-style oven, under a broiler, or on a barbecue grill, but none of them is quite satisfying; they either came out tough, or hardened if not eaten immediately, or lacked flavor. So I went back to my trusted griddle, and started experimenting with unconventional ingredients like cream and ground nuts. The result is these soft, moist ovals with a wonderful aroma and distinctive nutty flavor. They can be made in advance and warmed for tea or entertaining.

1. *To make the dough in a food processor:* Put the cashews in the work bowl and process until powdered. Add the cardamom, soda, sugar, salt, flour, and rose water and process until crumbly. With the machine running, gradually add the half-and-half through the feed tube in a steady stream. Process until the dough comes together and begins to clean the sides of the bowl. *By hand:* Grind the cashews to a powder in a blender or mortar. Mix with the other dry ingredients in a mixing bowl. Make a well in the center, add the rose water, and gradually add the half-and-half, mixing until the dough holds together.

2. Shape the dough into a smooth ball. Cover and let rest for 2 to 4 hours.

3. Lightly dust your hands with flour and knead the dough briefly on a work surface. Divide into 10 portions and roll each portion between your hands to form a smooth ball. Put on a plate.

4. Preheat a griddle or skillet over high heat for 2 minutes; reduce the heat to medium. Meanwhile, roll a ball of dough into a 4-inch oval, dusting with flour as necessary. Stretch one end of the dough by hand to create a teardrop shape. Transfer the nan to the hot griddle. Cover with a lid and cook for 1 minute. Remove the lid, flip the nan with a metal spatula, and continue cooking uncovered until the bottom is speckled lightly. Brush with butter while it cooks on the second side, and press the nan gently with the back of a spoon so the bread will puff evenly. Transfer to a plate. Repeat with the remaining dough. Put silver leaf on 5 of the nans and place alternately with other 5 nans slightly overlapping in a napkin-lined serving basket. Serve warm or at room temperature.

# Whole Wheat Puffy Bread
## (Poori)

Makes about 18 pooris
Preparation time:
  20 minutes, plus
  resting time

2 tablespoons mild
  vegetable oil
1 cup whole wheat flour
1 cup unbleached all-
  purpose flour
2 tablespoons quick
  cooking cream of
  wheat
½ teaspoon salt
¾ cup water
Whole wheat flour, for
  dusting
Mild vegetable or
  avocado oil, for frying

These delightful puffs are an enticing treat for family and friends. As long as the oil is hot enough (see Deep-Frying Tips, page 41), the pooris will absorb very little oil; at 120 calories each, a poori has only 30 calories more than a chapati. Serve with any vegetable or curry dish.

1. Heat 2 tablespoons oil in a wok or large skillet until it ripples when the pan is tilted. Turn off the heat.

2. *To make the dough in a food processor:* Combine the dry ingredients in the work bowl. Add the hot oil and process until crumbly. With the machine running, gradually add the water through the feed tube in a steady stream. Process until the dough comes together and begins to clean the sides of the bowl. *By hand:* Combine the dry ingredients in a mixing bowl. Make a well in the center, add the oil, and mix until crumbly. Gradually add water and mix until the dough holds together.

3. Form the dough into a smooth ball; cover and let rest for 10 minutes. Place on a work surface and knead until soft, 5 to 6 minutes. Divide into 3 balls and put on a plate.

4. Add oil to a depth of 1½ inches to the same wok or skillet and heat to 365°F. (To test the oil, drop in a tiny piece of the dough; if it comes to the surface immediately the oil is ready for frying.) Place a ball of dough on a floured work surface and roll it out to ⅛ inch thick. Using a 3½-inch biscuit cutter, cut out 4 rounds. Reserve the trimmings. Carefully slip one of the rounds into the hot oil; it will sink and pop up. Using a slotted spoon, gently submerge the poori in the oil until it puffs and cooks evenly, about 15 seconds. Turn and fry on the other other side until golden brown. Remove and drain on paper towels. Repeat with the other three rounds, then the remaining portions of dough. Gather all the trimmings, knead them together, and roll, cut, and fry one more batch of rounds.

5. Arrange the hot pooris in a single layer in a napkin-lined basket and serve immediately. Or place on a cookie sheet, tent with foil, and keep warm in a 250°F oven for up to 30 minutes.

**Note:** Pooris can be made ahead and stacked (they will deflate immediately); wrap with paper towels and then cover loosely with foil. Store at room temperature up to 8 hours; to reheat, see page 79.

# INDORE SPINACH PUFFY BREAD
## (Indori Palak Poori)

**Makes about 14 pooris**
**Preparation time:**
    15 minutes, plus resting time

2 cups packed chopped fresh spinach
1 cup whole wheat flour
½ cup unbleached all-purpose flour
½ teaspoon salt
1½ teaspoons mild olive oil
⅓ cup warm water
Whole wheat flour, for dusting
Mild vegetable or avocado oil, for frying

This pretty striped spinach puff is perfect for an elegant dinner. Make the dough and side dishes ahead of time, so you can fry the pooris as your guests arrive and serve them hot from the fryer. They are also well suited for a dinner for two by the fireside. Studded with delicate greens, the pooris can be served with Braised Paneer Cheese in Rich Tomato Sauce (page 167), Whole Kernel Corn Raita (page 175), a sweet chutney, and Royal Vegetable Basmati Rice (page 138). End the elegant meal with a platter of sliced seasonal fruits.

1. Cook the spinach in a skillet on medium heat with just the water clinging to the leaves, stirring occasionally, until completely wilted, about 6 minutes. Cool to room temperature. Place the flours and salt in a large mixing bowl. Make a well in the center, add the spinach and oil, and mix gently until crumbly. Gradually add water and mix until the dough holds together.

2. Form the dough into a smooth ball. Cover and let rest for 10 minutes. Place the dough on a floured work surface and knead briefly. Divide into 2 balls and put on a plate. Fill a wok or skillet with oil to a depth of 1½ inches and heat to 365°F. (To test the oil, drop in a tiny piece of the dough; if it comes to the surface immediately the oil is ready for frying.) Place a piece of dough on a floured work surface and roll it out to ⅛ inch thick. Using a 3½-inch biscuit cutter, cut out 6 rounds.

3. Carefully slip one round of dough into the hot oil; it will sink and pop up. Using a slotted spoon, gently submerge the poori in oil until it puffs and cooks evenly, about 15 seconds. Turn and fry on the other side until golden brown. Remove and drain on paper towels. Repeat with the other rounds, then the other portion of dough. Reknead and reroll the trimmings and cut out and fry a few more rounds. Arrange on a warm serving platter and serve immediately.

**Note:** See Deep-Frying Tips (page 41) before you start. The pooris can be made ahead and placed in a 250°F oven, covered loosely with foil, for up to 30 minutes; they will deflate.

Do not use a food processor to make the dough — instead of golden pooris with attractive green streaks you will have green pooris.

**Variation:** Substitute ½ cup of fresh tender fenugreek leaves (see page 18), kale, or collard greens for the spinach.

# YOGURT BALLOON BREAD
## (Bhatura)

Makes 20
Preparation time:
    25 minutes, plus 3 to
    4 hours resting time

4 cups unbleached
    all-purpose flour
1 teaspoon salt
2 teaspoons sugar
1 teaspoon baking soda
½ teaspoon cumin seeds
2 tablespoons desi ghee
    or unsalted butter
1 cup plain yogurt,
    stirred to blend
⅓ cup water
Mild vegetable or
    avocado oil, for frying
Flour for dusting

One creative version of fried poori is *bhatura,* in which a small amount of yogurt acts as a leavening agent. Traditionally it accompanies Garbanzo Beans in Tangy Tomato Sauce (page 160) with onion slices and lemon wedges passed at the side. Sometimes I serve this bread topped with a sweet chutney along with Vegetable Mulligatawny with Pink Lentils (page 50).

1. *To make the dough in a food processor:* Combine the dry ingredients in the work bowl, add the desi ghee, and process until crumbly. With the machine running, gradually add the yogurt, followed by the water in a steady stream. Process until the dough begins to clean the sides of the bowl. *By hand:* Combine the dry ingredients in a large mixing bowl. Add the desi ghee and mix until crumbly. Make a well in the center, add the yogurt and water, and mix until the dough holds together.

2. Form the dough into a smooth ball. Cover and let rest for 3 to 4 hours.

3. Lightly coat your hands with oil and place the dough on a work surface. Knead until smooth and elastic. Divide the dough in half. Roll each half into a log and cut the log into 10 equal pieces, to make 20 in all. Roll each portion between your hands to form a smooth ball. Put on a plate and cover.

4. Fill a wok or skillet with oil to a depth of 2 inches and heat to 365°F. (To test the oil, drop in a tiny piece of dough; if it comes to the surface immediately the oil is ready for frying.) Meanwhile, roll out a ball of dough on a floured work surface to a 4½-inch round, slightly thicker than ⅛ inch. Carefully slip the bhatura into the hot oil. As it rises, use a slotted spoon to gently submerge it in the oil until it puffs and cooks evenly, 15 to 20 seconds. Turn and fry on the other side until puffy and light brown. Remove and drain on paper towels. Repeat with the remaining dough. The oil temperature will drop at first but rise again as the bhaturas brown, so regulate the heat accordingly. Arrange the breads in slightly overlapping stacks in a basket and serve immediately.

# ONION-SESAME PUFFY BREAD
## (Poori Banjaran)

Makes about 20 pooris
Preparation time:
   20 minutes

Scant ¼ cup mild
   vegetable or avocado
   oil
2 cups unbleached
   all-purpose flour
½ tablespoon sesame
   seeds
1 teaspoon cumin seeds
2 fresh hot green chiles,
   stemmed and minced
½ cup finely chopped
   onion
½ teaspoon salt
Scant ½ cup water
Mild vegetable oil, for
   frying

When I visit India, one person I love to meet is my mother's maid Gangawwa, who has been with her for over 20 years. She still teases me about my childhood forays in the kitchen and how I would sniff around and exclaim, "Boy, does that smell delicious!" without ever offering to help or learn. These pooris, which she called "gypsy bread," were her favorites and she often made them as after-school snacks for us. They remain soft-textured and fresh for up to 3 days at room temperature. On a cold wintry evening, accompany the bread with Hearty Vegetable Soup (page 45).

1. Heat the ¼ cup of oil in a skillet until quite hot; remove from the heat.

2. *To make the dough in a food processor:* Combine the flour, sesame, cumin, chiles, onion, and salt in the work bowl. Add the hot oil and process until crumbly. With the machine running, gradually add the water through the feed tube in a steady stream. Process until the dough comes together and begins to clean the sides of the bowl. *By hand:* Combine the flour, sesame, cumin, chiles, onion, and salt in a large mixing bowl. Make a well in the center and add the hot oil. Mix until crumbly. Add water and mix until it comes together in a medium-soft, slightly sticky dough.

3. Place the dough on a work surface and knead 5 to 6 minutes. Divide into 3 balls and put on a plate. Fill a wok or skillet with oil to a depth of 1½ inches and heat to 365°F. (To test the oil temperature, drop in a tiny piece of the dough; if it comes to the surface immediately the oil is ready for frying.) Place a ball of dough on a floured work surface and roll it out to ⅛ inch thick. Using a 3½-inch biscuit cutter, cut out 4 rounds. Reserve the trimmings.

3. Carefully slip a round of dough into the hot oil; it will sink and pop up. Using a slotted spoon, gently submerge the poori in oil until it puffs and cooks evenly, about 15 seconds. Turn and fry the other side until golden brown. Remove and drain on paper towels. Repeat with the remaining dough; reknead and reroll the trimmings to cut out additional pooris. If the pooris brown instantly, reduce the heat to maintain a temperature of 355° to 365°F.

**Variation:** When Gangawwa made these, she used a mixture of millet and whole wheat flour, which gives a distinctive, "country" flavor. If you want to try it, substitute 1½ cups whole wheat pastry flour and ½ cup millet flour for the all-purpose flour.

# VEGETABLE DISHES

Roasted Eggplant Smothered with Tomatoes

Seasoned Potatoes with Peas and Raisins

Garlicky Smothered Bell Peppers

Anaheim Chiles Smothered with Sesame Seeds

Cauliflower and Pepper Stir-Fry

Crisp Okra with Crushed Peanuts

Sauteed Eggplant Slices with Sesame and Walnuts

Sauteed Potatoes with Crushed Nuts

Stuffed Eggplant with Shallots

Potato-Stuffed Anaheim Chiles in Cream Sauce

Hyderabad Stuffed Zucchini

Chayote Curry with Peanuts

Mushrooms Braised in Mustard Greens

Morel Mushrooms with Cashews and Dates

Veggies and Fruits in Fragrant Korma Curry Sauce

Mangalore Pineapple Curry

Tropical Green Papaya Roast

Gujarat-Style Baked Cabbage

Baked Bombay Potatoes

Royal Cabbage Packets in Saffron Sauce

Baked Swiss Chard Rolls with Apple-Tomato Sauce

"Melt-In-Your-Mouth" Pan Bread

Basil-Coconut Vegetable Casserole

Vegetable Koftas in Velvety Cream Sauce

Pumpkin Koftas in Rustic Swiss Chard Sauce

Baked Yam Koftas in Green Gravy

Acorn Squash Wadas in Garlicky Peanut Oil

Spinach Wadas in Aromatic Korma Sauce

Fresh vegetables, together with grains and legumes, make up the great triumvirate of the Indian vegetarian diet. In addition to supplying essential nutrients, vegetables provide the greatest diversity of flavors, textures, and colors. For thousands of years, Indian cooks have combined vegetables with herbs, spices, and dairy products in endless permutations to form the largest range of vegetable preparations in the world.

In India, my mother has a large garden, full of tropical plants and exotic introduced varieties. I remember as I was growing up spending most of our leisure time strolling or working in the garden. The kitchen garden and herb patch received special attention, and the vegetables in it were dearly loved and treated with respect. Planting a seed and observing it grow into a mature plant with juicy fruits and vegetables was very satisfying. By touching and feeling the young plants, my mother would say we were "talking" to them. We would eagerly reap baskets full of fresh fenugreek and dill, yellow and green string beans, and an assortment of eggplants and squashes with distinct shapes and colors.

What we did not grow ourselves, we typically purchased at the doorstep from the vendors who brought them from nearby villages. (Cooking frozen or canned vegetables was unheard of.) As a vegetarian, my mother would turn this daily harvest into two or three vegetable dishes for every meal, in contrasting colors, to be served with dal, bread, and rice.

When I came to America, I brought with me this love for fresh vegetable dishes. A cornucopia of produce from all over the world is available in American supermarkets. Now and then, I am asked by other shoppers about some of the more "curious" vegetables in my cart, such as okra, chayote, daikon, fresh dill, and kohlrabi. When they do make it to the counter finally, it is not uncommon to find the cashier staring at them, rolling them in hand, and hollering for help to look up the price. I find it quite amusing and take the opportunity to pass along recipes to anyone brave enough to ask.

But it is in my weekly tours of the farmers' market where I most clearly recall the garden-fresh produce of my childhood. Amid the familiar varieties, I have been fascinated by unusual treasures such as gold, blue, and purple potatoes, yellow baby zucchini, pear tomatoes, and morel mushrooms, and items which I had never seen before, like kumquats.

I also inherited my mother's love of gardening, and I have planted a vegetable and herb garden everywhere I have lived since then. Nothing is more gratifying than picking earth-speckled tubers, sun-ripened tomatoes, and dew-covered greens and cooking them with fragrant herbs and spices in their true and natural form. When we lived in Ohio, the cold winters limited my gardening to spring through fall, but here in California I enjoy a year-round growing season. Summer means tomatoes (to use both red and green), summer squashes, basil, and various types of eggplant, and in the cooler months I grown spinach, fenugreek, and other greens. Of course, there is always cilantro growing in the herb patch.

When it comes to cooking these and other vegetables, I fall back on my Indian background. Indian cooking provides an excellent selection of styles of vegetable dishes — sauteed, stir-fried, steamed, braised, baked, sauced, stuffed, and roasted. Vegetables combine well with myriad flavorings, from the most delicate herb to the spiciest of spices. Many vegetables marry happily with one another, and with fruits and nuts. They are nutritious and economical, and taste wonderful in different ways.

The following collection of vegetable recipes is organized by cooking method. We begin with the typically Indian technique of tossing roasted or otherwise precooked vegetables in oil seasoned with spices. Roasted Eggplant Smothered with Tomatoes (page 96) is the most familiar example of this style.

Stir-frying and sauteing — cooking cut-up vegetables briskly over high heat in a small amount of oil — are not as popular techniques in India as they are in China and Southeast Asia, but several regions have their stir-fried or sauteed vegetable specialties. In the Indian style, the evenly cut pieces (julienned, chopped, or diced) are cooked over moderately high heat, and are lifted and turned (gently, rather than briskly as in Chinese stir-frying) in spice-infused oil until tender-crisp and lightly browned. Nuts and seeds add texture, flavor, and nutritional value.

Stuffed vegetables are among the most important preparations in Indian vegetarian cuisine. The procedures and ingredients vary from region to region and household to household, but cooks all over India use blends of spices, onion, nuts, and coconut to add excitement to the already delicious flavors of vegetables. In a distinctive technique that is unique to Indian cooking, vegetables like eggplant and zucchini are often quartered lengthwise, making a cross-shaped opening that exposes a lot of the inner surface to the stuffing. The stem end is left intact to hold the quarters and the stuffing together. Bell peppers, large chiles, okra, tomatoes, other summer squash like pattypan and crookneck can all be used interchangeably for stuffing; adjust the amount of filling according to the length and width of the vegetables.

For most Westerners, "curry" is synonymous with Indian cooking, and probably suggests a single style of dish. To an Indian cook, on the other hand, it covers many widely different dishes: thin and soupy dishes like *rasam, saar,* and *kadhi* (discussed in the chapter on soups); thick, stewlike curries (which also include legume stews such as sambar); and *kormas* or "dry" curries.

What all these dishes have in common is that the vegetables, fruits, or legumes are cooked in a spiced sauce (*kari* in the Tamil language). The British borrowed the word in the colonial period, and "curry" has been part of the English language ever since, although it has taken on a rather narrow meaning (see page 22).

The vegetable curries in this chapter give a sense of the extraordinary and fascinating variations of the genre. The sauce can be abundant, thick, and velvety, as in the Mushrooms Braised in Mustard Greens on page 110; or it can be thick and almost dry, so it clings to the veggies, as in the *korma* on page 112. The choice of spices varies from one region to the next; southern cooks often use a "wet masala" of fresh chiles, onion, and kari leaves, while in the north, dry spices are more typical. Even how and when the spices are used varies. A spice blend may be tossed in the oil at the beginning, or drizzled in toward the end of cooking, or simply sprinkled on a finished dish, giving a different effect in each case. In the Mangalore Pineapple Curry on page 113, most of the spices are used to infuse the oil that is added to the simmered pineapple as the last step.

Baking as practiced by Westerners has a very limited role in the Indian subcontinent. Except in the north, where cooks use an old-fashioned clay oven (*tandoor*) for baking meats, vegetables, and breads, the typical Indian kitchen does not have an oven. Instead, most dishes are cooked on top of the stove.

The most common form of "baking" in India is to cook foods in an earthenware pot buried in live coals, with additional coals placed on top of the sunken lid. It's the same technique used in this country by campfire cooks using a cast iron Dutch oven.

Since moving to America, I have learned to rely on the convenience and reliable heat of a modern oven, and have adapted many traditional dishes to baking. The Gujarat-Style Baked Cabbage on page 115 is based on the buried-pot cooking of this state in western India, but you don't have to build a fire in the backyard or fireplace. The capacity of the oven has also inspired me to adapt the Western-style casserole to Indian flavors, creating innovative dishes like Baked Bombay Potatoes.

The chapter ends with the savory dumplings known as *koftas* and *wadas*. *Kofta* usually means meatball, and the word occurs in various forms from India to the Middle East. In yet another clever adaptation of a meat dish to a vegetarian style, Indian cooks make koftas with a variety of vegetables — potato, cauliflower, radish, cabbage, and squash, to name a few. Paneer cheese, chopped nuts, or dried fruits are added occasionally to make them rich. A little cornstarch or chick-pea flour is used to bind the ingredients together. Koftas are traditionally fried, but I have adapted one variety to baking. When steamed they become known as *wadas*.

Curried koftas make an attractive, hearty entree. The sauce can simply be spooned over the freshly cooked koftas, or for a different effect you can simmer them for a while in the sauce to soften and absorb additional flavors. I have recommended specific sauces that partner the koftas pleasingly, but you can improvise with other combinations. Serve as a main course with generous helpings of flatbreads and hot steamed rice when appetites are substantial.

Bite-size koftas make a tempting, tasty hors d'oeuvre that can easily be popped into the mouth. Feel free to pair koftas with chutneys or dips to serve with cocktails. Be sure to make plenty, because they will disappear quickly. If you have any left over, you can serve them as an entree another day, with your favorite sauce.

## STOVETOP ROASTING

One of the most typical cooking techniques of the traditional Indian kitchen is "roasting" vegetables. Whole eggplant, potatoes, squash, and similar vegetables are left in the dying embers of the cooking fire (this was always one of my father's favorite cooking tasks). After a few hours, they are retrieved from the ashes, dusted off, and peeled, and then they are ready to be cut up and seasoned with onion, tomatoes, oil, and chile. It may seem odd, but the easiest way to get the same rich, smoky "outdoor" flavor in a Western kitchen is by roasting the vegetables right on the stovetop. (This technique is also used in modern Indian kitchens.)

To catch the drippings from the roasting vegetables, lay a sheet of aluminum foil under the heating coil of an electric burner. Rub the surface of the whole vegetables with a little oil, set the heat control on medium-high, and place the vegetable stem side up directly on the burner. Roast for a few minutes, then turn it on its side. Turn the vegetable every few minutes (using the stem as a handle, or with a skewer or knife inserted near the stem end, or with tongs) until it is completely charred on the outside and butter-soft inside. Place on a dinner plate or in a bowl and cover with a lid to trap the steam, which helps loosen the skin.

After about 20 minutes, the vegetable should be cool enough to handle. Hold the stem with one hand and peel off the charred skin with the other. Dip your hand in a bowl or pan of cold water every now and then so that any skin sticking to your fingers will slip off in the water. Wash the peeled vegetable in cold running water to remove any remaining charred pieces. Place on a cutting board and cut off the stem. The pulp is now ready to be chopped and used as directed in the recipes.

If you have a large quantity of vegetables to roast, you can use a charcoal grill or broiler to save time. Or roast them in a hot oven. Whichever method you use, you can roast and peel the vegetables and store the pulp in the refrigerator for up to 5 days, or freeze it for 2 to 3 months.

# Roasted Eggplant Smothered with Tomatoes
## (Baingan Bharata)

Serves 4
Preparation time:
   50 minutes

¼ teaspoon plus 1 table-
   spoon mild vegetable
   oil
1 medium eggplant
   (1 pound)
¼ teaspoon mustard
   seeds
¼ teaspoon cumin seeds
½ cup finely chopped
   onion
½ fresh hot green chile,
   stemmed and finely
   chopped
⅛ teaspoon turmeric
½ cup chopped tomato
¼ teaspoon curry
   powder, homemade
   (page 22) or store-
   bought
½ teaspoon salt,
   or to taste
½ teaspoon sugar,
   or to taste
Chopped fresh cilantro

This dish is extremely popular in Indian restaurants, though it can be quite expensive considering the humble ingredients involved and the typically small servings. It is an easy and inexpensive dish for the home cook to serve as a side dish with breads or pilafs or as a relish on toasts or crackers.

1. Rub the eggplant on all sides with 1/4 teaspoon oil. Preheat the broiler, or prepare a charcoal grill, or line a stove burner with foil for stove-top grilling (see page 95). Roast the eggplant, turning occasionally, until the outside is completely charred and the pulp is soft, about 20 to 25 minutes. Cover and set aside briefly to cool.

2. As soon as the eggplant is cool enough to handle, remove and discard the charred skin. Rinse quickly in cold running water to wash away any remaining bits of skin. Set the eggplant on a cutting board and cut off and discard the stem end, plus any tough, stringy parts. Chop the pulp coarsely and set aside.

3. Heat the remaining 1 tablespoon oil in a medium skillet over medium-high heat. Add the mustard and cumin seeds. When the seeds begin to sizzle and splutter, add the onion, chile, and turmeric. Stir and cook 2 to 3 minutes. Add the tomato and cook another 2 minutes. Stir in the eggplant and curry powder. Reduce the heat to low, cover, and cook, stirring occasionally, until thick, 8 to 10 minutes. Season to taste with salt and sugar. Garnish with cilantro and serve hot.

**Microwave:** The eggplant will cook quickly in a microwave oven, but the skin will not char and the flavor will not be the same as with grilled or roasted eggplant. In step 1, place the oiled eggplant on a microwavable dinner or pie plate. Cook at full power for 9 minutes or until a knife pierces it easily. Cool briefly, then continue with step 2.

**Note:** In India, the favored eggplant for roasting is a dainty variety about 2 inches in diameter. Some markets here sell small round Thai varieties which are similar; however, any eggplant, from the slender Chinese and Japanese varieties to the large deep-purple Italian globe type can be roasted and served in the Indian style. Whichever type you choose, look for a taut, smooth skin and a green calyx, which indicates a fresh eggplant; avoid any with shriveled skin or soft spots.

# Seasoned Potatoes with Peas and Raisins
## *(Alu Sabji)*

Serves 10
Preparation time:
   30 minutes

5 medium boiling
   potatoes (about 1½
   pounds)
3 tablespoons mild
   vegetable oil
¼ teaspoon mustard
   seeds
¼ teaspoon cumin seeds
¾ cup finely chopped
   onion
2 fresh hot green chiles,
   stemmed and chopped
⅛ teaspoon turmeric
¼ cup frozen petite
   peas, thawed
1 tablespoon dark raisins
1 tablespoon chopped
   cashews
1 teaspoon salt
1 teaspoon lime juice
Chopped fresh cilantro

Whenever I use the pressure cooker to cook a batch of dal (see page 150), I toss in a few potatoes to make this side dish. Otherwise, simple boiled potatoes will work fine. Combined with favorite Indian seasonings, tender peas, golden raisins, and crunchy cashews, the potatoes can be served on their own as a vegetable dish, or try them with Whole Wheat Puffy Bread (page 87) for a special brunch. Or tuck them into hot buttered rolls for a wonderful travelling companion or brown bag lunch.

1. Boil the potatoes until tender, about 15 minutes. Peel and dice. Set aside to cool if time permits.

2. Heat the oil in a large heavy skillet over medium-high heat. Add the mustard and cumin. When the seeds begin to sizzle and splutter, add the onion, chiles, and turmeric. Stir and cook until the onion is soft, 3 to 4 minutes.

3. Add the potatoes, peas, raisins, cashews, and salt and mix gently but thoroughly. Reduce the heat to low, cover, and cook until heated through. Just before serving, sprinkle with lime juice and toss to mix. Serve garnished with cilantro leaves.

**Note:** If the potatoes are still warm in step 3, mix them with the seasonings very gently or they will get mashed. Cooking the potatoes ahead of time and refrigerating them for an hour makes them easier to handle.

   The whole dish can be made several hours ahead, covered, and set aside at room temperature, or up to 3 days in the refrigerator. Reheat on a moderate flame or in a microwave oven.

**Variation:** Leftover *alu sabji* is a favorite stuffing for *samosas* and *dosas* (see Paper-Thin Rice Crepes Udupi Style, page 72). Or mix it with whole wheat flour and cilantro in the food processor to make potato parathas (page 77).

# GARLICKY SMOTHERED BELL PEPPERS
## (*Simla Mirch Bharata*)

Serves 4
Preparation time:
  35 minutes

1 large green bell pepper
  (9 ounces)
1 large red bell pepper
  (9 ounces)
1 teaspoon plus 1 table
  spoon mild vegetable
  oil
½ teaspoon cumin seeds
½ cup finely chopped
  onion
1 teaspoon crushed garlic
1 teaspoon crushed fresh
  ginger
1 or 2 fresh hot green
  chiles, stemmed and
  minced
½ cup chopped tomato
⅓ teaspoon salt
¼ teaspoon sugar
Chopped fresh cilantro

These roasted bell peppers explode with the flavors of garlic and ginger. One red and one green pepper gives a nice color contrast. Serve with Tomato-Spinach Flatbread (page 81), a yogurt raita, and Curried Mixed Sprouts (page 158). Follow with a rice pilaf for a complete meal. This is also good over toast or as a canapé filling, and is a wonderful topping for noodles. The roasted peppers can also be combined with peas to extend their flavor to a larger dish.

1. Rub the peppers all over with 1 teaspoon oil. Preheat the broiler, prepare a charcoal grill, or prepare a stovetop burner for direct cooking (see page 95). Roast the peppers, turning often, until the skin is blistered and well charred on all sides, about 15 minutes. Wrap in paper bags or place in a covered bowl and let stand 10 minutes to steam. Peel off and discard the charred skins and split and core the peppers. Wash under running cold water and pat dry on paper towels. Chop the peppers very finely; there should be about 1½ cups.

2. Heat the remaining tablespoon of oil in a heavy 2-quart skillet over medium-high heat. Add the cumin, onion, garlic, ginger, and chile. Stir and fry 4 to 5 minutes. Add the tomato and roasted pepper and cook, stirring occasionally, until reduced by a third, 8 to 10 minutes. Add the salt and sugar, mix well, and remove from the heat. Garnish with cilantro.

**Note:** This dish can be prepared ahead and stored at room temperature for several hours or covered and refrigerated up to 2 days. Rewarm on a moderate flame or in the microwave.

# Anaheim Chiles Smothered with Sesame Seeds
## *(Mirch Masala Foogath)*

Serves 2 to 4
Preparation time:
    10 minutes

6 Anaheim chiles
    (12 ounces in all)
2 tablespoons mild
    vegetable oil
4 cloves garlic, minced
1 teaspoon sesame seeds
2 teaspoons light brown
    sugar, or to taste
½ teaspoon ground
    cumin
¼ teaspoon salt
2 teaspoons lime or
    lemon juice
2 teaspoons flaked
    sweetened coconut

My sister-in-law Uma introduced me to this simple stir-fry on a visit to India. Uma uses bell peppers, but I find it has a more interesting flavor when made with the long green Anaheim chiles. If you don't care about removing the seeds, you can slice the peppers crosswise into attractive ½-inch rings. For a change, try it on buttered toasts or serve with Calcutta Plain Flakybread (page 82). To expand the dish and vary the flavors and colors, add a large portobello mushroom cut into wedges.

1. Remove the chile stems, slit the chiles lengthwise, and discard the seeds. Cut into ½-inch squares. Heat the oil in a skillet or wok over medium-high heat until it ripples when the pan is tilted. Add the chiles and garlic. Stir-fry until the edges of the chiles start to brown, about 5 minutes.

2. Reduce the heat to low. Add the sesame, sugar, cumin, salt, and lime juice. Stir and cook until tender, 2 to 3 minutes. Transfer to a serving dish. Serve with a sprinkling of coconut.

**Note:** This dish can be made ahead and kept, covered, at room temperature for 2 hours or in the refrigerator up to 3 days. Reheat over a moderate flame or in the microwave oven.

# CAULIFLOWER AND PEPPER STIR-FRY
## (Kadai Phoolgobi)

Serves 4
Preparation time:
   15 minutes

2 tablespoons mild
   peanut or sesame oil
¼ teaspoon cumin seeds
1 fresh hot green chile,
   chopped
⅛ teaspoon turmeric
2 cups cauliflower cut
   into 1-inch florets
½ cup 2-inch julienne
   strips red bell peppers
½ cup 2-inch julienne
   strips yellow or green
   bell peppers
¼ cup fresh or thawed
   petite peas
½ teaspoon salt
1 tablespoon lemon juice
½ teaspoon My Mother's
   Spice Blend (page 23)
   or garam masala
1 tablespoon minced
   cilantro

Cauliflower is truly a versatile vegetable. Here it teams up with dainty peas and peppers for a pleasing side dish to serve with Whole Wheat Puffy Bread (page 87) and Tomato-Cucumber Raita (page 174) for a quick lunch. But that's only one of the possible uses. As a topping for barbecued foods, it makes a beautiful mosaic of colors. Stir in chunks of broiled paneer toward the end of cooking for a burst of tangy flavor. Or add it to cooked tortellini to make a spicy pasta entree.

1. Heat the oil in a heavy wok or saute pan over medium-high heat until it ripples when the pan is tilted. Toss in the cumin, chile, and turmeric. Stir and cook 1 minute. Add the cauliflower, peppers, and peas if fresh. Stir-fry until the edges of the florets start to brown on all sides, 6 to 8 minutes.

2. Reduce the heat to low. Add the peas now if using frozen. Sprinkle with salt, lemon juice, and the spice blend. Toss to mix. Transfer to a serving dish. Serve sprinkled with cilantro.

**Variation:** Trimmed and quartered Brussels sprouts can replace the cauliflower.

**Variation:** SPICY CAULIFLOWER FAJITAS (Anokhi Tukre)
Stir in a tablespoon of fajita seasoning mix and a few spoonfuls of salsa along with the spice blend in step 2. To serve, fold into warm tortillas and add cheese.

# CRISP OKRA WITH CRUSHED PEANUTS
## (Bhindi Masalewali)

Serves 4
Preparation time:
    25 minutes

3 tablespoons mild
    sesame or peanut oil
¼ teaspoon cumin seeds
1 small onion, peeled,
    halved, and thinly
    sliced
½ tablespoon minced
    garlic
1 or 2 fresh hot green
    chiles, stemmed and
    slit lengthwise
1 pound fresh okra,
    trimmed and sliced
    into ½-inch-thick rings
2 tablespoons crushed
    roasted peanuts (page
    239)
½ teaspoon garam
    masala, homemade
    (page 21) or store-
    bought (optional)
½ teaspoon salt
2 teaspoons lemon juice
1 tablespoon flaked
    sweetened or
    unsweetened coconut

Okra is extremely popular in India for its mild asparagus-like flavor. Like tomatoes and other hot-weather vegetables, it is available most of the year, but it is most plentiful and at its best in late summer. Buy tender and slender pods that snap easily at their tapered ends. Stir-frying takes away the slimy stickiness and renders the okra crisp and firm. Crushed peanuts add texture and flavor. Serve as a side dish with any of the curried main courses.

1. Heat the oil in a heavy skillet or saute pan over medium-high heat until it ripples when the pan is tilted. Toss in the cumin, onion, garlic, chiles, and okra. Stir and fry until the okra is no longer sticky and the edges start to brown, about 8 minutes.

2. Reduce the heat to medium. Stir in the peanuts and garam masala. Cook uncovered, stirring occasionally, for 5 minutes. Sprinkle with salt and lemon juice, toss to mix, and transfer to a heated serving dish. Serve with a sprinkle of coconut.

Note: This dish can be made ahead and kept, covered, at room temperature for 2 hours or up to 1 day in the refrigerator. Reheat on a moderate flame.

Sometimes, just before serving, I saute halved cherry tomatoes and mix them into the okra, adding another element of flavor and stretching the dish.

# SAUTEED EGGPLANT SLICES WITH SESAME AND WALNUTS
## (Sukhe Baingan)

Serves 4
Preparation time:
    20 minutes

Sauteed eggplant slices have been appearing more and more in vegetarian sandwiches and pastas in trendy restaurants. Here is an Indian-style variation on the theme. Serve with Shredded Green Cabbage Flatbread (page 81), Stewed Black-Eyed Peas with Cherry Tomatoes (page 153), and Lemon-Sesame Rice Crowned with Vegetables (page 136) for a complete meal.

1 pound Japanese or
   regular oval eggplant
4 teaspoons salt
4 tablespoons mild
   sesame or peanut oil
½ teaspoon cayenne
¼ teaspoon sugar
½ teaspoon sesame
   seeds
2 tablespoons chopped
   walnuts
2 teaspoons lemon juice
2 tablespoons chopped
   fresh cilantro or
   parsley

1. Cut the eggplant diagonally into ⅛-inch-thick slices. Place the slices in a colander and sprinkle with salt. Mix well so that each slice is coated with salt. Set aside for 10 minutes. Rinse thoroughly and pat dry.

2. Heat half the oil in a heavy 12-inch frying pan over medium heat. Add half the eggplant slices in single layer. Cover and cook until the bottoms are lightly browned, about 3 to 4 minutes. Turn and cook on the other side for 3 minutes. Remove and set aside. Repeat with the remaining oil and eggplant.

3. Return the cooked eggplant slices to the pan. Sprinkle in the cayenne, sugar, sesame, walnuts, and lemon juice and mix well. Transfer to a heated serving dish and garnish with cilantro.

**Note:** The eggplant can be sauteed and seasoned ahead, and kept covered in the refrigerator up to 3 days. Serve at room temperature, or reheat over moderate heat or in the microwave oven.

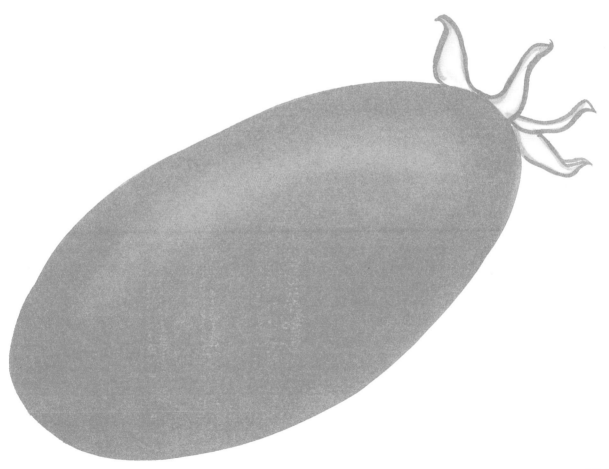

# SAUTEED POTATOES WITH CRUSHED NUTS
## (Alu Kadai)

Serves 4
Preparation time:
  25 minutes

½ pound all-purpose
  potatoes
1½ tablespoons mild
  corn or sesame oil
¼ teaspoon mustard
  seeds
¼ teaspoon cumin seeds
1 fresh hot green chile,
  stemmed and chopped
½ teaspoon salt
1 tablespoon crushed
  roasted peanuts (page
  238)
½ teaspoon fresh lime
  juice
1 teaspoon minced fresh
  cilantro

Potatoes can be cooked in a variety of ways, each with its own delectable and distinctive flavor. This dish is an excellent choice for home meals or a lunch box or picnic. (When my husband and I spent holidays in Pune, my mother-in-law would always pack some of these potatoes with chapatis for us to eat on the train journey back to Calcutta.) If the potato skins are thin and tender, do not peel them.

1. Peel the potatoes if desired and cut them into ¼-inch sticks about 1½ inches long, as for French fries. Heat the oil in a heavy wok or saute pan over medium-high heat until it ripples when the pan is tilted. Add the mustard and cumin seeds. When the seeds begin to sizzle and splutter, stir in the chile and potatoes. Stir-fry until the potatoes are coated with oil, about 4 minutes.

2. Sprinkle the potatoes with salt and peanuts. Stir and mix well. Cover, reduce the heat to medium, and cook, stirring occasionally, until the potatoes are tender, crisp, and lightly browned on the edges, 10 to 12 minutes. Add the lime juice and remove from the heat. Transfer to a serving dish, garnish with minced cilantro, and serve hot.

**Note:** The potatoes can be made ahead, and kept covered at room temperature for 4 hours or in the refrigerator up to 3 days. Reheat in a skillet over moderate heat, or in the microwave oven.

**Variations:** This dish lends itself to numerous variations. To further enhance the flavor, throw in a cup of chopped fresh dill when the potatoes are nearly done. For a more colorful presentation, use yellow Yukon Gold or purple potatoes or a combination, and add frozen petite peas at the end of cooking.

You can also use the potatoes as a topping for open-face sandwiches. Brush bread slices with Fresh Mint Chutney (page 192) and top with lettuce, sauteed potatoes, sliced tomatoes, cheese, and alfalfa sprouts.

# STUFFED EGGPLANT WITH SHALLOT
## *(Bharli Vangi)*

Serves 4 to 6
Preparation time:
   30 minutes

8 small Japanese
   eggplants (1 pound)
3 tablespoons mild
   peanut or vegetable oil
½ cup finely chopped
   shallots
2 or 3 fresh hot green
   chiles, minced
⅛ teaspoon turmeric
¼ cup grated coconut
   (fresh or dried)
½ cup crushed roasted
   peanuts
1½ teaspoons ground
   cumin
1 teaspoon ground
   coriander
1 teaspoon garam masala,
   homemade (page 21)
   or store-bought *or* 1
   teaspoon My Mother's
   Spice Blend (page 23)
1 teaspoon sugar (omit if
   using sweetened dried
   coconut)
1 teaspoon salt
2 tablespoons finely
   chopped cilantro

Eggplant is native to India, where it has always enjoyed wide popularity. In this version, they are stuffed with onion that has been slowly caramelized with peanuts, traditional seasonings, and fresh herbs, then gently cooked until exceptionally succulent. This low-calorie and healthful entree looks stunning served on a bed of freshly cooked basmati rice or even spaghetti.

1. Wash the eggplants and slit them lengthwise with 2 cuts perpendicular to each other, keeping the stem end intact. Put them in a bowl of cold water for about 10 minutes to open them up slightly (this also helps avoid discoloration).

2. Meanwhile, heat 1½ tablespoons oil in a small heavy skillet over medium heat. Add the shallots and chiles. Stir and fry until the shallots are soft, 6 to 8 minutes. Add the turmeric, coconut, and peanuts. Stir and fry 2 more minutes. Add the spices, sugar, salt, and cilantro and cook, stirring occasionally, until the spices are incorporated and aromatic, 2 to 3 minutes. Remove and set aside until cool enough to handle.

3. Remove the eggplants from the water and pat dry. Gently spread the cuts open and smear the filling inside, about 1 tablespoon of filling in each eggplant. Press together to enclose the filling.

4. Heat a nonstick skillet large enough to hold all the eggplants in a single layer over medium heat. Add 1 tablespoon oil; when the oil is hot transfer the stuffed eggplants gently to the skillet. Drizzle the remaining ½ tablespoon of oil over the eggplants. Cover and cook until lightly browned on one side, 6 to 8 minutes. Uncover and turn the eggplants gently, reduce the heat to low, cover and cook until tender, 10 to 12 minutes. Serve hot.

**Variation:** Green peppers may be used in place of eggplants. You may want to increase the quantity of the filling ingredients, or use only 4 large peppers.

# POTATO-STUFFED ANAHEIM CHILES IN CREAM SAUCE
## *(Mirchi Makhan Salan)*

Serves 4 to 6
Preparation time:
   25 minutes

1 pound (about 8)
   Anaheim chiles or
   other long peppers
1 cup warm mashed
   potato
½ teaspoon salt
½ teaspoon freshly
   ground pepper
2 tablespoons mild
   olive oil
1 medium onion, halved
   and sliced lengthwise
½ teaspoon crushed
   fresh ginger
Scant ½ teaspoon
   turmeric
½ teaspoon ground
   coriander
¼ teaspoon ground
   cumin
3 whole cloves, ground
1 cup half-and-half

Here Anaheim chiles take on a new character. Stuffed with potatoes and drenched in cream sauce, their heat is mellowed. Channa (page 164) or paneer (page 165) may be used in place of the mashed potatoes. Or, for a quick and dry version, stuff the chiles with ricotta cheese and saute without the cream sauce. Try this dish with Rustic Kidney Bean Flatbread (page 81), or in an international menu alongside your favorite Mexican or barbecued foods.

1. Slit the chiles lengthwise, leaving the stems intact, and discard the seeds. Season the potato with half the salt and pepper to taste; mix well. Stuff each chile with a generous portion of the potato mixture.

2. Heat the oil in a large heavy skillet over medium heat. Add the stuffed chiles, onion, ginger, and turmeric. Cook, stirring occasionally, until the chiles start to brown, about 6 minutes. Add the spices, remaining salt, and half-and-half. Bring to a boil, cover, and simmer until the sauce is thick and the chiles are tender, about 12 minutes. Transfer to a serving dish. Serve hot.

**Note:** The skins of the chiles are necessary to hold them together during cooking. If you find them too tough to eat, leave them behind at the table.

# HYDERABAD STUFFED ZUCCHINI
## (Hyderabadi Bhareli Lauki)

Serves 3
Preparation time:
35 minutes

3 small zucchini
(9 ounces total)
½ tablespoon sesame
seeds
2½ tablespoons mild
vegetable oil
1 large onion, grated
½ teaspoon ground
cumin
½ teaspoon curry
powder, homemade
(page 22) or store-
bought
¼ teaspoon tamarind
concentrate, dissolved
in 1 tablespoon water
1 tablespoon crushed
roasted peanuts (page
238)
½ teaspoon salt
½ teaspoon sugar

The cuisine of Hyderabad is unique in southern India, with a stronger influence from the Mughal occupation than that of other southern regions. Rich flavors of nuts and aromatic spices, together with the tamarind which grows abundantly in the region, make the cuisine as vibrant and distinct as the multi-cultural people themselves. Fresh and tender okra, bitter melon, green bananas, and many varieties of pumpkins and squashes are slashed open and cooked with stuffings of onion, tamarind, sesame, and peanuts. Zucchini is not available in India; however, it lends itself remarkably well to Indian-style spices. It is also rich in vitamin C and fiber, and relatively low in calories.

1. Trim off the flower ends of the zucchini and slice them in half. Slit each half lengthwise into fourths leaving ½ inch uncut at one end. Place in water and set aside.

2. Toast the sesame seeds in a small dry skillet over medium heat, shaking the pan often, until aromatic, about 6 minutes. Transfer to a grinder and grind to a fine powder. Set aside.

3. Heat 1 tablespoon oil in the same skillet over medium-high heat. Add the onion and cook, stirring occasionally, until it starts to brown, about 6 minutes. Reduce the heat to medium and add the cumin, curry powder, tamarind, peanuts, salt, sugar, and ground sesame. Stir and cook until all the liquid evaporates, about 5 minutes. Cool.

4. Remove the zucchini from the water and pat dry slightly. Gently spread the cuts open and smear the filling inside, about 2 teaspoons of filling in each squash. Press gently back together. Heat 1 tablespoon oil in a large nonstick skillet over medium heat. Place the zucchini side by side in a single layer. Drizzle with the remaining ½ tablespoon of oil. Cover and cook until lightly browned on one side, 6 to 8 minutes. Turn gently, reduce the heat to low, cover, and cook until tender, 10 to 12 minutes. Serve hot.

# CHAYOTE CURRY WITH PEANUTS
## (Sime Badnekai Rasa)

Serves 4
Preparation time:
     25 minutes

2 medium chayotes
     (1 pound total)
2 tablespoons mild
     vegetable oil
1 teaspoon mustard seeds
½ teaspoon cumin seeds
12 to 15 fresh kari leaves
     *or* 1 teaspoon crushed
     dried leaves
1 cup finely chopped
     onion
1 teaspoon crushed garlic
2 fresh hot green chiles,
     stemmed and slit
     lengthwise
½ teaspoon curry
     powder, homemade
     (page 22) or store-
     bought
¾ cup water
2 tablespoons fresh
     grated coconut
     (optional)
1 teaspoon salt
2 tablespoons crushed
     roasted peanuts
     (page 239)

Chayote is a pear-shaped tropical summer squash used extensively in southern Indian cooking. It has an edible delicate light green skin and moist flesh that tastes like a cross between zucchini and apple. Also called mango squash, vegetable pear, mirliton, and various other names, it is available the year around in supermarkets. Serve as a side dish accompanied by Whole Wheat Flatbread (page 79), Curried Mixed Sprouts (page 158), Asparagus Chaat with Hot Chile Oil (page 185), and Light Yogurt Rice (page 133) for a complete low-calorie meal. For a more colorful variation, or to stretch the dish if you have unexpected company, toss in halved cherry tomatoes at the end of cooking.

1. Halve the chayotes lengthwise and discard the pits. Cut the flesh into 1-inch pieces. Set aside.

2. Heat the oil in a small saucepan over medium-high heat. Add the mustard and cumin; when the seeds begin to sizzle and splutter, add the kari leaves, onion, garlic, and chiles. Cook, stirring occasionally, about 4 minutes. Add the chayote and curry powder and stir 2 minutes. Add the water, coconut, and salt and bring to a boil. Cover and simmer until the chayote is tender, 15 minutes. Just before serving, sprinkle with peanuts. (The chiles and kari leaves are not meant to be eaten; discard them before serving if you like.)

**Variation:** Other tender squashes such as green or yellow zucchini, pattypan, or yellow crookneck will yield good results, as will turnips, rutabagas, or parsnips.

# MUSHROOMS BRAISED IN MUSTARD GREENS
## (Dhingri aur Sarsoon ki Sabji)

Serves 4 to 6
Preparation time:
  30 minutes

2 cups (packed) chopped
  fresh spinach (leaves
  and tender stems from
  1 small bunch)
2 cups chopped mustard
  greens
½ cup water
3 tablespoons sesame or
  peanut oil
1 cup grated onion
1 teaspoon crushed garlic
1 teaspoon shredded
  fresh ginger, plus
  additional for garnish
2 fresh hot green chiles,
  stemmed and chopped
¼ teaspoon turmeric
½ pound chanterelles
  or button mushrooms,
  sliced
¼ teaspoon salt
½ teaspoon ground
  toasted cumin seeds
½ teaspoon ground
  toasted fennel seeds

Wild mushrooms grow in the Himalayan foothills in the north and east of India, and both wild and commercial mushrooms are common in northern cooking. Three of the most popular varieties, two wild and one cultivated, turn out to be the same as varieties found in North America. The trumpet-shaped chanterelle *(dhingri)* is enjoyed for its meaty bite, and is braised or stewed with spicy sauces. The cone-shaped morel *(guhchi)* is prized for its hearty flavor in vegetarian dishes. The familiar button-shaped agaricus *(khumbi),* grown commercially in India as it is here, is relished for its chewy texture, and is used in fritters and stir-frying.

In this light curry, mushrooms are simmered in a subtly seasoned sauce, with a peppery bite from mustard greens. It's delicious with ordinary button mushrooms, but even better with chanterelles and other wild varieties. Offer it as a side dish with breads. This is also good served over pasta, or baked in a puff pastry shell.

1. Wash the spinach and mustard greens well and put them in a medium saucepan with just the water clinging to the leaves. Cover and cook on medium heat until the leaves are soft, 5 to 6 minutes. Transfer to a blender or food processor, add ½ cup water, and blend to a smooth puree.

2. Heat the oil in a large skillet over medium heat. Add the onion, garlic, ginger, and chile. Cook, stirring, until the onion softens and starts to brown, about 5 minutes. Stir in the turmeric and mushrooms and cook 5 minutes more, stirring occasionally. Add the spinach puree and salt. Cook uncovered until piping hot.

3. Transfer to a heated serving dish. Just before serving, sprinkle with the cumin and fennel. Garnish with shreds of ginger and serve hot.

# MOREL MUSHROOMS WITH CASHEWS AND DATES
## (Guhchi Ki Meethi Saas)

Serves 6
Preparation time:
  20 minutes

½ pound fresh morels
  *or* 3 ounces dried
  morels, reconstituted
  (see note)
2 tablespoons mild
  vegetable oil
½ cup grated onion
1 teaspoon grated fresh
  ginger
¼ teaspoon turmeric
½ teaspoon garam
  masala, homemade
  (page 21) or store-
  bought
½ cup peas, fresh or
  thawed
½ cup chopped dates,
  soaked in ¼ cup water
  for 10 minutes and
  pureed
¼ teaspoon cayenne
2 tablespoons chopped
  cashews
½ teaspoon salt

Morel mushrooms (*guhchi*) are harvested in summer in Kashmir. They are expensive, therefore they are used only for specific occasions such as religious and wedding feasts. Their hearty flavor enlivens pilafs and other meatless dishes. Fresh morels are available in America from March through May in farmers' markets, specialty food stores, and some supermarkets. The dried variety is available year round. In this stew, dates act both as a thickener and to lend a distinct sweetish taste, and cayenne and garam masala round out the flavors. It's also delicious with cultivated button mushrooms. Try it with a pilaf, or as a "mushroom sauce" to top your barbecued foods or roasts.

1. Rinse the mushrooms and drain. Trim off the bases of the stems. Slice and set aside.

2. Heat the oil in a small skillet over medium-high heat. Add the onion, ginger, and turmeric. Stir and fry until lightly browned, about 4 minutes. Add the mushrooms, garam masala, and peas if fresh. Stir and cook on medium heat for 3 to 4 minutes. Stir in the remaining ingredients (add the peas now, if frozen), reduce the heat to low, cover, and cook until thick, 6 to 8 minutes. Serve hot.

**Note:** Dried mushrooms have to be rehydrated before use. Soak in enough warm water to cover the mushrooms for 30 minutes. Lift them out of the water, rinse under cold water, and scrub gently with a stiff brush to remove any grit. Pat dry with paper towels, and discard any tough stems.

# VEGGIES AND FRUITS IN FRAGRANT KORMA CURRY SAUCE
## (Shahi Navratna Korma)

Serves 6
Preparation time:
    35 minutes

1 tablespoon desi ghee
    or unsalted butter
½ tablespoon crushed
    garlic
Seeds from 4 green
    cardamom pods,
    ground
¼ teaspoon cinnamon
¾ teaspoon ground
    coriander
1 tablespoon tomato paste
¼ cup cauliflower, cut
    into 1-inch florets
¼ cup sliced carrots
¼ cup diagonally
    chopped green beans
¼ cup chopped zucchini
5 Brussels sprouts,
    trimmed and cut in half
¼ cup broccoli florets
⅓ cup julienned red and
    green bell pepper
2 tablespoons peas,
    fresh or thawed
½ cup whipping cream
    or half-and-half
½ teaspoon salt
½ teaspoon sugar
¼ cup plain yogurt
¼ teaspoon cayenne
¼ teaspoon paprika
2 tablespoons chopped
    blanched almonds
1 tablespoon raisins
½ cup pineapple
    chunks (fresh or
    canned), drained
Orange sections, for
    garnish

Korma, a splendid sauce, evolved in the magnificent kitchens of the Mughals. *Navratna* translates as "nine diamonds," and superstitious Indian women believe possessing a piece of jewelry studded with navratna brings luck. Here, the nine jewels are an assortment of healthful vegetables, steeped in a soothing yogurt sauce. You can add some diced paneer cheese to the vegetable mix. Precede this specialty with Classic Mixed Greens Soup (page 51). For a complete Mughal-style meal, accompany with Rose-Cashew Skillet Nan (page 86), Nectarine and Currant Chutney with Pecans (page 199), and a rice pilaf such as Shahjahan Corn Pilaf (page 140). Serve Yogurt Mango Cooler (page 229) to drink.

1. Melt the desi ghee in a heavy medium saucepan over moderate heat. Add the garlic and cook until light brown. Add the cardamom, cinnamon, and coriander; stir and cook until aromatic, about 1 minute. Add the tomato paste and cook, stirring occasionally, 1 more minute. Add all the vegetables. Stir and cook about 5 minutes.

2. Add the cream, salt, sugar, yogurt, cayenne, paprika, almonds, and raisins. Cover and cook until the vegetables are just tender, about 10 minutes. Gently stir in the pineapple chunks. Transfer to a heated serving bowl. Garnish with orange sections and serve hot.

# MANGALORE PINEAPPLE CURRY
## (*Aamtekai Rasa*)

Serves 3 to 4
Preparation time:
   20 minutes

1 can (20 ounces)
   pineapple chunks in
   unsweetened juice (or
   chunks and juice from
   1 medium fresh
   pineapple)
Scant ¼ teaspoon
   turmeric
1 teaspoon brown sugar
½ teaspoon salt
2½ tablespoons
   Aromatic Spice
   Powder (page 25)
1 tablespoon mild
   vegetable oil
Scant 1 teaspoon
   mustard seeds
15 fresh kari leaves *or*
   1 tablespoon chopped
   fresh cilantro

During one of our visits to India, my sister-in-law Keertilata prepared a classic Mangalorean curry with *aamtekai,* an inch-long subtropical oval fruit that resembles loquats (it is also used in chutneys and pickles) with a taste reminiscent of raw mango. My sister and I were discussing which other fruit might be harmonious with the curry sauce; finally we chose pineapple. I tried it, and it became an instant hit.

This dish is a snap to make with canned pineapple chunks. However, when fresh pineapples are in season, I like to use them both for their flavor and for presentation. I cut the fruit in half lengthwise, leaving the crown portion attached to each half, and using a small sharp knife I hollow out the halves. The chunks of fruit go into the curry, which is then served at room temperature in the pineapple "boats." Serve it with Whole Wheat Puffy Bread (page 87), Raw Papaya Salad with Walnuts (page 183), Pickled Baby Carrots (page 207), and Royal Vegetable Basmati Pilaf (page 138) for an elaborate dinner. Round off with Rose-Scented Ricotta Patties in Cream (page 219).

1. Combine the pineapple chunks and juice, turmeric, brown sugar, salt, and spice powder in a small saucepan. Cover and cook on medium heat until slightly thick, 8 to 10 minutes.

2. Heat the oil in a small frying pan over medium heat. Add the mustard seeds; when they begin to sizzle and splutter, stir in the kari leaves or cilantro. Remove and pour over the pineapple mixture. Serve hot.

**Note:** This dish can be prepared several days ahead and kept covered in the refrigerator. Rewarm over moderate heat or in a microwave oven.

# TROPICAL GREEN PAPAYA ROAST
## (Malai Papita)

Serves 6
Cooking time:
    25 minutes, plus 25
    minutes baking

1 green papaya, 1¼
    pounds
½ teaspoon salt
¼ teaspoon pepper
1 tablespoon mild
    vegetable oil
½ cup chopped onion
½ teaspoon crushed
    garlic
½ cup chopped tomato
4 slices day-old bread,
    cut into cubes
¾ teaspoon curry
    powder, homemade
    (page 22) or bought
14 whole cloves
¼ cup whipping cream

Papaya is best known in the West as a sweet fruit, but the green (unripe) version tastes less sweet and is used more like a vegetable all over southern Asia. The taste is somewhere between that of an acorn squash and the white part nearest the rind of a watermelon, and it takes on spices very gracefully. Real green papayas are sometimes available here; if you can't find them, ask your grocer for the least ripe papayas which may be ripening back in the storeroom — most of the papayas sold here are picked pretty green to survive the trip from the tropics. They will be slightly sweeter, but the flavor of the dish will still be good.

In this preparation the whole papaya is first cooked until tender, then stuffed with home-style seasonings and bread for an interesting textural contrast, and finally baked in a golden cloud of cloves and cream. In place of the bread stuffing, you might try one based on fragrant wild rice, spiced couscous, quinoa, or kasha. Serve with Light Yogurt Rice (page 133) and a fruit chutney.

1. Prick the papaya all over with a fork. Under running cold water, rinse away the milky juice that oozes out of the holes. Peel. Combine ¼ teaspoon of the salt and the pepper and rub the mixture over the papaya. Set aside.

2. Bring 1½ quarts of water to a boil in a large pot. Immerse the papaya gently and cook until a knife pierces it easily, about 15 minutes. Drain and set aside.

3. Meanwhile, heat the oil in a nonstick skillet over medium-high heat. Add the onion and garlic and cook until translucent, about 3 minutes. Stir in the tomato and cook until soft, about 5 minutes. Add the bread cubes, curry powder, and remaining salt. Stir and mix well. Turn off the heat.

4. Place a rack in the middle of the oven and preheat the oven to 350°F. Split the papaya lengthwise and remove the seeds. Stuff the cavity of one half with the tomato-bread mixture. Poke 4 whole cloves into the cut surface around the edge, cover with the other half, and press the halves together gently so the halves are secured together by the clove "dowels." Stud the outer surface with the remaining cloves.

5. Place the stuffed papaya in a 2-quart (8 x 8 x 2-inch) baking dish. Pour the cream on top and bake uncovered until the cream is golden brown. Transfer to a serving platter and cut into neat wedges to serve.

# GUJARAT-STYLE BAKED CABBAGE
## *(Patta Gobi Wadi)*

Serves 8
Preparation time:
    10 minutes, plus 45
    minutes baking

2 cups firmly packed
    finely shredded green
    cabbage
1 medium onion, halved
    and finely sliced
¼ cup grated coconut,
    fresh or thawed
¾ cup chick-pea flour
1 teaspoon grated fresh
    ginger
1 or 2 fresh hot green
    chiles, chopped
1 teaspoon ground
    coriander
1 teaspoon salt
3 tablespoons mild
    vegetable oil
¼ cup water
1 teaspoon sesame seeds

Countless varieties of healthful steamed and baked creations have originated in Gujarat state in western India. Although some preparations are time-consuming, this one, which comes from my friend Kusum in West Virginia, is easy to make yet delectable, and will fit today's busy lifestyle. You just combine the ingredients, pop them in the oven, and bake to a texture somewhere between a crisp potato pancake and dinner hash browns. Serve as an accompaniment to bread and rice dishes, or cut it into smaller pieces for a pleasing hors d'oeuvre.

1. Position a rack in the middle of the oven and preheat the oven to 350°F.

2. Combine the cabbage, onion, coconut, chick-pea flour, ginger, chile, coriander, and salt in a large mixing bowl. Toss to mix. Add the oil and water and mix thoroughly. Pour the mixture into an ungreased 8 x 8 x 2-inch baking pan or earthenware baking dish. Press lightly to spread into an even layer. Sprinkle the sesame seeds on top. Bake until the top is lightly browned, about 45 minutes. Let it rest for 5 minutes. Cut into 2-inch squares. Serve hot or at room temperature.

**Note:** The baked cabbage can be made 2 days ahead and kept, covered, in the refrigerator. To reheat, place the pan in a cold oven and turn the heat to 350°F. Bake until heated through, about 12 to 15 minutes.

# BAKED BOMBAY POTATOES
## *(Alu-Malai Bake)*

Serves 4 to 6
Preparation time:
  15 minutes, plus 30
  minutes baking

2 medium new potatoes
  (¾ pound total)
1 medium onion, halved
  and finely sliced
12 to 15 whole cashews
½ tablespoon dried
  black or red currants
5 whole cloves, ground
¼ teaspoon freshly
  ground pepper
Seeds from 4 green
  cardamom pods,
  ground
½ tablespoon minced
  garlic
½ tablespoon grated
  fresh ginger
2 tablespoons minced
  cilantro
¾ teaspoon salt
1 cup whipping cream

This casserole is an exceptional choice for entertaining. Bake it ahead of time, reheat it in a hot oven, and run it under the broiler for a minute or two just before serving for a golden color. It will serve a crowd, and can easily be doubled for a larger crowd. Partner with Fresh Cilantro Pilaf (page 134) and Yellow Mung Bean Salad with Walnuts (page 182).

1. Position a rack in the center of the oven and preheat the oven to 375°F.

2. Scrub the potatoes and slice into ⅛-inch-thick rounds. Immerse the slices in cold water and pat dry.

3. Place one layer of potato rounds slightly overlapping in a 3-quart baking dish. Add a layer of onion and sprinkle in a few cashews and currants. Repeat until the remaining potato and onion slices are used. Top with the remaining nuts and currants.

4. Combine the spices, garlic, ginger, cilantro, and salt in a small bowl. Add the cream and mix well until blended. Pour this mixture over the potatoes. Bake uncovered until the potatoes are tender, about 30 minutes. Before serving, run the dish under the broiler for a minute to get a golden color on the top. Serve hot.

**Note:** This dish can be baked one day ahead and kept covered in the refrigerator. To reheat, place the dish in a cold oven and bake at 350°F for 15 minutes or until heated through.

# ROYAL CABBAGE PACKETS IN SAFFRON SAUCE
## *(Palak Bhari Patta Gobi Patra)*

Serves 4
Preparation time:
   30 minutes, plus 25
   minutes baking

2 tablespoons corn or
   vegetable oil
1 cup finely chopped onion
2 teaspoons sliced garlic
2 fresh hot green chiles,
   stemmed and chopped
Leaves and tender stems
   from 2 bunches (10
   ounces each) fresh
   spinach (6 cups in all,
   loosely packed)
½ recipe paneer cheese
   (page 165), crumbled
1 teaspoon garam masala,
   homemade (page 21)
   or store-bought
¾ teaspoon salt
1 medium head (1¼
   pounds) green cabbage

*Saffron Sauce*
¼ teaspoon nutmeg
¼ teaspoon cinnamon
Seeds from 4 cardamom
   pods, ground
8 whole cloves, ground
⅓ cup (24) whole cashews
   or shelled pistachios
½ recipe khawa milk
   (page 238) *or* ½ cup
   dry milk (optional)
1 cup milk
⅛ teaspoon salt (optional)
Pinch of freshly ground
   white pepper
¾ teaspoon saffron
   threads dissolved in 2
   tablespoons boiling
   milk

High-protein paneer cheese and iron-rich spinach combine in the filling for these neat cabbage packets. Not only are they tasty and highly nutritious, they are pretty to look at, cloaked in a light golden and delicately perfumed sauce. It's a dish you can serve with pride to company. For an elaborate dinner, precede it with Mughal Chaat Salad with Pistachios (page 184) and follow with a rice pilaf.

1. Heat the oil in a large nonstick saucepan over medium-high heat. Add the onion, garlic, and chiles and cook until the onion is lightly browned, about 4 minutes. Add the spinach and cook, stirring occasionally, until it wilts, about 5 minutes. Reduce the heat to medium and add the paneer, garam masala, and salt. Mix well. Cover and cook until heated through. Remove from the heat and set aside.

2. Remove and discard any wilted outer leaves from the cabbage. Rinse and drain. Cut out the core, cutting about 1 inch deep. Bring a pot of water to a boil, add the cabbage, and cook over high heat for 10 minutes. Remove and drain on paper towels. Pull off 8 large outer leaves; trim off the thick center ribs of each leaf and set aside for filling. Shred the remaining cabbage coarsely and spread over the bottom of a 2-quart (8 x 11½ x 2-inch) baking dish.

3. Divide the spinach mixture into 8 portions. Place a portion in the center of each prepared cabbage leaf. Wrap the leaf sides and ends around the filling to enclose, and fold into a neat package. Place the packets seam side down on top of the shredded cabbage in the baking dish.

4. Position a rack in the center of the oven and preheat the oven to 375°F. Meanwhile, combine the sauce ingredients in a blender and blend until smooth. Pour the sauce over the cabbage packets, cover the dish with foil, and bake until the sauce is bubbly and very thick, about 25 minutes. Place the cabbage packets on heated plates, spoon the sauce and shredded cabbage over them, and serve hot.

**Note:** The cabbage packets and sauce may be made a day ahead and stored separately in the refrigerator. Bring to room temperature before assembling and baking.

   If you don't have paneer cheese on hand, use ½ cup ricotta, pressing it between your palms to drain off the excess whey.

# BAKED SWISS CHARD ROLLS WITH APPLE-TOMATO SAUCE
## (*Alu Bhari Patra*)

Serves 4
Preparation time:
   15 minutes, plus 20
   minutes baking

1 bunch green Swiss
   chard
2 medium potatoes,
   boiled, peeled, and
   mashed
½ cup chopped onion
   (optional)
¼ teaspoon toasted
   cumin seeds
⅛ teaspoon cayenne
1 tablespoon crushed
   toasted peanuts
¼ teaspoon dried basil
   or mixed dried herbs
1 teaspoon salt
1 cup tomato puree,
   homemade or canned
¼ cup coarsely chopped
   walnuts
2 tablespoons chopped
   dates
1 small cooking apple,
   cored, grated and
   dressed with ½ table-
   spoon lemon juice
Sour cream (optional)
Tomato wedges, for
   garnish

A specialty of the state of Uttar Pradesh in northern India, these rolls are made with a variety of edible leaves, and fillings ranging from vegetables to paneer cheese or even cooked lentils. In this version, chard leaves with a spiced potato stuffing are richly napped in a wholesome sauce infused with sweet walnuts and apple and slowly baked until they absorb the delicate sauce and become soft as silk. Choose crisp and unblemished chard leaves, each about 6 to 8 inches in length. If you have smaller ones you may require more, so keep a few extra leaves handy. Top them with the pan juices and serve with Daikon Salad with Aromatic Oil (page 188), and round off the menu with Glazed Garbanzo-Milk Confection (page 218).

1. Select 6 large perfect chard leaves. Trim off all but 1/2 inch of the stem. Wash the leaves well.

2. In a large saucepan, bring 6 to 8 cups of lightly salted water to a boil over high heat. Push the leaves gently down into the boiling water and cook uncovered until limp, 1 to 2 minutes. Lift out carefully and immerse at once in ice water to seal in the brilliant green color and prevent further cooking. Drain and set aside.

3. Position a rack in the center of the oven and preheat the oven to 375°F. In a small mixing bowl, combine the mashed potato, onion, cumin, cayenne, peanuts, dried herbs, and ½ teaspoon salt. Mix well. Divide the mixture among the chard leaves, roll up the leaves, and tuck in the ends to enclose the stuffing. Place seam side down in a 3-quart (13 x 9-inch) baking dish.

4. Combine the tomato puree, walnuts, dates, apple, and remaining ½ teaspoon salt. Stir well and pour over the chard rolls to moisten the entire surface. Cover the pan and bake until the filling is hot, about 15 minutes. Transfer to a heated serving dish. Top with a dollop of sour cream, if desired, and garnish with tomato wedges.

**Note:** The rolls can be made a day ahead and kept, covered, in the refrigerator. Prepare the sauce and bake just before serving.

   Do not discard the chard stems; use them in soups or curry sauces for their delicate celery-like taste and texture.

# "Melt-in-Your-Mouth" Pan Bread
## (Handi La Jawab)

Serves 4 to 6
Preparation time:
   15 minutes, plus 4
   hours soaking and 30
   minutes baking

½ cup cream of rice
   cereal
1 cup plain nonfat or
   low-fat yogurt
½ cup mung bean
   sprouts (page 239)
1 cup packed finely
   shredded cabbage
2 tablespoons chopped
   fresh cilantro
1 teaspoon grated fresh
   ginger
2½ tablespoons mild
   vegetable oil
⅛ teaspoon mustard
   seeds
2 or 3 dried red chiles,
   stemmed and broken
⅛ teaspoon turmeric
Pinch of asafetida
   (optional)
¾ teaspoon salt
½ teaspoon sugar
½ teaspoon baking soda
¼ cup chopped cashews

Versatile mung bean sprouts and cabbage combine with readily available cream of rice cereal and plain yogurt in this feathery-light baked dish with a texture like baked polenta or spoonbread. For a light lunch, serve it as a main course accompanied with a big green salad. For a heartier meal, precede with Aromatic Lentil Soup (page 46).

1. Combine the cream of rice and yogurt. Mix well, cover, and let stand for 4 hours.

2. Mix the bean sprouts, cabbage, cilantro, ginger, and 2 tablespoons oil in a large mixing bowl. Toss gently and set aside.

3. Position a rack in the center of the oven and preheat the oven to 350°F. Heat the remaining oil in a small skillet over medium-high heat. Add the mustard and chiles. When the seeds begin to sizzle and splutter, add the turmeric and asafetida. Remove from the heat and pour over the bean sprout mixture. Toss gently. Add the cream of rice mixture, salt, sugar, and baking soda and mix thoroughly. Pour into an ungreased 8-inch cake pan or earthenware baking dish. Sprinkle the cashews on top. Bake until the top is lightly browned, 30 to 35 minutes. Remove from the oven and let rest for 5 minutes, then cut into 1-½-inch diamonds. Serve warm or at room temperature.

Note: This dish can be made 3 days ahead and kept covered in the refrigerator. To reheat, place the pan in the cold oven and turn it to 350°F. Bake until heated through, about 12 minutes.

# BASIL-COCONUT VEGETABLE CASSEROLE
## (Tarkari Handi)

Serves 8
Preparation time:
  15 minutes, plus 2 to
  4 hours resting and 1
  hour and 15 minutes
  baking

¾ cup coconut milk,
  homemade (page 236)
  or canned
½ cup cream of rice
  cereal
1 cup cauliflower, cut
  into ½-inch florets
½ cup petite peas, fresh
  or thawed
½ cup diced carrot
¼ cup chick-pea flour
1 or 2 fresh hot green
  chiles, stemmed and
  minced
¼ teaspoon ground
  coriander
1 teaspoon salt
½ teaspoon sugar
½ teaspoon baking soda
½ cup tomato puree,
  fresh or canned
¼ cup (loosely packed)
  fresh basil leaves,
  chopped
⅛ teaspoon freshly
  ground black pepper
1 teaspoon mild
  vegetable oil, for
  greasing
Caramelized Onion and
  Garlic Shreds (page
  141)
Toasted whole cashews
Fresh basil sprigs, for
  garnish

In India, basil is valued much more as a medicinal herb than a culinary one. But my taste for this herb goes back to childhood, when my brother and I would pluck and chew on leaves of the *tulsi* (holy basil) plant my grandmother grew for herbal teas. I have remained fond of the flavor, and with fresh basil so widely available here in America, now I use it as often as cilantro.

This easy casserole goes with almost everything for parties or buffets. Once again, cream of rice provides a perfect binder for an assortment of colorful vegetables, this time in combination with coconut milk. Minimally spiced and fragrant with fresh herbs, the resulting dish is meltingly soft, rich, and feather-light. For an elegant presentation, make it in attractive molds, and top with caramelized onion and garlic shreds and cashews.

1. Combine the coconut milk and cream of rice in a large bowl and mix gently. Cover and set aside for 2 to 4 hours.

2. Add the vegetables, chick-pea flour, chiles, coriander, salt, and sugar to the coconut-rice mixture. Mix thoroughly. Stir in the baking soda and blend well. Set aside.

3. Position a rack in the center of the oven and preheat the oven to 350°F. Stir the basil and pepper into the tomato puree. Rub a 1½-quart ovenproof glass bowl (or a decorative mold) with oil. Pour the tomato puree into the bowl, then spoon the vegetable mixture on top of the puree. Bake uncovered for 1 hour. Cover loosely with foil and bake until lightly browned, about 15 minutes longer. (If there is any liquid at the top, it will firm up as it cools.)

4. Set the bowl on a wire rack to cool for about 15 minutes. Run a plastic spatula around inside the bowl and unmold onto a warmed serving platter. Garnish with onion and garlic shreds, cashews, and basil sprigs. Cut into wedges to serve.

**Note:** The casserole can be baked up to 3 days ahead; cover loosely and refrigerate. Reheat in a 350°F oven until heated through, about 12 to 15 minutes.

**Variation:** In place of the fresh vegetables, use 2 cups frozen mixed vegetables.

# VEGETABLE KOFTAS IN VELVETY CREAM SAUCE
## (Makhmalai Kofta)

Makes 20 koftas
(4 servings)
Preparation time:
45 minutes

### Koftas
2 large russet potatoes
(1 pound), boiled,
peeled, and mashed
½ cup green peas, fresh
or thawed
⅓ cup shredded
Cheddar cheese
1½ fresh hot green
chiles, stemmed and
finely chopped
½ teaspoon ground
coriander
½ teaspoon ground
cumin
1 teaspoon salt
¼ cup cashews, finely
chopped
1 tablespoon raisins

### Batter
¾ cup chick-pea flour
½ cup water
Mild vegetable oil,
for frying

### Cream Sauce
8 whole cashews or
¼ cup cashew bits
4 whole cloves, ground
⅛ teaspoon nutmeg
¼ teaspoon cinnamon
1 clove garlic, minced
2 tablespoons desi ghee
or unsalted butter
1 large onion, grated
⅛ teaspoon turmeric
2 teaspoons paprika

Makhmalai translates as "velvety cream"; in this dish, regularly featured in restaurants under the name malai kofta, the koftas are lavishly napped with a velvety sauce perfumed with warm seasonings. Traditionally the koftas are made from paneer cheese or khawa milk, but I have substituted cheddar cheese, which is more readily available and makes koftas with a moister texture and a crisp crust. Since this entree is filling, I like to serve it with Whole Wheat Flatbread (page 79), accompanied by Spinach Raita with Sesame Oil Seasoning (page 176). Serve this hearty dish to give an Indian flavor to one of your holiday meals.

1. Combine the kofta ingredients in a bowl and mix well. Form the mixture into 1-inch balls. In another bowl, combine the chick-pea flour and water to make a batter.

2. Fill a deep fryer, wok, or deep heavy skillet with oil to a depth of 2 inches and heat to 345°F. Dip the balls into the batter to coat completely. Fry a few at a time (do not crowd) until brown on all sides, about 6 minutes. After you add koftas to the oil, do not turn them for at least half a minute or they may break apart. Drain on paper towels and keep warm in a 250°F oven while frying the remaining koftas, or up to 30 minutes.

3. Combine the cashews, cloves, nutmeg, cinnamon, and garlic in a food processor or blender with 1 to 2 tablespoons water. Process until smooth.

4. Heat the desi ghee in a large heavy saucepan over medium-high heat. Add the onion and cook, stirring, until light brown, 3 to 4 minutes. Reduce the heat to medium and add the cashew mixture. Stir and cook until fragrant, about 4 minutes. Add the turmeric, paprika, coriander, cayenne, and salt. Stir until aromatic, about 2 minutes. Add the water, bring to a boil, reduce the heat, cover, and simmer until the sauce is slightly thick, about 10 minutes. (The sauce can be prepared to this point 2 days ahead, covered and refrigerated.)

5. Stir the cream and koftas into the sauce. Cook until heated through. Transfer to a heated shallow serving dish. Garnish with cilantro.

**Note:** If you prefer the koftas to remain crisp, keep them separate in a serving

½ teaspoon ground
  coriander
½ teaspoon cayenne
1 teaspoon salt
1 cup water
2 cups whipping cream
2 tablespoons chopped
  fresh cilantro

bowl tented with foil while you finish the sauce, then pour the hot sauce over them at the last minute.

**Variation:** You can also float these koftas in Hot Yogurt Soup with Roasted Kari Leaves (page 55).

# PUMPKIN KOFTAS IN RUSTIC SWISS CHARD SAUCE
## (Mughlai Kofta Motimahal)

Makes about 24 koftas
(6 servings)
Preparation time: 45
minutes

*Pumpkin Koftas*
1¼ pounds fresh ripe
pumpkin, peeled and
grated (4 cups)
2 to 4 fresh hot green
chiles, stemmed and
finely chopped
½ teaspoon cumin seeds
1 teaspoon salt
1 tablespoon fresh lime
juice
⅔ cup chick-pea flour
❁
Mild vegetable or
avocado oil, for frying

*Swiss Chard Sauce*
4 tablespoons mild olive
or peanut oil
1 2-inch piece fresh
ginger, roughly
chopped
2 fresh hot green chiles,
slit lengthwise
4 cups chopped green
Swiss chard (6 large
leaves)
1 bunch (¾ pound)
fresh spinach,
trimmed and
chopped, *or* 10 ounces
frozen spinach,
thawed
1 cup lightly packed
chopped fresh mint
leaves
1½ cups water
1 teaspoon salt

Mildly flavored and slightly sweet, these golden pumpkin koftas look wonderful in a sea-green sauce. Serve with Calcutta Plain Flakybread (page 82) and Fragrant Baby Dill with Mung Beans (page 152) and pass plain yogurt at the side. For a complete meal, serve with Tanjore Tamarind Garlicky Rice (page 145). I make this with pumpkin in October, when they are most abundant; later in the winter, when pumpkins disappear, use other hard-shelled squash such as butternut or banana. These sweetish koftas also pair exceptionally well with the piquant Tamarind-Apple Dipping Sauce on page 39.

1. Combine the kofta ingredients in a large mixing bowl. Form the mixture into 1-inch balls. The moisture from the pumpkin and lime juice should be just right to bind the koftas; if the mixture is too moist, stir in a little more chick-pea flour.

2. Fill a wok or deep fryer with oil to a depth of 2 inches and heat to 340°F. Fry the pumpkin balls in batches, turning them occasionally, until lightly browned, 3 to 4 minutes. The oil temperature will drop at first but rise again as the koftas brown, so regulate the heat accordingly. Remove with a slotted spoon and drain on paper towels. Set aside or serve as an appetizer.

3. For the sauce, heat the oil in a large skillet on medium-high heat. Toss in the ginger and chiles and cook 2 minutes. Add the chard, spinach, and mint leaves; stir and cook until the leaves start to wilt, about 5 minutes. Add the water and salt. Reduce the heat to medium, cover, and simmer 15 minutes. Remove from the heat.

4. Puree the chard mixture in a food processor or blender until smooth. Pour the sauce into a heated shallow dish and place the koftas in the center.

**Note:** The sauce can be made 2 days ahead and kept, covered, in the refrigerator. Reheat on moderate heat or in the microwave.

**Variation:** Kale, a prized cruciferous vegetable, can be substituted for chard. Rinse the leaves well before use — the curly leaves can hide a lot of debris.

# BAKED YAM KOFTAS IN GREEN GRAVY
## *(Ratalu Kofta Hara Bhara Saas Me)*

Serves 4 (16 koftas)
Preparation time:
    15 minutes plus 25
    minutes baking

Oil or vegetable spray

*Yam Koftas*
2 medium yams (12
    ounces), boiled,
    peeled, and mashed
½ cup peas, fresh or
    thawed
1 teaspoon minced garlic
2 fresh hot green chiles,
    stemmed and minced
2 tablespoons chopped
    fresh cilantro
½ teaspoon sesame
    seeds
½ teaspoon salt
Pinch of freshly ground
    pepper
2 tablespoons cornstarch
¼ teaspoon baking
    powder

*Green Gravy*
¼ cup frozen peas,
    thawed and steamed
    for 4 minutes
½ cup green pepper
½ cup cilantro
1½ fresh hot green
    chiles, stemmed
1 clove garlic
1 tablespoon oil
¼ teaspoon mustard
    seeds
½ teaspoon ground
    cumin
½ teaspoon ground
    coriander
¾ teaspoon salt
1 teaspoon sugar

These koftas are at their best hot and slightly puffed from the oven. You may add these to your parade of hors d'oeuvre with cocktails. Or turn them into a hearty main dish by simmering them in a sauce of fresh peas and green peppers sparked with garlic and chiles. As an entree, accompany with Peasant Cucumber Flatbread (page 81) and a raita (pages 174-179). For a more substantial meal serve with Jahangir Pilaf with Yellow Mung Beans (page 144).

1. Position a rack in the center of the oven and preheat the oven to 400°F. Brush a cookie sheet with oil or coat with cooking spray.

2. Combine the kofta ingredients in a mixing bowl and mix thoroughly. Form into 1-inch balls and place them 1 inch apart on the cookie sheet. Bake until puffed and golden, about 30 minutes.

3. Meanwhile, make the gravy: Combine the peas, green pepper, cilantro, chiles, and garlic in a blender or food processor. Process until finely pureed. Heat the oil in a small saucepan on medium-high heat. Add the mustard seeds; when the seeds sizzle and splutter, stir in the puree. Cook, stirring constantly, until slightly thickened, about 5 minutes. Stir in the cumin and coriander and simmer 1 minute. Add 1 cup water and bring to a boil. Reduce the heat to low, cover, and simmer until thick, about 10 minutes. Stir in the salt and sugar.

4. Remove the koftas from the oven and set the pan on a wire rack to cool for 5 minutes, then ease the koftas off the pan with a metal spatula onto a plate. Reheat the green gravy in a saucepan or in the microwave until heated through. Turn into a serving dish, add the koftas, and serve hot.

# ACORN SQUASH WADAS IN GARLICKY PEANUT OIL
## (*Doodhi Na Modhiya*)

Makes 18 dumplings
(4 to 6 servings)
Preparation time:
15 minutes

*Squash Dumplings*
1 small acorn squash
(10 ounces)
1 fresh hot green chile,
stemmed and minced
½ cup whole wheat
flour
2 tablespoons chick-pea
flour
½ teaspoon ground
coriander
½ teaspoon ground
cumin
½ teaspoon salt
⅛ teaspoon baking soda
❀
2 tablespoons mild
peanut or vegetable
oil, plus more for
brushing the steamer
½ teaspoon mustard
seeds
2 or 3 garlic cloves cut
into slivers
1 tablespoon minced
fresh cilantro

The "sauce" for these steamed dumplings is simply oil flavored with garlic and cilantro, a specialty of Gujarat. Other winter squashes — butternut, banana, buttercup, or spaghetti — may be substituted for acorn squash. Serve these dumplings as a side dish with pilaf and dal; or cut them in half and toss them into Lentil Sprouts Salad with Tomatillo Dressing (page 181); or float them in Aromatic Lentil Soup (page 46); or fold them gently into Fresh Cilantro Pilaf (page 134).

1. Peel and seed the squash. Grate and measure 1½ cups of squash. Combine with the remaining dumpling ingredients and mix well.

2. Brush a steamer basket with oil, or line a bamboo steamer with cheesecloth. Bring at least 1 inch of water to a boil in the steaming pot. Place heaping tablespoonfuls of the squash mixture ½ inch apart in the steamer basket. Place over the boiling water, cover, and steam until a knife inserted in the middle comes out clean, about 4 minutes. (You may have to steam them in batches, depending on the size of your steamer; add more boiling water for the second batch if necessary.) Ease out gently with a metal spatula and turn into a shallow serving dish.

3. Heat 2 tablespoons oil in a small skillet over medium heat. Add the mustard seeds; when the seeds begin to sizzle and splutter, stir in the garlic. Cook until the garlic is lightly browned, 3 to 4 minutes. Turn off the heat and add the cilantro. Pour the seasoned oil over the dumplings, scraping the skillet with a rubber spatula. Toss well to coat. Serve immediately.

**Variation:** Squash wadas are also delicious served with the Korma Sauce from the following recipe, in place of or in addition to the oil seasoning.

# SPINACH WADAS IN AROMATIC KORMA SAUCE
## (Palak-Wadi Korma)

Serves 4 to 6
Preparation time:
  30 minutes

*Dumplings*

4 cups packed finely
  chopped fresh spinach
  (leaves and tender
  stems from 1 large
  bunch)
1 recipe paneer cheese
  (page 165), crumbled
2 tablespoons chopped
  raw almonds, with
  skin
¼ teaspoon curry
  powder, homemade
  (page 22) or bought
½ teaspoon ground
  coriander
½ teaspoon salt
¼ teaspoon baking soda
¼ cup unbleached all-
  purpose flour
❀
Mild vegetable oil, for
  brushing the steamer
1 cup coarsely chopped
  onion
½ cup fresh cilantro
  leaves with stems
2 tablespoons flaked
  coconut
1 or 2 fresh hot green
  chiles, stemmed
½ cup water
2 tablespoons desi ghee
  or unsalted butter
6 to 8 whole cloves
2 cups plain nonfat yogurt
½ teaspoon ground fennel
½ teaspoon salt
Sweet paprika

Steaming is one of the most wonderful cooking techniques, used in all the regional cuisines of India. This healthful, low-calorie dish from northern India is a real delight. The dumplings, made from spinach, paneer cheese, and almonds infused with the scent of curry, explode with flavor. A smooth yogurt sauce provides an interesting textural contrast. For a low-calorie meal, precede the wadas with Aromatic Lentil Soup (page 46) and accompany them with Toasted Lentil Wafers (page 30); follow with Fresh Cilantro Pilaf (page 134).

1. Steam the spinach for 3 minutes. Remove to a colander, let cool, and squeeze lightly. Place the spinach in a mixing bowl. Add the paneer, almonds, curry powder, coriander, and salt. Mix the baking soda and flour and sprinkle over the spinach mixture. Mix well.

2. Lightly oil a 9-inch steamer basket, or line a bamboo steamer with cheese-cloth. Bring at least 1 inch of water to a boil in the steaming pot. Scoop table-spoonfuls of the dumpling mixture into the steamer basket ½ inch apart, to make about 20 dumplings. Place over the boiling water, cover, and steam until a knife inserted in the middle comes out clean, about 5 minutes. (You may have to steam them in batches, depending on the size of your steamer; add more boiling water for the second batch if necessary.) Cover and set aside.

3. Combine the onion, cilantro, coconut, and chiles in a blender or food processor. Process until coarsely chopped. Add ¼ cup water and blend to a smooth paste.

4. Heat the desi ghee in a heavy medium saucepan over medium heat. Add the cloves and fry until they are plump, about 2 minutes. Add the onion puree and cook, stirring constantly, until the onion loses its raw aroma and the sauce is thick, about 10 minutes. Stir the yogurt and add it to the pan. Add the fennel, salt, and remaining ¼ cup water. Cover and cook until heated through.

4. Place the dumplings in a serving bowl, pour the sauce on the top, and serve hot with a pinch of paprika.

**Note:** Both the dumplings and the sauce can be made 3 hours ahead and stored separately at room temperature. Just before serving, place the dumplings in hot water for 2 minutes. Lift with a slotted spoon, squeeze gently, and place in a serving bowl with the reheated sauce.

# PILAFS

## AND OTHER RICE DISHES

Plain Basmati Rice

Microwave Basmati Rice

Nutty Rice with Shredded Mango

Peas Pilaf with Almonds

Light Yogurt Rice with Cucumber

Fresh Cilantro Pilaf

Quick Savory Rice with Peas and Peanuts

Lemon-Sesame Rice Crowned with Vegetables

Malabar Coconut Rice

Royal Vegetable Basmati Rice (Biryani)

Shahjahan Corn Pilaf

Fragrant Spinach Pilaf with Baby Carrots

Tomato Pilaf with Yellow Split Peas

Jahangir Pilaf with Yellow Mung Beans

Tanjore Tamarind Garlicky Rice

Rice is the most important staple food in much of India. In some parts of the subcontinent it appears at every meal, while in other regions it alternates with bread as the main dish. Rich in carbohydrates but deficient in proteins and vitamins, rice provides the bulk of the diet for vegetarians and non-vegetarians alike, with legumes, nuts, and vegetables providing the missing nutrients to create a balanced diet.

The various regions of India have developed a wide variety of rice dishes, and they go by various names, including pilaf (a mixture of stir-fried rice and vegetables) and *biryani* (a more elaborate layered rice dish). Some are everyday favorites, others are elaborate presentations to honor a special guest. Perhaps because it is so important, rice is also the choice for religious celebrations and other festive occasions.

For millions of vegetarians in southern India, rice is the center of every meal. It may be eaten as often as three times a day, and may appear several times in the same meal; a typical menu might include rice and hot lentil soup *(sambar),* followed by rice and a smooth soup *(rasam),* followed by rice and yogurt. A superb southern Indian cook, it is said, can produce a different rice dish for each day of the year.

In the north, where wheat is the more important staple, rice serves as a supplement to main courses of bread and legumes. Rice dishes are flavored with dried fruits and nuts. The classic layered *biryanis* are the result of Mughal influence. Even the simpler rice pilafs often take a more intricate, stunningly decorated form in the north.

The beautiful landscape of the east is a mosaic of hundreds of acres of rice fields and date and coconut palms. There, plain boiled rice serves as the main staple. The pure, mild flavor of the steaming hot rice forms the background for more flavorful legume and vegetable dishes.

Rice and flatbreads are equally important in the classic vegetarian cuisine of western and southwestern India; breads appear early in the meal, and rice typically comes later. Western Indian cooks prepare plain white rice with the same veneration that the Italians have for their pastas. In a perfect rice dish, each grain of rice is separate and perfectly cooked. In a typical meal, a bowl of steaming rice topped with desi ghee and dal follows the main course of breads and vegetables, and finally a small portion (about a quarter of a cup) of rice topped with plain yogurt rounds off the meal.

All of the recipes in this chapter call for genuine Indian basmati rice, the world's finest gourmet rice. Basmati has its own unique delicate fragrance and wonderful texture. When cooked, it extends to almost twice its original length. Basmati is available in America in most supermarkets, but it can be quite expensive in small packages; to save money, look for it in bulk, or in larger bags in warehouse-type stores. Indian markets may offer basmati in several grades and prices. The Dehradun brand, named for a place in northern India, is more expensive than other brands but superior.

If you cannot find basmati rice, other fragrant long-grain varieties of rice can be used interchangeably. Some relatives of basmati are grown domestically in Texas and California. Texmati is flavorful and does not require rinsing or soaking prior to cooking. Fragrant Thai jasmine rice will also make a good substitute. Other long-grain varieties are similar in texture, though they lack the special aroma and flavor of basmati.

In America, a lot of vegetarians favor brown rice for its nutrients as well as for its nutty, robust flavor and satisfying texture. Brown rice is rarely used in Indian cooking. If you prefer brown rice, you might look for Calmati, a fragrant variety grown in California's Sacramento Valley which cooks fluffy and separate, with a nice bite. I've even started to use wild rice, a grain unheard of in India, in some of my recipes. Experiment with different varieties to develop your own personal tastes.

# PLAIN BASMATI RICE
## (Basmati ki Khusbu)

Makes 4 cups
Preparation time:
    20 minutes, plus 10
    minutes soaking

1 cup raw basmati rice
1¾ cups water
1 teaspoon desi ghee or
    unsalted butter
    (optional)
1 teaspoon fresh lime
    juice
½ teaspoon salt

This is the basic method of cooking basmati rice, to be served as is or used to make a variety of other rice dishes in the chapter. You can easily double or triple the recipe in a larger pot. A sprinkle of fresh lime juice will help the grains to remain fluffy and white. Serve this fragrant rice with legumes and vegetable dishes.

Basmati cooks relatively quickly. As a general rule Indian basmati requires a little less than two parts water to one part rice. Cooking time may vary depending on the brand and the age of the rice; older rice may require longer cooking and more water than freshly harvested rice.

The recipe begins with a cleaning step, to rid the rice of any small stones or other foreign matter, although most basmati these days is pretty clean. Washing is necessary in any case. Soaking the uncooked rice briefly (10 minutes to an hour) before cooking helps to "relax" the grains; the little bit of water they absorb reduces the tendency for individual grains to stick to each other. If you don't have time, you can skip the soaking step; it does not affect the cooking time nor the amount of water needed. Use cold water for rinsing and soaking; hot water can wash away valuable vitamins and break the delicate grains. If you want to preserve all the vitamins, reserve the soaking water and use it for cooking.

1. Place the rice on a dinner plate. Work a small portion of the rice across to the opposite side of the plate, picking out any stones and unhulled rice grains. Repeat with the remaining rice. Place the rice in a bowl and wash two or three times in cold running tap water, stirring the grains with your fingertips. Drain, add water to cover by at least 2 inches, and let soak for 10 minutes.

2. Drain the rice and place it in a medium saucepan. Add all the remaining ingredients and bring to a boil. Reduce the heat to low, cover, and simmer until the rice is tender and all the liquid is absorbed, about 15 minutes.

3. Turn off the heat and let the rice stand, covered, for 5 minutes. Fluff the rice lightly with a fork before serving.

**Note:** Plain rice can be prepared 5 days ahead and kept, covered, in the refrigerator or frozen up to 1 month. To reheat, bring to room temperature first, then cook on moderate heat or in the microwave until piping hot. If the rice appears dry from storage, sprinkle it with some water before reheating.

**Variation:** MICROWAVE BASMATI RICE

With the addition of a little extra water, the microwave oven cooks basmati rice as well as the stovetop. This is the method I use every day to prepare plain rice. Wash, soak, and drain 1 cup raw basmati rice as directed in step 1. Place in a 3-quart microwavable bowl with 2⅓ cups water and ½ teaspoon salt. Cook uncovered at full power for 12 minutes. Remove from the oven, stir once, cover, and cook at full power for 5 more minutes. Remove the rice from the oven and let stand covered for 5 minutes before fluffing and serving.

# NUTTY RICE WITH SHREDDED MANGO
## (*Nagpuri Kairi Bhat*)

Serves 4 to 6
Preparation time:
   15 minutes

1 medium-size (10 ounce)
   green mango
2 cups freshly cooked
   basmati rice, cooled to
   room temperature
½ cup flaked unsweet
   ened coconut
½ teaspoon salt
1 teaspoon sugar
1½ tablespoons mild
   vegetable or olive oil
1 teaspoon white gram
   beans (urad dal)
   (optional)
½ teaspoon mustard
   seeds
2 or 3 dried red chiles,
   stemmed and broken
¼ cup chopped cashews
½ cup coarsely crushed
   peanuts

In this tantalizing dish from Nagpur in central India, the rice grains are perfectly counterpoised with nuts and tinged with the tropical sweetness of coconut and the sour tang of green mango. It makes for a wonderful picnic meal or tailgate party accompanied by Gujarat-style Baked Cabbage (page 115), Sweet Lime Pickles in Peppercorn Syrup (page 202), vegetarian sandwiches, and plenty to drink. It would also make a great filling for crepes.

1. Wash the mango well, wipe it dry, and cut off the stem end. Grate the skin and the flesh with a hand grater; discard the seed. Measure 1 cup, loosely packed. Place the rice in a mixing bowl, sprinkle with the mango, coconut, salt, and sugar, and toss gently but thoroughly.

2. Heat the oil in a small saucepan over medium heat. Add the urad dal and mustard seeds. Fry until the dal is lightly browned and the mustard seeds begin to sizzle. Toss in the dried chiles, cashews, and peanuts. Stir and fry until the nuts begin to brown, 4 to 5 minutes. Pour the contents of the pan onto the rice and mix gently. Mound the rice on a heated serving platter. Serve at room temperature.

**Note:** This rice dish can be made 3 hours ahead and set aside, covered, at room temperature.

# PEAS PILAF WITH ALMONDS
## (Matar Badaam Pulao)

Serves 2 to 4
Preparation time:
   25 minutes, plus 10
   minutes soaking

1 cup raw basmati rice
2 tablespoons desi ghee
   or mild vegetable oil
8 almonds, blanched,
   peeled, and slivered
½ teaspoon cumin seeds
Seeds from 3 green
   cardamom pods,
   ground
½ teaspoon ground
   coriander
½ cup fresh or thawed
   petite peas
1¾ cups water
½ teaspoon salt

With the rich taste of almonds and cardamom, this pilaf is an all-time favorite throughout India. It is a good choice for any party table or buffet dinner, and it can easily be doubled or tripled. Present it with wholesome appetizers like Quick Spinach Bites (page 38), and one or two side dishes such as Morel Mushrooms with Cashews and Dates (page 111) or Spinach Wadas in Aromatic Korma Sauce (page 127), and a good Chardonnay.

1. Wash, soak, and drain the rice (see step 1, page 130). Set aside.

2. Heat the desi ghee in a medium saucepan on moderate heat and fry the almonds until lightly browned, about 4 minutes. Remove with slotted spoon and set aside.

3. Add the cumin, cardamom, and coriander to the same pan. Stir until the spices are fragrant and begin to brown, about 30 seconds. Add the peas (if fresh) and rice. Stir-fry until the rice begins to glisten, about 5 minutes. Add the water and salt and bring to a boil. Reduce the heat to low, cover, and cook 10 minutes (stir in thawed peas at this point). Cook until the rice is tender and the liquid is absorbed, 5 more minutes.

4. Turn off the heat and let the rice stand covered for 5 minutes to allow the grains to firm up. Uncover, fluff the pilaf lightly with a fork, and serve garnished with the fried almonds.

Note: This pilaf can be prepared 2 days ahead and kept covered in the refrigerator. Rewarm on moderate flame or in the microwave oven. The almonds are best if freshly cooked. Black cumin seeds (see page 17) are especially good in this dish.

# LIGHT YOGURT RICE WITH CUCUMBER
## (Dahi Bhat)

Serves 2 to 3
Preparation time:
   5 minutes

1 teaspoon grated fresh
   ginger
1 teaspoon minced garlic
1 fresh hot green chile,
   stemmed and minced
½ teaspoon ground
   cumin
1½ cups cooked
   basmati rice, cooled to
   room temperature
1 cup chopped English
   hothouse cucumber
½ teaspoon salt
1 teaspoon sugar
1 cup plain nonfat or
   low-fat yogurt, stirred
1 tablespoon chopped
   cashews (optional)
½ tablespoon chopped
   fresh cilantro
2 clusters green grapes

My teenage son Kailash loves rice dishes. When he returns home from his base-ball games, I make this quick cooling "rice salad" as he prefers to call it. Zesty, flavorful, and low in calories, this dish is a refreshing choice for warm summer evenings. Packed in a cooler, it makes a wonderful side dish for a picnic or lunchbox. For a dieter's lunch, accompany this light entree with Fragrant Baby Dill with Garlic and Mung Beans (page 152), and Asparagus Chaat with Chile Oil (page 184).

1. Combine the ginger, garlic, chile, and cumin in a large mixing bowl. Add the rice and cucumber and toss gently to mix. Sprinkle in the salt and sugar and mix well. Fold in the yogurt and cashews. Transfer to a serving bowl. If not serving immediately, cover the bowl and chill up to 4 hours. Garnish with cilantro and grapes just before serving.

**Note:** The yogurt rice can be made a day ahead and kept, covered, in the refrig-erator. You may want to add more yogurt before serving.

**Variation:** Drizzle the rice with a little oil seasoning (see page 13) made with mustard seeds, kari leaves, and a pinch of asafetida.

# FRESH CILANTRO PILAF
## (Hara Dhania Pulao)

Serves 6 to 8
Preparation time:
    30 minutes, plus 10
    minutes soaking

2 cups raw basmati rice
2 tablespoons desi ghee
    or unsalted butter
1-inch piece cinnamon
    stick
½ teaspoon whole black
    peppercorns
5 whole cloves
5 whole cardamom pods
1 cup finely chopped
    fresh cilantro
3¾ cups water
1 teaspoon salt
¼ cup whole cashews

Cilantro is one of my favorite fresh herbs for garnishing and more. Here it marries well with delicately scented basmati rice to create an elegant entree. For a quick and light supper, serve it with Garbanzo Beans in Tangy Tomato Sauce (page 160) and Tomato Cucumber Raita (page 174). Celery leaves or parsley may be substituted for cilantro, but the flavor will not be the same.

1. Wash, soak, and drain the rice (see step 1, page 130). Set aside.

2. Heat the desi ghee in a large saucepan or Dutch oven over medium heat. Add the spices. Stir and cook until aromatic, about 2 minutes. Add the rice and stir-fry gently until the grains begin to glisten, about 4 minutes.

3. Add the cilantro, water, and salt. Bring to a boil, reduce the heat to low, cover, and simmer until the rice is tender, about 15 minutes. Let the rice stand, covered, for 5 minutes.

4. Meanwhile, toast the cashews in a small skillet over medium heat until lightly browned, 5 minutes.

5. Fluff the rice gently into a serving dish. Garnish with toasted cashews and serve hot.

**Note:** The pilaf can be made 2 days ahead and kept covered in the refrigerator. Since storage tones down the herbal fragrance, enliven the pilaf with 2 tablespoons chopped cilantro when reheating.

**Variation:** WILD RICE WITH CILANTRO (Phirangi Bhat)
I recently tasted wild rice for the first time (this grain is unknown in India) at a restaurant in San Francisco. Inspired by its distinctive nut-like flavor, now I use it in place of basmati in various rice dishes. For a wild rice version of Fresh Cilantro Pilaf, wash 2 cups wild rice in 2 or 3 changes of cold water. Measure 5 cups water and soak the rice in it for 10 to 30 minutes. Drain and reserve the water. Continue as above, using the reserved soaking water in step 3 and increasing the cooking time to 45 minutes.

# QUICK SAVORY RICE WITH PEAS AND PEANUTS
## (Chitranna)

Serves 6 to 8
Preparation time:
  15 minutes

¼ cup mild sesame or
  vegetable oil
½ teaspoon mustard
  seeds
½ teaspoon cumin seeds
1 teaspoon yellow chick
  peas (chana dal)
  (optional)
1 large onion, finely
  chopped
3 fresh hot green chiles,
  stemmed and chopped
¼ teaspoon turmeric
10 fresh kari leaves
  (optional)
2 tablespoons roasted
  peanuts, salted or
  unsalted
5 cups day-old cooked
  basmati rice
2 tablespoons frozen
  peas, thawed
1 teaspoon salt
1 teaspoon sugar
1 tablespoon fresh lime
  juice
1 tablespoon chopped
  fresh cilantro

When rice is the main course, quite often you will find that there is some left over in the pot, and every rice-based cuisine has various ways of using leftover rice. As children, my cousins, brother, sister, and I definitely had our favorite — Amma's chitranna. Amma (mother), as we fondly called our maternal grandmother, would cook rice the previous day to make this superb specialty. Chitranna is perfect for a buffet, potluck, or even picnic. In India it is sometimes cooked with yogurt, and I like it with plain or lightly flavored (vanilla or strawberry) yogurt on the side.

1. Heat the oil in a large heavy saute pan or Dutch oven over medium-high heat. Add the mustard and cumin seeds and chana dal. When the seeds begin to sizzle and splutter, stir in the onion, chiles, turmeric, kari leaves, and nuts. Cook, stirring occasionally, until the onion is soft, about 4 minutes. Reduce the heat to low.

2. Combine the rice, peas, salt, and sugar and toss to mix. Add to the pan and mix thoroughly until each grain is stained yellow from the turmeric. Sprinkle in the lime juice and mix well. Cover and cook until very hot, 6 to 8 minutes. Transfer to a heated serving platter. Garnish with a sprinkling of cilantro and serve hot, warm, or at room temperature.

**Note:** The chitranna can be made ahead and set aside several hours at room temperature or up to 2 days in the refrigerator. Reheat on moderate heat.

# LEMON-SESAME RICE CROWNED WITH VEGETABLES
## (Limbu-Til Bhat)

Serves 4
Preparation time:
    20 minutes

2 tablespoons sesame
    seeds
2 cups freshly cooked
    basmati rice, cooled to
    room temperature
1 tablespoon chopped
    fresh dill
¼ cup chopped toasted
    cashews or pecans
2 tablespoons lemon
    juice, preferably fresh
½ cup peeled, sliced
    carrots
1 cup broccoli, cut in
    1-inch florets
¾ cup julienned sweet
    red bell pepper
½ cup cauliflower, cut
    in 1-inch florets
1 tablespoon mild olive
    oil
¼ teaspoon mustard
    seeds
2 or 3 small dried chiles,
    stemmed and broken

I love gardening. The greatest satisfaction to me is to reap the garden bounty — mounds of fresh, glistening vegetables, vine-ripened peppers, and aromatic herbs. When the freshly cut vegetables are cooked, they have a wonderful sweet taste, quite unlike store-bought. To serve them at their crunchy and colorful best, I prefer to steam them and toss them into tasty, nutty flavored rice. Visually attractive and wonderfully seasoned, this rice dish makes a hearty and satisfying meal accompanied by a legume dish such as Garlicky Curried Whole Mung Beans (page 156) and a quick yogurt-based salad like Whole Kernel Corn Raita (page 175). Substituting freshly cooked brown rice for basmati will add a chewy texture and robust flavor. If you prefer this dish spicy, saute the veggies in oil sprinkled with some curry powder instead of steaming.

1. Toast the sesame seeds in a small frying pan over medium heat, shaking the pan frequently, until lightly browned, about 4 minutes. Transfer to a grinder and grind to a coarse powder. Add to the rice with the dill, nuts, and lemon juice and toss gently to combine.

2. Combine the carrots, broccoli, bell pepper, and cauliflower in a steamer basket over boiling water. Steam until tender, about 4 minutes.

3. Meanwhile, heat the oil in a small skillet over medium-high heat and add the mustard. When the seeds begin to sizzle and splutter, add the chiles. Stir 1 minute and remove from the heat.

4. Mound the rice on a warmed serving platter. Top with the steamed vegetables. Toss gently to mix. Drizzle the seasoned oil on top, scraping the skillet with rubber spatula. Serve at room temperature.

**Note:** This rice dish can be made 3 hours ahead and set aside covered at room temperature.

# MALABAR COCONUT RICE
## (Tengai Sadam)

Serves 6
Preparation time:
  30 minutes

1½ cups raw basmati
  rice
1½ tablespoons mild
  vegetable oil
2 tablespoons whole
  cashews
½ teaspoon mustard
  seeds
1 or 2 fresh hot green
  chiles, stemmed and
  slit lengthwise
10 kari leaves, preferably
  fresh
2 cups coconut milk,
  fresh (page 236) or
  canned
¾ cup water
¾ teaspoon salt
2 tablespoons grated
  fresh or flaked
  coconut, for garnish

The Malabar Coast, a historic center of the spice trade, is a verdant land of swaying coconut palms in southern India, now part of the state of Kerala. Keralite cooks use coconut milk and meat in all sorts of dishes, including rice. Coconut milk has gotten something of a bad name in recent years because it is so high in saturated fat; however, as long as you stick to light dishes for the rest of the menu, it will make a balanced meal. Try it with Cauliflower and Pepper Stir-Fry (page 101) and Classic Madras Lentil Stew (page 154), and add Warm Tomato Relish (page 194) to spice up the meal.

1. Wash, soak, and drain the rice (see step 1, page 130). Set aside.

2. Heat the oil in a medium saucepan over moderate heat. Fry the cashews until lightly browned, 4 to 5 minutes. Remove with a slotted spoon and set aside. Add the mustard; when the seeds begin to sizzle and splutter, add the chiles and kari leaves. Stir 1 minute and add the rice. Stir and fry the rice for 5 minutes. Add the coconut milk, water, and salt. Bring to a boil, reduce the heat to low, cover, and simmer until the rice is tender and the liquid is absorbed, about 15 minutes.

3. Turn off the heat and let the rice stand covered for 5 minutes. Uncover and fluff the rice. Transfer into a serving dish and garnish with fried cashews and coconut. Serve hot or warm.

# ROYAL VEGETABLE BASMATI RICE
## (Biryani)

Serves 5
Preparation time:
  40 minutes, plus 20
  minutes baking

*Biryani* is an elaborate northern Indian dish in which common ingredients — rice and vegetables — are given an elegant presentation. Biryanis made with lamb or chicken are better known in the West, but this vegetarian version is equally traditional. The rice and veggies are first cooked separately, then they are arranged in layers in a large pot and sprinkled with saffron and milk. The pot is covered and sealed (traditionally with a wheat flour paste, though foil works just as well), then baked in the oven. The result is unexpectedly subtle, with essence of sweet saffron. Lavishly decorated with gold or silver leaves and a bouquet of mint, it serves to honor both the guest and the food itself. For an elaborate dinner, precede the biryani with a soup such as Vegetable

1 cup raw basmati rice

3 cups plus 2 tablespoons water

½ teaspoon salt

4 whole cloves, ground

Seeds from 4 green cardamom pods, ground

1 tablespoon grated fresh ginger

1¼ cups coarsely chopped onion

10 fresh mint leaves

2 tablespoons desi ghee or unsalted butter, plus additional for brushing

1 tablespoon dark raisins

2 tablespoons slivered pistachios

3 cups fresh or frozen diced mixed vegetables (carrots, cauliflower, green beans, zucchini, and red or green bell pepper)

1 cup chopped tomato

½ teaspoon saffron threads dissolved in 2 tablespoons hot milk

2 4-inch squares silver or gold leaf (*varak,* optional)

Mint sprigs, for garnish

Mulligatawny with Pink Lentils (page 50), accompany it with Baked Yam Koftas with Green Gravy (page 125) and Pickled Baby Carrots (page 207), and follow with Fudge Balls in Rose-Perfumed Syrup (page 216).

1. Wash, soak, and drain the rice (see step 1, page 130). Place in a medium saucepan with 3 cups of water and the salt. Bring to a boil, reduce the heat, cover partially and cook until barely tender, about 10 minutes. Drain the rice (you may save the water to use in soups or vegetable dishes) and set aside.

2. Combine the cloves, cardamom, ginger, onion, mint and 2 tablespoons water in a blender container. Process until smoothly pureed, scraping the sides of the bowl as necessary. Set aside.

3. Heat the desi ghee in a large saute pan over medium heat. Add the raisins and fry until plump, about 1 minute. Remove with a slotted spoon and set aside. Add the pistachios and fry until lightly browned, about 4 minutes. Remove and set aside along with the raisins. Add the spice-onion puree to the pan and cook, stirring constantly, about 4 minutes. Add the vegetables, cover, and cook, stirring occasionally, until tender, about 8 minutes.

4. Meanwhile, place a rack in the middle of the oven and preheat to 350°F.

5. Brush a 1½-quart heatproof glass bowl with desi ghee or butter. Spread a quarter of the rice in the bowl, top with a third of the vegetable mixture, and continue with alternate layers of rice and vegetables, finishing with a layer of rice. Sprinkle the saffron-milk mixture over the top. Cover tightly with foil and bake for 20 minutes.

6. Remove the rice from the oven and let stand covered for 5 minutes. Just before serving, place a heated serving platter upside down over the baking dish. Invert the dish over the platter holding both securely, and let the biryani slide down onto the platter. Garnish with the silver or gold leaves. Sprinkle the raisins and nuts on top and arrange the mint sprigs neatly. Serve hot, cut into wedges.

**Note:** The biryani can be prepared 1 day ahead. Let cool in the baking dish, cover, and refrigerate. Rewarm in the oven or microwave oven.

**Variation:** If you are short on time, use frozen mixed vegetables.

# SHAHJAHAN CORN PILAF
## (Shahjahan Biryani)

Serves 4
Preparation time:
    40 minutes, plus 15
    minutes baking

1 cup raw basmati rice
1¼ cups water
½ cup low-fat or whole
    milk
¾ teaspoon salt
3 ears fresh corn, husks
    and silk removed
1 tablespoon mild
    vegetable oil
2 bay leaves
½ cup chopped onion
1 teaspoon crushed garlic
⅛ teaspoon turmeric
2 tablespoons chopped
    cashews
1 tablespoon currants
    or raisins
½ teaspoon ground
    cumin
½ teaspoon ground
    coriander
½ cup chopped tomato
Caramelized Onion and
    Garlic Shreds (oppo-
    site), for garnish

Here is my own variation on the classic biryani, with a subtle stew of sweet corn and tomato replacing the vegetable mix in the previous recipe. I have added some other new twists, including steaming the rice in low-fat milk. Covered with a blanket of caramelized onion and garlic shreds, it makes a superb entree for entertaining. Since the pilaf has a slightly sweet taste, I like to accompany it with Potato-Stuffed Anaheim Chiles in Cream Sauce (page 106), Curried Mixed Sprouts (page 158), and Daikon Salad with Aromatic Oil (page 188). Round off the meal with Glazed Garbanzo Milk Confection (page 218). Serve sparkling white wine.

1. Wash, soak, and drain the rice (see step 1, page 130). Bring the water and milk to a boil in a medium saucepan. Add the rice and ½ teaspoon salt. Reduce the heat to low, cover, and cook until just tender, about 10 minutes.

2. Meanwhile, grate the corn on the coarse side of a box grater, or use a small sharp knife to cut off just the tips of the kernels, then scrape the milky centers out of the kernels into a bowl.

3. Heat the oil in a heavy saute pan over medium-high heat. Add the bay leaves, onion, and garlic. Stir and cook until the onion is lightly browned, 3 to 4 minutes. Add the turmeric, cashews, raisins, cumin, and coriander. Cook, stirring, 2 to 3 minutes. Add the tomato, corn, and remaining ¼ teaspoon salt and mix well. Reduce the heat to medium, cover, and cook until soft, 6 to 8 minutes.

4. Position a rack in the center of the oven and preheat to 350°F. Make alternate layers of rice and spicy-corn mixture in a 2-quart heatproof glass baking dish, finishing with a layer of rice. Cover tightly with foil and bake for 15 minutes. Remove the rice from the oven and let stand covered for 5 minutes. Uncover and serve from the baking dish, garnished with caramelized onion and garlic shreds.

**Note:** The pilaf can be made 1 day ahead. Let cool in the baking dish, cover, and refrigerate. Reheat in the oven or microwave oven.

*Caramelized Onion and Garlic Shreds*

These golden brown slivers of onion and garlic are wonderful sprinkled over stews, pilafs, salads, and chaats. For a delicious appetizer, serve them warm, piled in a napkin-lined basket and sprinkled with toasted cumin seeds and salt.

Peel 1 large onion and cut it in half. Thinly slice each half and separate the slices into half rings. Separate and peel the cloves from 2 heads garlic and slice thinly. Pour 1½ inches of oil into a large frying pan or wok and heat it to 300°F. Add the onion and garlic and cook, stirring constantly, until they are golden and crisp. The oil temperature will drop at first but will rise again as the onion browns. Regulate the heat to keep it at 300°F. Lift the onion and garlic from the pan with a slotted spoon and drain on paper towels. Discard any scorched bits.

Serve warm, or cool completely and store in an airtight container for up to 1 week at room temperature or 1 month in the refrigerator. To reheat, spread in a single layer on a cookie sheet and heat in 300°F oven for 5 minutes. You can use the leftover oil for frying again, or to flavor stews and dal dishes. Let cool, then strain and cover tightly.

# FRAGRANT SPINACH PILAF WITH BABY CARROTS
## (Palak Pulao)

Serves 4
Preparation time:
    30 minutes

1 cup raw basmati rice,
    cleaned
½ cup chopped spinach,
    fresh or thawed
1½ cups water
1 tablespoon desi ghee or
    unsalted butter
4 whole cloves, ground
⅛ teaspoon cinnamon
8 baby carrots
½ teaspoon salt
Caramelized Onion and
    Garlic Shreds (page
    141)

A delicious aroma would fill the kitchen when my mother cooked rice, and as the fragrance infiltrated our neighbor's yard, they would frequently ask what was the new theme in rice. In this preparation rice is delicately infused with sweet, soothing spices — cinnamon and cloves — and cooked in spinach puree. Elegantly studded with petite baby carrots, the pilaf makes a wholesome meal in itself. Accompany with simple earthy Stewed Black-eyed Peas with Cherry Tomatoes (page 153) and Smoky Eggplant Raita (page 179). For a more substantial meal include any of the flatbreads.

1. Wash, soak, and drain the rice (see step 1, page 130). Set aside.

2. Place the spinach in a small dry skillet. Stir and cook on medium heat until wilted, about 5 minutes. Transfer to a food processor or blender with ½ cup water and blend into a smooth puree. Set aside.

3. Heat the desi ghee in a medium saucepan over moderate heat. Add the cloves and cinnamon. Stir until aromatic, about 30 seconds. Immediately add the carrots and rice and stir-fry for 4 minutes. Add the spinach puree and salt and 1 cup water. Bring to a boil, reduce the heat to low, cover, and simmer until the rice is tender, 15 minutes.

4. Turn off the heat and let the rice stand covered for 5 minutes. Fluff gently and transfer to a heated serving platter. Garnish with onion and garlic shreds. Serve hot or warm.

**Note:** The spinach pilaf can be made 2 days ahead and kept covered in the refrigerator. Reheat on moderate heat or in the microwave.

**Variation:** Like my mother, I make numerous variations on this dish with the plentiful leafy greens from the market or my garden. Choose fresh bunches of red or green Swiss chard, sorrel, chicory, kale, or collard or turnip greens. A particularly attractive version (choti makkai pulao) uses beet greens, with a mixture of baby corn and baby carrots for color contrast.

# TOMATO PILAF WITH YELLOW SPLIT PEAS
## (*Khichari*)

Serves 4 to 6
Preparation time:
    35 minutes, plus
    soaking time

1 cup raw basmati rice
½ cup dried yellow
    split peas
2 tablespoons mild
    vegetable oil
1 tablespoon desi ghee
    or unsalted butter
¼ teaspoon cumin seeds
3 cloves garlic, minced
10 to 12 whole black
    peppercorns
1 cup peeled and
    chopped tomato (fresh
    or canned), with juices
2¾ cups water
½ teaspoon salt

*Khichari* refers to a dish made of rice and dal with numerous seasonings. There are two styles, one moist and stew-like and the other dry. This is the dry rendition; if you prefer it more stew-like, add two more cups of water and a little sambar powder and cook to the consistency of porridge. Mildly seasoned with whole spices, this specialty is good with Morel Mushrooms with Cashews and Dates (page 111), Stuffed Eggplant with Shallots (page 105), and a cool soothing yogurt-based salad such as Baked Potato Raita with Walnuts (page 178).

*Khichari* is traditionally served in the south as part of Pongal, the feast of thanksgiving that follows the rice harvest in January. The newly harvested rice is cooked in new earthenware pots and first offered to God before being served. In celebration of Mother Earth's bounty, villagers decorate their cattle in brilliant colors, and the animals are led in procession to the joyous sounds of music and drums. Bullfights, cockfights and bullock-cart races are all part of the exhilarating occasion.

1. Combine the rice and split peas in a bowl. Wash in several changes of water. Add enough water to cover by at least 2 inches and soak for 10 minutes. Drain and set aside.

2. Heat the oil and desi ghee in a medium saucepan over moderate heat. Add the cumin, garlic, and peppercorns. Stir and cook until aromatic, about 2 minutes. Add the tomatoes, rice and peas, water, and salt. Bring to a boil, reduce the heat, cover and cook until the rice and split peas are tender and all the water is absorbed, 20 to 25 minutes. (Sprinkle in a little more water if necessary.) Turn off the heat and let the rice stand covered for 5 minutes. Fluff lightly and transfer to a serving platter. Serve hot.

**Note:** The khichari can be made ahead and kept several hours at room temperature or up to 5 days in the refrigerator.

**Variation:** SUN-DRIED TOMATO PILAF (*Sukhe Tamatar Bhat*)
Replace the fresh tomatoes with chopped sun-dried tomatoes. Fry 1 to 2 minutes along with the spices and garlic and continue with the recipe.

# JAHANGIR PILAF WITH YELLOW MUNG BEANS
## (Khichari Jahangiri)

Serves 4
Preparation time:
    35 minutes

1 cup raw basmati rice
2 cups water
⅓ cup yellow mung
    beans, cleaned and
    rinsed
¾ teaspoon salt
1½ tablespoons mild
    vegetable oil
1 small potato, peeled
    and cut into 1½-inch
    sticks
1 tablespoon dark raisins
1 tablespoon slivered
    pistachios
2 bay leaves
½ cup chopped onion
½ teaspoon crushed
    fresh ginger
½ teaspoon ground
    cumin
½ teaspoon ground
    coriander
½ teaspoon cinnamon
¼ teaspoon ground
    cardamom

It is believed that the Mughal cuisine reached a height of excellence during the time of Emperor Akbar. Jahangir, Akbar's son, followed in his father's gourmet footsteps. This healthy and easy-to-digest rice pilaf with mung dal, warm northern-style spices, nuts, and raisins was his favorite dish. I like to fold in potato sticks toward the end of cooking to help it hold its shape. Serve it with Garlicky Smothered Bell Peppers (page 98), Mangalore Pineapple Curry (page 113), and No-Cook Spicy Lime Pickles (page 203). Pass plain yogurt at the table.

1. Wash, soak, and drain the rice (see step 1, page 130). Bring the water to a rolling boil in a medium saucepan. Add the rice, mung beans, and salt. Reduce the heat to low, cover, and simmer for 10 minutes.

2. Meanwhile, heat the oil in a 10-inch skillet over medium-high heat. Add the potato and stir-fry until lightly browned and easily pierced with a knife, 6 to 8 minutes. Remove with a slotted spoon and set aside. Add the raisins and fry until plump; remove and set aside. Toss in the pistachios, fry until lightly browned, remove and set aside.

4. Add the bay leaves, onion, and ginger to the skillet. Cook until the edges of the onion start to brown, about 4 minutes. Add the ground spices and stir until aromatic, 1 minute. Pour this mixture onto the rice. Add the potato and mix gently with a fork. Cover and simmer until the beans are tender but still hold their shape, 5 minutes.

5. Remove the pilaf from the heat and let stand covered for 5 minutes. Uncover and fluff lightly with a fork. Just before serving, discard the bay leaves. Garnish with pistachios and raisins. Serve hot.

Note: The khichari can be kept covered for several hours at room temperature or up to 3 days in the refrigerator. Reheat on moderate heat or in the microwave. Sprinkle with a little water first if it seems dry.

Variation: GARBANZOS PILAF (Kabuli Chana Chawal)
Omit the mung dal; when you are ready to add the potatoes, stir in 1 cup canned garbanzos, drained and rinsed.

# TANJORE TAMARIND GARLICKY RICE
## (Puliyogare)

Serves 8
Preparation time:
   40 minutes

½ tablespoon coriander
   seeds
1 teaspoon dried yellow
   split peas
¼ teaspoon fenugreek
   seeds
½ teaspoon cumin seeds
1 or 2 dried red chiles,
   stemmed
Pinch of cinnamon
2 cups raw basmati rice
3 cups water
1 teaspoon salt
1½ tablespoons mild
   vegetable or peanut oil
½ teaspoon mustard
   seeds
½ tablespoon sliced
   garlic
¼ teaspoon turmeric
20 fresh kari leaves
2 teaspoons yellow chick-
   peas (chana dal)
   (optional)
½ teaspoon tamarind
   concentrate, dissolved
   in ¾ cup water
2 tablespoons chopped
   cashews
½ teaspoon brown
   sugar

Tanjore is a rich delta area in southern India, where rice dominates the menu. It is cooked with numerous flavors and always served steaming hot, topped with a trickle of desi ghee. Tamarind and a blend of spices give a pleasant tang and aroma to the rice in this southern house-special. Serve with Pumpkin Koftas in Rustic Swiss Chard Sauce (page 124), accompanied by a fruit chutney. You may also include Shredded Green Cabbage Flatbread (page 81) and a vegetable side dish for a substantial meal.

1. Toast the coriander, split peas, fenugreek, cumin, and chiles in a frying pan on medium heat until the spices are aromatic and the seeds start to darken, about 5 minutes. Transfer to a grinder and grind to a fine powder. Stir in the cinnamon and set aside.

2. Wash, soak, and drain the rice (see step 1, page 130). Place in a Dutch oven. Add 3 cups water and bring to a boil. Stir in the salt, reduce the heat to low, cover, and simmer until barely tender, about 12 minutes.

3. Meanwhile, heat the oil in a small saucepan on medium-high heat. Add the mustard. When the seeds begin to sizzle and splutter, reduce the heat and stir in the garlic, turmeric, kari leaves, and dal. Stir and cook until the garlic is aromatic and light brown, 3 to 4 minutes. Add the tamarind liquid and stir in the spice blend. Bring to a boil, reduce the heat, and simmer for 6 to 8 minutes.

4. Stir in the nuts and sugar and remove from the heat. Pour the mixture over the rice and mix gently with fork. Cover and cook until all the liquid is absorbed and the rice is tender, 5 to 8 minutes. Turn off the heat and let the rice stand covered for 5 minutes. Serve hot. Store any leftover spice mixture in a screw-top jar.

Note: This rice dish can be prepared ahead and kept, covered, up to a week in the refrigerator, or frozen up to 1 month. Bring to room temperature; reheat on moderate heat or in a microwave.

    The spicy tamarind concentrate (step 3) can be made ahead and frozen up to a year. Cool and pour into ice cube trays and set in the freezer for 4 hours. Then transfer the cubes into plastic bags and freeze.

# LEGUMES

## PEAS, BEANS, AND LENTILS

PRESSURE COOKER METHOD FOR LEGUME PUREE

STOVE-TOP METHOD

FRAGRANT BABY DILL WITH GARLIC AND MUNG BEANS

STEWED BLACK-EYED PEAS WITH CHERRY TOMATOES

CLASSIC MADRAS LENTIL STEW (SAMBAR)

GARLICKY CURRIED MUNG BEANS

CHILE LIMA BEANS WITH FRESH DILL

CURRIED MIXED SPROUTS WITH POTATOES

PASTA INDIAN STYLE WITH LENTILS

GARBANZO BEANS IN TANGY TOMATO SAUCE

BRAISED LEEKS WITH SPLIT PEAS

In India, an infant's first solid food is invariably *dal* and rice. Although *dal* properly refers to a specific type of legumes (see A Shopping Guide, next page), it also serves as a generic name for all dried legumes — split peas, beans, and lentils — and the dishes cooked with them.

Legumes have been valued since ancient times in the subcontinent, and are a mainstay of the everyday diet for their healthful benefits, for religious reasons, and because they are undeniably delicious. Dried beans and dals are found in practically every kitchen cupboard in India. In contrast to their role in the West, where legumes have often been relegated to the status of "poor man's meat," in India dals are favored by everyone from the poorest peasants to royalty. When Emperor Shahjahan, who built the Taj Mahal, was deprived of his throne and imprisoned by his ambitious son Aurangzeb, his captor asked him, "What will you have for food?" Shahjahan promptly replied, "Dal!" The son exclaimed in contempt, "Oh! Even in prison, royal tastes still persist!"

I am often asked how I get adequate protein from a vegetarian diet. One key is India's vast collection of delicious, inexpensive legume dishes. In combination with grains, legumes provide plenty of dietary protein. Although neither grains nor legumes can supply complete protein all by themselves — each is deficient in one or more of the essential amino acids that constitute protein — together they complement each other, providing millions of vegetarians in India and around the world all the protein we need without eating meat.

Legumes are also termed "Nature's broom" because of their high amount of dietary fiber. They contain no cholesterol (they have been shown to lower cholesterol levels in the blood), and only a trace of fat (of the polyunsaturated variety). They have the same amounts of vitamin B complex and iron as beef. No wonder doctors and nutritionists are urging us to include them in our diet.

Dals provide not only important nutrients but also a wholesome, satisfying earthy taste. The recipes in this chapter illustrate varied flavors and endless culinary combinations. Most of them use the common Indian seasoning of mustard- and cumin-infused oil (see page 13), which enhances both flavor and appearance and helps stimulate digestion.

A word about flatulence: Legumes contain complex sugars called oligosaccharides which are indigestible by humans. Bacteria in the intestinal tract consume the sugars, emitting gas as a byproduct. For centuries, cooks have tried dozens of procedures to prevent gas but with limited success. However, there are two ways to deal with it.

First, eat beans frequently; people who consume legumes regularly seem to have less discomfort. Start with small quantities, then gradually increase the serving size. If you are just starting to add legumes to your diet, mung dal is one of the most easily digestible varieties. Also, fluids help in the digestion of beans, so drink plenty of liquids when eating legumes.

Second, discard the water in which you have soaked them and replace it with fresh water for cooking; some of the oligosaccharides are released into the soaking water. Some of the protein and vitamins also leach into the water, but the loss is minimal — 1 to 3 percent.

Another way to deal with the oligosaccharide problem is to turn the dry legumes into sprouts. The sprouting process consumes most of the oligosaccharides, and increases the level of vitamins B, C, and E three to five times. Directions for sprouting legumes are found on page 240.

# A Shopping Guide

The following is a brief guide to the dried legume varieties used in this book. Many of them can be purchased in supermarkets, but for others you may need to go to Indian or other ethnic markets. When selecting, especially in bulk, look at them closely; choose plump, whole, and unbroken legumes, and avoid any batches with broken, moldy, shriveled, or spotted beans or lentils. Small pebbles, bits of soil, or other agricultural products are perfectly okay, though you will have to sort and discard them. Store dried legumes in an airtight container in a cool, dry place for up to a year or in your freezer indefinitely.

The Indian names for the various legumes tell you not only the variety, but in what form it is sold. Split and hulled forms are called *dal,* while those sold whole are known as *saabat.* Some legumes, such as mung beans, are sold in both forms, for different uses.

## BROWN LENTILS *(Saabat Masoor)*

These pale greenish-brown lentils from India are smaller than the American brown lentils found in supermarkets, but the two are similar in flavor and can be used interchangeably. They do not require soaking.

## PINK LENTILS *(Masoor Dal)*

These hulled and split lentils do not require soaking. They cook quickly to a velvety yellow puree, and are therefore excellent for soups, sauces, and stews. Available in supermarkets.

## YELLOW LENTILS *(Toovar, Toor or Arhar Dal)*

Also known as "pigeon peas," these thin, bright yellow lentils cook quickly. Their mild, earthy flavor is a natural for soups, sauces, pilafs, and sweets. Yellow lentils sometimes come in an oil-coated

form, to prevent insect infestation. I recommend the plain form if you have a choice, but if not, wash the oil-coated lentils in several changes of hot water to remove the oil.

## SPLIT PEAS *(Pardesi Dal)*

The yellow split peas widely available in supermarkets are similar in diameter to Indian *toovar dal,* but are somewhat thicker. They are not quite as sweet, but otherwise make a fine substitute.

## GARBANZO BEANS *(Chole)*

Also called chick peas or ceci beans, garbanzos have a pleasant, nutty flavor. The recipes in this book can be made with dried garbanzos, but I highly recommend using the canned version widely available in supermarkets; dried garbanzos take a long time to soak and cook. Two varieties are available in Indian markets: the pale yellow type called *safed* or *kabuli channa,* and the smaller, dark brown *kala channa.* They can be used interchangeably and can also be sprouted.

## YELLOW CHICK PEAS *(Chana Dal)*

Cousins of garbanzo beans, yellow chick peas are sold split and hulled. These small, thick, bright yellow, lens-shaped beans are frequently used in thick velvety purees and soups, and a little ground chana dal adds thickening power to Sambar Powder (see page 24). When chana dal is milled, the resulting flour is called *besan* (see Chick-pea Flour, page 237). Available in Indian markets.

## MUNG BEANS *(Saabat Mung)*

These oval beans with aqua-green skins, native to India, are among the most versatile legumes. Cooked whole, or milled into flour for use in breads and fritters, or sprouted, their rich, earthy flavor blends well with many foods. Whole mung beans can be cooked without prior soaking. Dried mung beans are available in the Oriental section of supermarkets and in Indian markets. There is also a split version with the skins intact called *mung ki chilke dal,* available in Indian markets; these can be used interchangeably with whole mung beans.

## YELLOW MUNG BEANS *(Mung Dal)*

These petite, golden-yellow legumes are not a separate variety of mung bean, but the same variety hulled and split. Lighter and easier to digest than other beans and relatively quick to cook, they have many uses in Indian cuisine such as curries, soups, pilafs, and dumplings.

## WHITE GRAM BEANS *(Urad Dal)*

These tiny, hulled and split ivory-white ovals are extensively used in south Indian cooking. Soaked and ground, they are combined with ground rice or *chana dal* to accelerate the fermenting of batters. They are also used in making lentil wafers. Available in Indian markets. Indian markets may also carry black gram beans in whole form *(saabat urad)* or split with the skin on *(urad ki chilke dal),* neither of which can be substituted for urad dal.

## BLACK-EYED PEAS *(Lobhia)*

These are distinguished by their small kidney shape, beige color, and distinctive black spots. They have an earthy flavor. They are used in stews combined with vegetables and chaats. Dried, frozen, or fresh black-eyed peas are available in supermarkets; the dried form needs soaking and cooking like other dried beans, while the fresh and frozen forms cook much more quickly.

## BASIC COOKING OF LEGUMES

Many of the recipes in this and the Soups chapter call for precooked or pureed legumes. They can be cooked by several methods, including stove-top simmering, pressure cooking, and microwave. The table on page 151 shows the cooking and soaking times for various legume varieties and cooking techniques.

Legumes need to be cleaned before soaking or cooking. Sort through the beans to remove any small rocks, beans with holes or cavities indicating insects, and wrinkled, undersized, or discolored beans. Packaged dried legumes purchased at the supermarkets usually need just rinsing. Beans purchased in bulk at health food or Indian stores may not have been presorted.

Cooking times given here are approximate, and depend on the age of the legumes, how they were stored, and other variables. To test for doneness, remove one from the pan and press it between your thumb and finger. If it is soft, they are done, but if there is a hard core they need further cooking. Add water if required.

Once the legumes are cooked, they can be refrigerated, ready to be turned into a variety of soups, stews, and side dishes. Most of them begin with oil seasoned with spices, onion, and garlic. In the simplest and most common form, the seasoned oil is poured over the cooked legumes (particularly mung and toovar dals) and the mixture is cooked gently until slightly thick to serve as a side dish. The exact combination of dal and spices varies from region to region; one of my favorites is the Maharastrian version called *varan,* flavored with turmeric and a pinch of asafetida.

The finished legume dishes in this chapter can be made ahead of time and stored up to 4 hours at room temperature, or for 3 to 5 days in the refrigerator, or they may be frozen for longer storage. Reheat over moderate heat or in the microwave oven.

# GOOD OLD PRESSURE COOKER METHOD FOR LEGUME PUREE

Makes 1¾ cups
Preparation time: 15
  minutes, plus cooling
  time

½ cup dried yellow
  lentils (toovar dal),
  yellow split peas, or
  split yellow chick peas
  (chana dal)
1 cup water
1 teaspoon oil
¼ teaspoon turmeric
  (optional)

Pressure cooking is an ideal method for preparing legume purees. In half the time (or less) it takes to cook them on the stovetop, lentils and split peas cook butter-soft, ideal for soups and stews. The shorter cooking time makes this method more energy-efficient, and the yield is slightly greater. Twice a week, I use my pressure cooker to make an assortment of legume purees that I keep in the refrigerator, ready to whisk together a stew or soup at a moment's notice.

Cooking legumes this way is even more efficient when you use the special stacking containers sold in Indian stores. A three-layer stand will fit comfortably in a 6-quart pressure cooker. Each variety sits in its own container with its cooking liquid, and additional water in the bottom of the cooker provides the pressurized steam that cooks them quickly. Don't worry about cooking different varieties with different cooking time requirements; with the exception of garbanzos, they all seem to come out consistently cooked in about the same time.

Pressure cookers vary in size and other details, so be sure to follow the manufacturer's directions. The recipes in this chapter were tested in a 6-quart cooker. Whatever size you use, it should not be filled more than halfway (including water). Some beans have a tendency to froth and clog the vent; adding a teaspoon of vegetable oil to a cup of dried beans will help prevent frothing and expedite the simmering. If the vents do get clogged, turn off the heat and set the cooker on a cold burner to allow it to depressurize on its own, or place it in a sink and run cold water over it. Tilt the weight and release pressure gradually.

The cooking time and proportions for several popular dals are given here. Consult the table on the opposite page for other varieties suitable for pressure cooking. If the dal is uncooked at the end of the prescribed time, either reseal the pot and cook longer or finish cooking uncovered by the conventional stovetop method.

1. Sort the lentils or peas and remove any debris. Wash in several changes of running tap water. Place in a 4- to 6-quart pressure cooker. Add the water, oil, and turmeric. Cover and cook at full pressure on high heat about 10 minutes.

2. Turn off heat. Allow the cooker to cool gradually, about 15 minutes, then open. Whisk the lentils or peas into a puree. The puree is now ready to use in recipes; or cool, cover, and store up to 4 days in the refrigerator or up to 1 month in the freezer.

150

# STOVE-TOP METHOD

Makes 2½ cups
Preparation time:
35 minutes

1 cup dried yellow lentils
(toovar dal) or yellow
split peas
2 cups water
1 teaspoon oil (optional)
¼ teaspoon turmeric
(optional)

In this method, lentils are fully cooked on the stove top. Other varieties of dal can be cooked by the same method; consult the table below for the amount of water and cooking time.

1. Sort the lentils and remove any debris. Wash in several changes of running tap water.

2. Transfer the lentils to a Dutch oven and add the water, oil, and turmeric if desired. Bring to a boil. Reduce the heat to medium, cover (partially at first, until the foam settles, then snugly), and cook until the lentils are tender and still hold their shape, 30 minutes. Turn off the heat and let the lentils stand, covered, for 5 minutes. Whisk into a puree and use or store as described above.

| DRIED LEGUMES | SOAKING TIME FOR STOVE-TOP COOKING (HOURS) | WATER FOR COOKING (CUPS) | STOVE-TOP COOKING (MINUTES) | PRESSURE COOKING (MINUTES) | APPROXIMATE YIELD AFTER COOKING (CUPS) |
|---|---|---|---|---|---|
| ½ cup black-eyed peas | 4 | 1½ | 30 | 15 | 1½ |
| ½ cup brown lentils | — | 1½ | 45 | 12 | 1¼ |
| ½ cup pink lentils | — | 1¼ | 22 | 8 | 1 |
| 1 cup garbanzo beans | 8 | 4 | 2½-3 hours | 25 | 2½ |
| 1 cup yellow chick-peas (chana dal) | — | 2 | 50 | 12 | 2¼ |
| ½ cup kidney beans | 8 | 1½ | 1½ hours | 20 | 1½ |
| ½ cup lima beans | 8 | 1 | 20 | 12 | 1½ |
| ½ cup whole mung beans | 4 | 1½ | 20 | — | 1½ |
| ¼ cup yellow mung beans (mung dal) | — | 1 | 20 | 8 | 1 |
| 1 cup split peas (yellow or green) or yellow lentils (toovar dal) | — | 2 | 32 | 10 | 2½ |

# FRAGRANT BABY DILL WITH GARLIC AND MUNG BEANS
## *(Shepuchi Bhaji)*

Serves 3
Preparation time:
    35 minutes

2 tablespoons mild
    peanut oil
⅓ cup chopped onion
3 large cloves garlic,
    minced
1 fresh hot green chile,
    stemmed and chopped
1 bunch (6 ounces) fresh
    dill, trimmed and fine-
    ly chopped
3 tablespoons yellow
    mung beans (mung
    dal), cleaned, rinsed,
    and drained
1 cup water
Heaping ¼ teaspoon
    salt
Tomato wedges, for
    garnish

Fresh dill is used in India as a vegetable as well as a garnish. Here the herb is simmered with mung dal in essence of garlic and onion and perked up by a fresh hot chile. The result is a low-calorie stew, light and easy on the palate, and especially attractive with the tiny yellow mung dal against the delicate needle-like dark green leaves. Accompany it with Spicy Sesame Flatbread (page 81) and Cool Onion and Tomato Raita (page 174) for a light luncheon. For a more substantial meal, serve Tanjore Tamarind Garlicky Rice (page 145). Round off with a platter of sliced fresh fruits and vanilla ice cream. Or try the stew as a stuffing for crepes or puff pastry.

1. Heat the oil in a medium saucepan over medium-high heat. Add the onion, garlic, and chile. Cook until the onion is soft, 3 to 4 minutes.

2. Add the dill and cook, stirring constantly, until aromatic, about 2 minutes. Add the mung dal, water, and salt. Bring to a boil, reduce the heat to medium, cover, and cook until the mung dal is tender but still holds its shape, 20 minutes. Let stand covered for 5 minutes. Transfer to a serving bowl, garnish with tomato wedges, and serve hot.

**Note:** If you prefer a drier texture, uncover the pot toward the end of cooking and simmer until all liquid is absorbed.

To trim fresh dill, pinch off the tender stems and leaves with your thumb and forefinger and discard the tough stems.

**Variation:** Use ⅓ cup of yellow split peas in place of the mung dal and increase the water to 2 cups.

# STEWED BLACK-EYED PEAS WITH CHERRY TOMATOES
## (Lobhia Rasedar)

Serves 6
Preparation time:
25 minutes

1 tablespoon mild peanut
or vegetable oil
¼ teaspoon mustard
seeds
⅓ cup finely chopped
onion
¼ teaspoon turmeric
1 small russet potato,
peeled and diced
1 cup (8 to 10) cherry
tomatoes, rinsed,
stemmed, and cut in
half
1½ cups cooked black-
eyed peas
1 cup water
½ tablespoon Aromatic
Spice Powder (page
25)
½ teaspoon salt

Humble black-eyed peas are glorified in this spicy stew. If you have the cooked peas in the refrigerator and a spice blend ready in the rack, this is a snap to make. You may substitute fresh or frozen black-eyed peas for dried; steam them 6 to 8 minutes or until just tender. I like to partner this stew with Whole Wheat Flatbread (page 79) or Whole Wheat Puffy Bread (page 87) accompanied by a stir-fried side dish of vegetables and Crisp Okra Raita (page 176). Follow it with plain basmati rice or pilaf for a complete meal.

1. Heat the oil in a medium saucepan over medium-high heat until it ripples when the pan is tilted. Add the mustard seeds; when they sizzle and splutter, add the onion. Stir and cook until soft, about 3 minutes. Add the turmeric and potato. Stir and fry 2 minutes longer.

2. Add half of the cherry tomato halves, reserving the other half for garnish. Stir in the peas, water, spice powder, and salt. Bring to a boil, reduce the heat to low, cover, and simmer for 15 minutes. Turn into a heated shallow bowl. Garnish with the remaining cherry tomato halves and serve.

# CLASSIC MADRAS LENTIL STEW
## *(Sambar)*

Serves 6 to 8
Preparation time:
  30 minutes

2½ cups cooked yellow
  lentils (toovar dal) or
  yellow split peas
1½ cups water
1 cup chopped tomato
½ cup cauliflower, cut
  into ½ inch pieces
¼ cup sliced carrots
¼ cup green beans,
  stem ends snapped off
  and cut into ½ inch
  lengths
½ teaspoon tamarind
  concentrate dissolved
  in ½ cup water
1 tablespoon sambar
  powder, homemade
  (page 24) or bought
¼ teaspoon cayenne
1 teaspoon salt
¼ teaspoon sugar
2 tablespoons chopped
  fresh cilantro, plus
  additional for garnish
1 tablespoon mild
  vegetable oil
½ teaspoon mustard
  seeds
½ teaspoon cumin seeds
⅛ teaspoon turmeric
15 fresh kari leaves
2 dried red chiles,
  stemmed and broken

Sambar, an everyday dish in southern India, is kind of a cross between soup and stew. Lentils and assorted vegetables are slowly stewed with tamarind and spices until the lentils reduce to a smooth, velvety puree. The characteristic blend of spices for this dish is sold in Indian markets as sambar powder, but for a really authentic flavor, you can make your own (see page 24). If you use a store-bought version, you might need to reduce the amount of cayenne, as some brands are quite hot. Paired with Paper-Thin Rice Crepes Udupi Style (page 72), sambar is perfect fare for a cool autumn night. For a dieter's lunch, serve the sambar with Madras Spongy Cakes (page 64). Follow with Warm Cream of Wheat Pilaf (page 59). For a quick light lunch, simply serve sambar generously spooned over plain basmati rice.

1. Combine the lentils, water, tomato, cauliflower, carrots, and beans in a large saucepan. Bring to a boil over high heat. Reduce the heat to medium and cook, covered, until the vegetables are tender, about 10 minutes. Add the tamarind liquid, sambar powder, cayenne, salt, sugar, and cilantro. Cover and simmer for 10 minutes longer. Transfer to a large tureen, cover, and set aside.

2. Heat the oil in a small frying pan over medium-high heat. Add the mustard and cumin seeds. When the seeds sizzle and splutter, immediately add the turmeric, kari leaves, and chiles. Stir for half a minute, remove, and pour over the sambar.

3. Serve the sambar in individual bowls or custard cups. Garnish each bowl with a sprinkling of cilantro.

**Note:** Any combination of vegetables such as Brussels sprouts, pearl onions, broccoli, eggplant, turnips, or parsnips make excellent substitutes for the ones given here.

The sambar can be prepared 5 days ahead and kept covered in the refrigerator or frozen up to 1 month. Reheat on moderate heat or in the microwave.

# GARLICKY CURRIED MUNG BEANS
## (Rasedar Saabat Mung Dal)

Serves 4 to 6
Preparation time:
   30 minutes, plus 4
   hours soaking

½ cup dried whole
   mung beans
1½ cups water
½ tablespoon minced
   garlic
2 teaspoons minced fresh
   ginger
¼ teaspoon turmeric
1 tablespoon mild peanut
   oil
½ teaspoon mustard
   seeds
1 teaspoon cumin seeds
1½ fresh hot green
   chiles, stemmed and
   chopped
1 teaspoon salt
½ teaspoon sugar
½ cup chopped tomato
Chopped fresh dill

Earthy whole mung beans, garlic, and ginger make a classic and delicious combination, and the ginger makes the beans easier to digest. A mixture of aromatic spices, chiles, and tomatoes cooked in peanut oil and stirred in at the last minute further rounds out the flavor. This versatile preparation goes well with breads or pilafs accompanied by a cool yogurt raita. Or serve it over pasta.

1. Sort the mung beans to remove any debris. Rinse 2 or 3 times in running tap water. Add enough water to cover by at least 2 inches and soak for 4 hours.

2. Drain the beans and place them in a large saucepan with the water, garlic, ginger, and turmeric. Bring to a boil, reduce the heat to medium, cover (partially at first, until the foam settles, then snugly), and cook until the beans are tender but still hold their shape, about 15 minutes. (If you prefer the beans very soft, cook them for a few more minutes.) Transfer to a heated shallow bowl. Cover and set aside.

3. Heat the oil in a small heavy skillet on medium-high heat. Add the mustard and cumin seeds. When the seeds sizzle and splutter, add the chiles. Stir and cook for 1 minute. Add the salt, sugar, and tomato; cook, stirring occasionally, until the tomato is soft, about 5 minutes. Pour the tomato mixture over the beans and mix lightly. Serve garnished with fresh dill.

# CHILE LIMA BEANS WITH FRESH DILL
## (Sime Avarekai Rasa)

Serves 4 to 6
Preparation time:
  45 minutes, plus 6 to
  8 hours soaking

¾ cup large dried lima
  beans, picked clean
½ tablespoon mild
  vegetable oil
¼ teaspoon cumin seeds
½ cup chopped onion
½ teaspoon crushed
  garlic
1 teaspoon crushed fresh
  ginger
½ cup chopped tomato
2 tablespoons unsweet-
  ened flaked coconut
  or grated fresh
  coconut
2 tablespoons chopped
  cilantro
2½ cups water
⅛ teaspoon cayenne
½ teaspoon paprika
½ teaspoon salt
1 tablespoon Caramelized
  Onion and Garlic
  Shreds (page 141)
  (optional)
1 tablespoon chopped
  fresh dill

Sometimes referred to as butter beans, lima beans have been termed the "aristocrats" of the bean family for their nice appearance and buttery taste. Although they are not available at markets in India, I remember my mother growing this "exotic" creeper in her garden. She had a penchant for novel plants and would frequently mail order seeds from abroad. She called lima beans "double beans" because of their size. As my sister and I would help shell these gorgeous, glistening beans, we could hardly resist biting into them while they were still raw.

Unfortunately, in the West lima beans are usually restricted to salads and soups. Here, they are bathed in a subtly spiced onion-tomato sauce and garnished with fried onion and garlic shreds and a sprinkling of fragrant fresh dill. (If you are lucky enough to find fresh lima bean pods in a farmers' market, simply shell them and add them to the tomato sauce in step 3. Frozen green limas can be used in the same way.) I like to serve this dish with Fresh Cilantro Pilaf (page 134) and Whole Kernel Corn Raita (page 175). For a more substantial course, precede with a bread and soup combination such as Spicy Sesame Flatbread (page 81) and Zippy Cucumber and Mint Soup (page 53).

1. Wash the lima beans 2 or 3 times in running tap water. Place in a bowl and add water to cover by at least 2 inches. Soak for 6 to 8 hours. Drain, rinse again, and set aside.

2. Heat the oil in a small heavy skillet over medium-high heat. Add the cumin seeds. When the seeds sizzle, immediately add the onion, garlic, and ginger. Stir and cook until the edges of the onion start to brown. Add the tomato, coconut, and cilantro and cook until the tomato is barely soft, 3 to 4 minutes. Remove from the heat. Transfer to a blender, add 1/4 cup water, and blend until smooth. Set aside.

3. Combine the lima beans, tomato-onion puree, and remaining water in a large heavy pot. Bring to a boil, reduce the heat to medium, cover, and cook until the beans are tender but still hold their shape, about 30 minutes. Add the cayenne, paprika, and salt. Mix well and let stand covered for 5 minutes.

4. Turn the beans into a heated serving bowl. Garnish with onion and garlic shreds and dill. Serve hot.

# CURRIED MIXED SPROUTS WITH POTATOES
## *(Matki Usal)*

Serves 4
Preparation time:
    30 minutes

1 tablespoon mild
    vegetable oil
½ cup coarsely chopped
    onion
4 whole cloves, ground
½ cup coarsely chopped
    tomato
1 tablespoon sweetened
    flaked coconut
1¼ cups water
¼ teaspoon mustard
    seeds
⅛ teaspoon turmeric
¼ cup sprouted brown
    lentils (page 240)
¼ cup mung bean
    sprouts (page 240)
1 medium-size russet
    potato, peeled and
    diced into ½-inch
    pieces
¼ teaspoon cayenne
½ teaspoon salt
½ teaspoon paprika
Chopped fresh cilantro

When I was in school, our dabbawallah (lunch box man), a middle-aged man named Babu, would deliver homemade lunches to me and about 25 other students. Every day he arrived on his bicycle in time to greet us with a smile at the stroke of the noon bell. My mother would always pack surplus of this zesty sprouts dish, as it was such great favorite with my friends.

When beans are sprouted, their starches turn into slightly sweet sugars. The mild, pleasantly sweet flavor may be enhanced by a horde of complementary ingredients. In this case, lentil and mung bean sprouts are combined with moist potatoes and embellished with a palate-teasing sauce of coconut and tomato infused with cloves. If you make your own sprouts, add a tablespoon of fenugreek seeds along with the beans for a unique flavor. For a low-calorie meal, serve with Whole Wheat Flatbread (page 79), Roasted Eggplant Smothered with Tomatoes (page 96), and a herb chutney such as Cilantro Onion Chutney (page 193). Follow with Light Yogurt Rice with Cucumber (page 133) or offer plain yogurt at the dinner table.

1. Heat half the oil in a small skillet over medium-high heat. Add the onion and cloves. Stir and fry until the edges of the onion start to brown, about 5 minutes. Stir in the tomato and coconut. Cook until the tomato is barely soft, about 3 minutes. Add ¼ cup water to the tomato-onion mixture and puree in a blender or food processor. Set aside.

2. Heat the remaining ½ tablespoon oil in a medium saucepan over medium heat. Add the mustard seeds. When the seeds sizzle and splutter, stir in the sprouts and potato. Cook, stirring occasionally, 2 minutes longer.

3. Add the cayenne, salt, paprika, tomato-onion puree, and remaining 1 cup water. Bring to a boil, reduce the heat to low, cover, and cook until the potato is tender and the sauce is thick, about 15 minutes. Turn off the heat and let stand covered for 5 minutes. Transfer to a heated serving dish and serve garnished with cilantro.

# PASTA INDIAN STYLE WITH LENTILS
## (Chakoli)

Serves 6
Preparation time: 1 hour
    and 10 minutes

3 tablespoons mild
    vegetable oil
1 teaspoon mustard seeds
¼ teaspoon turmeric
1 tablespoon fenugreek
    seeds
¼ cup yellow lentils
    (toovar dal) or yellow
    split peas, cleaned,
    rinsed and drained
4 cups water
½ recipe Whole Wheat
    Flatbread dough (page
    79)
Whole wheat flour, for
    dusting
¾ to 1 teaspoon cayenne
1 teaspoon My Mother's
    25-Ingredient Spice
    Blend (page 23) *or*
    curry powder, home-
    made (page 22) or
    store-bought
1¼ teaspoons salt
Grated Swiss cheese or
    melted desi ghee

In this dish, one of my very favorites since childhood, delicate whole wheat pasta diamonds team up with slowly simmered lentils in a dish so satisfying that non-vegetarians will never miss the meat. The pasta is simply chapati dough rolled especially thin and cut into shapes that cook instantly in the fragrant lentil stew. This entree is both substantial and nourishing, and should be enjoyed all by itself. Though not essential, Mughal Chaat with Pistachios (page 184) makes a nice accompaniment. If you are going to serve this steaming hot on a cold winter night by fireside, a soft, lush, aromatic red wine makes an excellent choice.

1. Heat the oil in a large skillet or Dutch oven on medium heat and add the mustard seeds. When the seeds sizzle and splutter, immediately add the turmeric and fenugreek seeds. Stir and cook until aromatic and the fenugreek seeds start to brown, 1 to 1½ minutes. Add the lentils and water and bring to a boil. Reduce the heat to medium.

2. While the lentil mixture is coming to a boil, divide the chapati dough into 4 equal portions; roll each portion between your hands into a smooth ball and put it on a plate. Place a ball of dough on a floured surface and roll it into a 5-inch circle about ⅛ inch thick, dusting with flour as necessary. With a sharp knife, cut the dough into 1-inch diamonds (or ½-inch wide strips). Lift the diamonds with your hands and drop them carefully into the simmering lentil mixture. Repeat with the remaining dough.

3. Add the cayenne, spice blend, and salt. Cook uncovered, stirring occasionally, for 10 minutes. Reduce the heat to low, cover, and cook, stirring occasionally, until most of the liquid is absorbed and the lentils are soft, about 45 minutes. Turn off the heat and let stand covered for 5 minutes. To serve, spoon into deep plates. Serve piping hot with a sprinkling of cheese or a trickle of desi ghee.

**Variation:** For a wonderful herbal flavor and visual appeal you may add two cups chopped fresh fenugreek leaves as a substitute for fenugreek seeds.

Linguine, tortellini, ravioli, or other pasta can take the place of the chapati dough for an Italian pasta dish with an Indian twist.

# GARBANZO BEANS IN TANGY TOMATO SAUCE
## (Chole)

Serves 4 to 6
Preparation time:
    40 minutes

2 tablespoons mild
    vegetable oil
1 cup coarsely chopped
    onion
2 large cloves garlic,
    minced
1-inch piece fresh ginger,
    crushed (1 tablespoon)
6 whole cloves, ground
½ teaspoon ground
    coriander
½ teaspoon ground
    cumin
1 teaspoon mango
    powder (amchur) *or* 2
    teaspoons fresh lime
    juice
½ teaspoon cayenne
1 large (6 ounces) tomato,
    coarsely chopped
10 cilantro sprigs, plus
    additional for garnish
½ cup water
1 tablespoon desi ghee or
    unsalted butter
⅛ teaspoon turmeric
1 (15½-ounce) can
    garbanzo beans,
    drained and rinsed
½ teaspoon salt
1 medium red or white
    onion, peeled and
    sliced
1 lime or lemon cut into
    wedges

When my son Kailash's seventh grade class at Martinez Junior High School was studying India, the teacher suggested that they get introduced to Indian cuisine as well. I was more than happy to oblige, serving the 30-strong class this tantalizing curry accompanied with chapati, mango lassi, and carrot pudding. The result was astounding. Not only did the kids empty the pans, but the following week they sent me touching "thank you" letters. I was proudest of all when I received recipe requests from some of the girls in the class.

*Chole* is popular in Punjab in northern India, where it is offered by street vendors and fast-food restaurants. Other varieties of garbanzo bean, including the small black *kala channa* sold in Indian stores, can be prepared the same way. Just as bread-and-soup suppers are popular in the West, Indians like to pair this zesty stew with Yogurt Balloon Bread (page 90). I like to serve it with Whole Wheat Flatbread (page 79), along with a cool yogurt salad such as Spinach Raita with Sesame Oil Seasoning (page 176).

1. Heat the oil in a medium skillet or saucepan over medium-high heat until it ripples when the pan is tilted. Add the onion, garlic, and ginger and cook until the onion is lightly browned, about 4 minutes.

2. Add the cloves, coriander, cumin, amchur (if you are using lime juice, don't add it yet), and cayenne. Stir and cook 1 minute. Add the tomato, lime juice (if used), and cilantro. Reduce the heat to medium, cover, and cook, stirring occasionally, until the tomato is soft, about 5 minutes. Transfer to a blender or food processor, add ¼ cup water, and process until smooth.

3. Heat the desi ghee in a medium saucepan over moderate heat. Add the turmeric and onion-spice puree. Cook, stirring constantly, until fragrant, 2 to 3 minutes. Add the beans and salt. Raise the heat and bring to a boil. Reduce the heat to low, cover, and simmer 15 minutes. Serve in custard cups or individual bowls. Garnish each serving with cilantro sprigs. Offer with slices of onion and lemon wedges.

# BRAISED LEEKS WITH SPLIT PEAS
## (Kaanda Chi Paati Chi Bhaji)

Serves 4 to 6
Preparation time:
   45 minutes

1 pound leeks (about 4)
2 tablespoons mild
   vegetable oil
½ teaspoon mustard
   seeds
2 fresh hot green chiles,
   stemmed and minced
Pinch of asafetida
   *or* ½ teaspoon minced
   garlic
¼ teaspoon turmeric
¼ cup yellow split peas
   or yellow lentils
   (toovar dal), cleaned,
   rinsed and drained
2 cups water
1 teaspoon salt
1 tablespoon chick-pea
   flour (optional)

In India this stew is prepared with green onions, but the onions are larger and juicier than the slender ones available in the West. American leeks taste delicious cooked this way, braised with split peas in rustic seasonings of oil, mustard, chiles, turmeric, and asafetida. If you prefer the dish thickened, stir in the chick-pea flour toward the end of cooking. For a village-style combination, serve this as a side dish with Peasant Cucumber Flatbread (page 81) and Whole-Kernel Corn Raita (page 175).

1. Trim off and discard the roots and dark green ends of the leeks. Wash the leeks to remove sand and grit. Chop into ¼-inch pieces and set aside.

2. Heat the oil in a medium saucepan over medium-high heat and add the mustard. When the seeds sizzle and splutter, immediately add the chiles, asafetida, and turmeric. Cook, stirring constantly, for 1 minute. Add the split peas and leeks; stir and cook 3 minutes. Add the water and bring to a boil. Reduce the heat to medium, cover, and cook until the peas are tender but still hold their shape, about 25 minutes.

3. Stir in the salt. The dish will be the texture of a thin curry at this point; if you prefer it thickened, uncover the pan, stir in the chick-pea flour, cover, and cook 5 minutes more. Turn off the heat and let stand covered for 5 minutes. Transfer to a serving dish and serve hot.

**Variation:** STEWED GREEN GARLIC *(Hara Lasun aur Dal)*
My encounters with novel bounty at the farmers' market have given me a wider scope in my kitchen experiments. One of my recent discoveries is fresh green garlic, which appears in early spring. You can substitute it (both the white and green parts) for all or part of the leeks in this recipe with excellent results.

# PANEER CHEESE

Fresh Homemade Cheese (Paneer)

Flavored Paneer Cheese

Homemade Soft Curd Cheese (Channa)

Paneer Cheese in Creamy Spinach Sauce

Braised Paneer Cheese in Rich Tomato Sauce

Roasted Paneer Cheese "Sandwich" in Silky Chard Sauce

Scrambled Paneer Cheese in Cucumber Boats

Paneer Cheese Simmered with Aromatic Peas

When American friends visit us, I always have a paneer dish on the menu. They seem to love this homemade cheese and its remarkable flavor. Paneer is used as a main ingredient in grilled kababs, vegetable dishes, and desserts, and is mixed with other ingredients in breads, salads, curries, pilafs, and lentil dishes. In vegetarian cooking it also makes a good substitute for meat.

Paneer is a fresh white cheese with a mellow flavor and creamy texture. Like all cheeses, it started as a way to preserve fresh milk, and has become a favorite food in its own right. Several stories are told in India about the discovery of paneer cheese. A favorite is about a daughter-in-law who was heating milk and accidentally dropped in a piece of fresh lime. The milk curdled as it was being heated. For fear of her mother-in-law, the woman tied the curd in a piece of cloth torn from her *saree* and hid it in a corner under a heavy object. The mother-in-law found it anyway — but she was delighted at the taste.

In India, paneer is sold in markets, but it is nearly impossible to find here; however, it's a breeze to make at home from either whole or skimmed milk (see recipe, page 165). Whole milk produces a creamy texture, while skim milk makes a cheese with a slightly rubbery texture and lower fat content.

The first step in making paneer is to add an acidic ingredient to the fresh milk to cause it to curdle (separate into semisolid curds and liquid whey). Traditional starters include lime or lemon juice, yogurt, vinegar, or a citric acid solution. Each of these starters will give a different body, flavor, and texture to the curd. I prefer to use the commonly available cultured low-fat buttermilk, which has a milder acid flavor than the others, but still contains enough lactic acid to curdle the milk. The resultant cheese emerges with an extraordinarily mellow taste and silky texture. Paneer made with some of the other acid agents may need to be rinsed in water to remove excess acidic flavor; rinsing is unnecessary with buttermilk paneer, which comes out with its tangy flavor perfectly balanced.

Paneer is widely used in northern regions of India. Braised with vegetables, it makes a delicious entree. Crumbled and mixed with seasonings, it can be shaped like sausages, threaded on skewers, and grilled or roasted in a *tandoor* (see page 36). For dessert, it is rolled into discs and simmered gently in sugar syrup. Paneer cubes also make an exquisite garnish for non-Indian foods such as omelets, fajitas, enchiladas, soups, pizza, pasta, and tacos.

Paneer's cooking qualities differ considerably from other types of cheese; it has enough body to broil, saute, or deep-fry without crumbling, softening, or getting stringy. Sliced paneer is usually fried in oil before it is combined with vegetables. To create lighter and healthier dishes, however, I brush cubes of paneer with oil and broil them 4 inches from the heat source for 2 to 3 minutes per side until they are lightly browned all over. A toaster oven can also be used for broiling small quantities of paneer. If you do not have a broiler you can saute or pan-fry the pieces in a little oil in a heavy nonstick skillet.

Paneer dishes are superb for entertaining or formal dinners as they make very appealing and colorful entrees. Most can be assembled and cooked ahead of time which is a boon to a modern cook. The following recipes give a sense of the range of paneer cheese dishes. Paneer Cheese in Creamy Spinach Sauce and Paneer Cheese Simmered with Aromatic Peas are typical examples of dishes beginning with broiled chunks of cheese, which take on an elegant appearance and richer flavor under the broiler. Try the southern-style Scrambled Paneer in place of scrambled eggs with toasted muffins. Braised Paneer Cheese in Rich Tomato Sauce and Roasted Paneer Cheese Sandwich in Fragrant Silky Sauce are my own inventions. You can improvise on the sandwich theme with your choice of ingredients.

## FLAVORED PANEER CHEESE
### (Masalawali Paneer)

Paneer can be flavored in a variety of ways. To incorporate the flavor throughout the cheese, stir herbs or spices (roasted cumin seeds, mixed fresh or dried herbs, crushed green peppercorns, dried oregano, carum seeds, or grated lemon peel) into the milk before curdling. (Don't worry if they fall to the bottom; the cheesecloth will catch them when you drain off the whey.) Or, for more of a surface effect, press the spices gently on top of the cheese after draining and pressing. I like to sprinkle roasted ground cumin and coriander over broiled paneer while it is still warm, then arrange the cubes in a napkin-lined basket and serve them as an appetizer with sweet-and-sour tamarind sauce. I sometimes spoon paneer into little molds and ripen it until it is firm enough to be unmolded, then roll the cheese in garam masala or paprika and add it to vegetable dishes such as Cauliflower and Pepper Stir-Fry (page 101), or simply toss it with salad greens. My sons Kailash and Kedar roll paneer cubes in cinnamon and sugar and offer them to their friends as "Indian marshmallows." As you become familiar with paneer cheese you can create your own variations.

## QUICK RICOTTA PANEER

Many Indian families here make a quick version of paneer by squeezing or draining ricotta cheese in a cheesecloth and then pressing it under a heavy weight for 2 to 4 hours. The cheese can then be cut into desired shapes and sizes like regular paneer. Ricotta paneer cubes can be baked, or gently sauteed in oil and folded into a sauce, but do not cook them for too long or the cheese might crumble. This type won't hold up to the rigors of broiling, skewering, or the "sandwiches" on page 169.

## THE TOFU ALTERNATIVE

Tofu (bean curd) does not have the wonderful silky texture and pleasant taste of paneer. But it is an excellent alternative nevertheless, and can be used in the recipes given here for paneer. Either the firm or the extra-firm type can be broiled much like paneer. Cut or slice the drained tofu as suggested in the recipe, place the cut pieces between several layers of paper towels, and press lightly to remove excess moisture. Broil if desired, or simply cut up and use in place of paneer cubes in the recipes.

## HOMEMADE SOFT CURD CHEESE
### (Channa)

In addition to paneer, Indian cooks make a softer, moister relative called channa. Channa is simply paneer that has been pressed for a shorter time, so it retains more moisture and a softer texture. It can be as creamy as Brie or as crumbly as feta, depending on how many hours it is drained.

To make channa, follow the recipe for Fresh Paneer Cheese, but reduce the pressing time in step 3 to 30 to 45 minutes. Transfer the soft cheese to a container and refrigerate until ready to use, up to 3 days. The yield is slightly higher than paneer, 1¼ to 1½ cups.

Channa is used frequently in desserts. For a savory dip, whisk in some minced chives or garlic and a few teaspoons catsup or Dijon mustard, and serve sprinkled with paprika. To make a cheese log for crackers, press the channa for a little over an hour, then shape it into a cylinder (I occasionally mix in a little brandy before shaping). Sprinkle a large sheet of plastic wrap with carum seeds, minced cilantro, finely chopped walnuts, and minced red bell pepper or fresh chile, place the cylinder on top, and roll to coat completely using the plastic wrap as an aid. Seal tightly and chill overnight.

# FRESH HOMEMADE CHEESE
## (Sada Paneer)

Makes 1 cup (about 8
ounces)
Preparation time: 15
minutes

1½ quarts (6 cups)
whole or low-fat milk
1½ cups cultured low-
fat buttermilk

1. Bring the milk to a boil in a medium saucepan. Add the buttermilk and reduce the heat to medium. Let the mixture return to the boil and cook, stirring gently, until the milk curdles and separates from the translucent whey, 4 to 5 minutes. Turn off the heat and let the pan stand uncovered for 10 minutes.

2. Line a colander with a double thickness of cheesecloth. If you want to reserve the whey for cooking, or for future batches of cheese, place the colander over a pan or bowl. Gently pour the contents of the saucepan into the colander. Gather the four corners of the cheesecloth and twist them together. Tie the corners with twine and hang the cheese from a faucet to drain into the sink for 2 hours.

3. Place the cheese in its cheesecloth on a plate. Place a 12 x 15-inch baking pan on top of the cheese. Fill an empty 1-gallon plastic milk container with water and stand it in the pan for 1½ hours. Its weight will form the cheese into a 4-inch circular disc. Unwrap the cheese and place it on a cutting board. Using a sharp, thin-bladed knife, cut the cheese into 16 wedges or into 1-inch cubes. If not using the cheese immediately, store it whole in a tightly covered container in the refrigerator for up to 4 days.

**Note:** Paneer can be made with other coagulating agents. Any of the following proportions will do for 1½ quarts of milk: 3 tablespoons distilled white vinegar; ¾ cup plain yogurt (be sure to use one without gelatin, which could affect the texture); ¼ cup fresh lemon juice; a citric acid solution made by dissolving ¾ teaspoon citric acid in ⅓ cup hot water; or 2 cups of the whey reserved from a previous batch of paneer. Whichever you use, add it gradually; sometimes the curd forms before all of the coagulant is added. If so, do not add any more, or it might harden and toughen the delicate cheese. If, on the other hand, you have added all of the curdling agent and curds are not formed sufficiently, add a little more (about a teaspoon at a time) until the whey separates.

All of these coagulants make a cheese with a slightly different flavor than using buttermilk. Yogurt paneer is a little more sour, lemon juice will add a citrus aroma, and vinegar or citric acid gives a strong tangy flavor. If the paneer is too sour, rinse the undrained cheese (still wrapped in its cheesecloth) in several changes of cold water to reduce the acidity, then drain and press as suggested above.

# PANEER CHEESE IN CREAMY SPINACH SAUCE
## (Palak Paneer)

Serves 4 to 6
Preparation time:
  30 minutes

1 recipe paneer cheese
  (page 165)
2 tablespoons mild
  vegetable oil
2 cups packed chopped
  fresh spinach
2 fresh hot green chiles,
  stemmed and roughly
  chopped
½ teaspoon crushed
  garlic
½ teaspoon crushed
  fresh ginger
½ tablespoon desi ghee
  or unsalted butter
½ cup finely chopped
  onion
¼ teaspoon turmeric
½ cup chopped tomato
1 cup low-fat milk
¼ cup cream
1 teaspoon salt
½ teaspoon sugar

Broiling paneer cheese and folding it into a creamy spinach sauce creates a dish rich in protein, iron, and unbeatable flavor. For an elegant dinner, serve it with Rose-Cashew Skillet Nan (page 86), Cool Onion and Tomato Raita (page 174), Peas Pilaf with Almonds (page 132), and Tropical Pineapple Chutney (page 198).

1. Using a sharp knife, cut the paneer into 16 wedges or 1-inch cubes. Place on a greased boiler pan. Using a pastry brush, lightly coat with 1 teaspoon oil. Place the pan 4 inches away from heat source and broil until lightly browned, 2 to 2½ minutes per side. Watch carefully because they scorch easily. Cover with foil and set aside.

2. Place the spinach in a steamer basket and steam over boiling water for 6 minutes. Transfer to a blender with the chiles, garlic, and ginger and blend until smooth. Set aside.

3. Heat the remaining oil and desi ghee in a medium-size nonstick saucepan on medium-high heat. Add the onion and turmeric and stir-fry for 4 minutes. Add the tomato and cook until soft, about 4 minutes.

4. Add the milk and spinach puree. Bring to a boil, reduce the heat, and simmer until piping hot, about 12 minutes. Add the cream, salt, sugar, and paneer. Mix gently and cook until the cheese is heated through. Serve hot.

**Microwave:** In step 2, the spinach can be cooked in the microwave oven. Place in a 1-quart microwave-safe dish, cover, and cook at full power for 5 minutes.

# BRAISED PANEER CHEESE IN RICH TOMATO SAUCE
## (Paneer Pasanda)

Serves 4
Preparation time:
   30 minutes

1 recipe paneer cheese
   (page 165)
1 tablespoon mild
   vegetable oil
2 tablespoons desi ghee
   or unsalted butter
1 large onion, grated
4 cloves garlic, minced
2 teaspoons grated fresh
   ginger
16-ounce can peeled
   tomatoes, with juices
½ teaspoon My Mother's
   Spice Blend (page 23)
   *or* garam masala,
   homemade (page 21)
   or store-bought
½ teaspoon salt
1 teaspoon sugar

You must try this elegant dish of golden brown and white wedges of cheese sitting on a carpet of fragrantly spiced red velvety sauce. I was amazed when this sauce tasted so wonderful made with canned tomatoes; it's even better with fresh tomatoes in season. You can also team the same sauce with steamed asparagus spears, Brussels sprouts, and cooked baby potatoes instead of paneer.

For a dinner for two, serve this dish with Whole Wheat Flatbread (page 79), Whole Kernel Corn Raita (page 175), any of the fruit chutneys, and Royal Vegetable Basmati Rice (page 138). Offer Pineapple Pistachio Cooler (page 233) to drink.

1. Cut the paneer into 2 x ½ x ¼-inch strips or into 8 wedges. Brush with oil. Place on a greased broiler pan and broil 4 inches from the heat until lightly browned, 2 to 3 minutes per side. Tent with foil and set aside.

2. Melt the desi ghee in a heavy skillet over medium-high heat. Add the onion, garlic, and ginger. Cook, stirring constantly, until the onion is lightly browned and imparts an herbal aroma, about 6 minutes. Drain the tomatoes, reserving their juice, and chop finely. Add the tomatoes and juice, spice blend, salt, and sugar to the skillet. Reduce the heat to medium, cover, and cook, stirring occasionally, until the tomato loses its raw aroma and the sauce is thick, about 15 minutes.

3. Spoon the sauce into a 1-quart casserole. Arrange the paneer strips or wedges attractively in a petal pattern. Serve hot or warm.

**Note:** The sauce can be prepared up to 3 days ahead and stored in the refrigerator. Rewarm on moderate heat while you broil the cheese. You can even broil the paneer on the day you make the sauce, then simply assemble the dish and reheat in the oven or microwave just before serving time.

The mixture of cooked onion, ginger, and garlic is known as a "wet masala." I make it in quantity and always keep a supply on hand frozen, making it a breeze to fix this kind of dish.

# Roasted Paneer Cheese "Sandwich" in Silky Chard Sauce
## (Paneer-E-Mumtaz Mahal)

Serves 2
Preparation time:
  20 minutes

4 cups packed chopped
  fresh red Swiss chard
  (leaves and tender
  stems)
½ cup water
4 tablespoons chopped
  cashews or Mughal
  Ready Mix (page 25)
½ teaspoon ground
  cumin
½ teaspoon ground
  coriander
½ teaspoon salt
½ cup half-and-half
2 8-ounce rounds (double
  recipe) paneer cheese
  (page 165)
1 recipe khawa milk,
  crumbled (page 238)
1 tablespoon dried red
  or black currants
2 fresh hot green chiles,
  minced
2 tablespoons finely
  chopped fresh cilantro
2 tablespoons mild
  vegetable oil, for
  brushing

This dish was created in honor of the empress Mumtaz Mahal, the beloved wife of Shahjahan, the emperor who built the monumental Taj Mahal in her memory. Slices of paneer cheese are the "bread" around a "sandwich" filling of khawa milk, currants, and a bit of chile, and the whole thing is blanketed in a delicate sauce. Partner it with Calcutta Plain Flakybread (page 82) and a cool yogurt raita for a less spicy and soothing meal. You can substitute other sweet or savory fillings with a spreadable texture.

1. Steam the chard for 5 minutes in a steamer basket. Combine in a blender with the water and cashews and blend into a smooth paste (if using Mughal ready mix, add it after blending). Transfer into a medium saucepan. Add the cumin, coriander, and salt. Bring to a boil on medium heat, add the half-and-half, and cook until heated through. Cover and set aside.

2. Slice the paneer discs horizontally in half. You will have four ½-inch thick discs. Cut each half into a semicircle. Combine the khawa milk, currants, chile, and cilantro in a small bowl. Spread this mixture on half of the cheese slices. Cover with the remaining slices.

3. Place the "sandwiches" on a greased broiler pan. Brush the tops with oil. Broil 4 inches from the heat until lightly browned, 2½ to 3 minutes.

4. Transfer to a heated serving dish. Pour the sauce on top of the sandwiches and serve immediately.

**Variation:** Replace the chard with other greens such as dandelion, kale (green, white, or purple), mustard, or chicory, individually or in combination.

169

# SCRAMBLED PANEER CHEESE IN CUCUMBER BOATS
## *(Paneer Bhurji)*

Serves 4
Preparation time:
    35 minutes

1 medium cucumber
    (8 ounces)
2 tablespoons mild
    vegetable oil
1 small onion, finely
    chopped
1 recipe paneer cheese
    (page 165), crumbled
1 medium tomato,
    chopped
½ teaspoon curry
    powder, homemade
    (page 22) or bought
½ teaspoon salt
2 teaspoons chopped
    fresh cilantro or pars-
    ley *or* ½ teaspoon dried
    mixed herbs
Butter lettuce leaves,
    washed and crisped

Scrambled paneer is the vegetarian version of scrambled eggs with only a tiny fraction of the cholesterol. Whole milk ricotta cheese may be substituted for paneer; just squeeze the water from the ricotta by placing it in a cheese cloth and use as paneer. Serve as a light main course with a salad of seasonal greens. For variation, serve it on top of buttered toasts or baked potatoes. My sister Smita makes a colorful buffet platter by spooning this mixture into various vegetables, including bell peppers, tomatoes, cooked plantains, and mushroom caps, and sets it out for the guests to choose.

1. Split the cucumber lengthwise and scoop out the seeds with a melon baller. Slice into 2-inch lengths. Set aside.

2. Place a rack in the middle of the oven and preheat to 350°F. Heat the oil in a heavy medium skillet (preferably nonstick) on medium-high heat. Add the onion and paneer. Stir-fry until lightly browned, about 4 minutes. Add the tomato, curry powder, and salt. Fry until the tomato is soft, about 5 minutes. Add the herbs and mix well. Remove from the heat.

3. Spoon a generous tablespoonful of the paneer mixture into each cucumber piece. Place on a baking dish and bake uncovered for 20 to 25 minutes. Transfer to a lettuce-lined platter to serve.

# PANEER CHEESE SIMMERED WITH AROMATIC PEAS

## (Matar Paneer)

Serves 6
Preparation time:
30 minutes

1 recipe paneer cheese
(page 165)
2 tablespoons mild
vegetable oil
1 large onion, grated
1 teaspoon grated fresh
ginger
1 teaspoon ground
coriander
½ teaspoon ground
cumin
1 cup tomato puree,
fresh or canned
½ cup water or reserved
paneer whey
¼ teaspoon cayenne
¾ cup petite peas,
fresh or thawed
½ teaspoon salt
1 teaspoon sweet paprika
¼ cup whipping cream
1 teaspoon minced fresh
cilantro

This popular restaurant dish, browned cubes of cheese simmered in a faintly perfumed sauce of peas and tomatoes, is probably the most familiar paneer dish to Westerners. Pay special attention when broiling the cheese, because it scorches easily. If you do not have a broiler, I recommend sauteing. Lemon-Sesame Rice (page 136) is a good accompaniment, with the sauce generously spooned over the rice.

1. With a sharp knife, cut the cheese into 1-inch cubes. Place on a lightly greased broiler pan and brush with 1 tablespoon oil. Broil 4 inches from the heat until browned on top, 2 to 2½ minutes; turn and brown on the other side.

2. Heat the remaining 1 tablespoon of oil in a skillet over medium-high heat. Add the onion and ginger. Cook, stirring constantly, until the onion is lightly browned, 6 to 8 minutes. Add the coriander and cumin and cook, stirring, until it is aromatic, another 2 minutes. Add the tomato puree and cook, stirring occasionally, until the tomato loses its raw aroma, 5 to 6 minutes. Add the water, cayenne, peas (if fresh), and salt. Bring the mixture to a boil, reduce the heat, cover, and simmer until the peas are tender and the sauce is thick, 10 to 12 minutes.

3. Add the paneer, peas (if using frozen), paprika, and cream. Cook until heated through. Spoon into a serving bowl, garnish with cilantro, and serve hot.

# SALADS

## RAITAS, CHAATS, AND KACHUMBERS

TOMATO AND CUCUMBER RAITA

COOL ONION AND TOMATO RAITA

WHOLE-KERNEL CORN RAITA

SPINACH RAITA WITH SESAME OIL SEASONING

CRISP OKRA RAITA

BAKED POTATO RAITA WITH WALNUTS

WARM CABBAGE SALAD WITH CRACKED PEPPER

SMOKY EGGPLANT RAITA

LENTIL SPROUTS SALAD WITH TOMATILLO DRESSING

SWEET ONION SALAD IN TOMATO BASKETS

YELLOW MUNG BEAN SALAD WITH WALNUTS

RAW PAPAYA SALAD WITH PINE NUTS

MUGHAL CHAAT WITH PISTACHIOS

ASPARAGUS CHAAT WITH CHILE OIL

BOMBAY CHOWPATTY BEACH CHAAT

KASHMIR MIXED FRUIT CHAAT

TANDOORI SALAD CHAAT

DAIKON SALAD WITH AROMATIC OIL

LUCKNOW-STYLE POTATO CHAAT

Indians are great salad lovers. Their meals always include some sort of raw vegetables: perhaps only sliced onions with a drizzle of salt, or chopped cucumber with a dollop of yogurt, or rings of tomatoes with a splash of fresh lime juice and a sprinkle of toasted ground cumin. There is an infinite variety of salads in the subcontinent, including yogurt-based *raitas,* boldly spiced *chaats,* and *kachumbers* drizzled with spice-infused oil. Any of these can be served in an Indian menu as a first course, as exotic partners to Western meals, or on their own as a light luncheon salad.

Raitas are refreshing salads of raw or cooked vegetables folded into smooth yogurt. The typical mustard-cumin infused oil imparts an exotic aura. *Raita* is derived from *rai,* the word for mustard seeds, and cooks of Gujarat in western India add a generous amount of this spice. Northerners flavor their raitas with a grinding of toasted cumin seeds. Raitas are called *pachadis* in the southern region, and are typically seasoned with *ogarne* (seasoned oil — see page 13). Crushed nuts add a mealy texture and contrast. Raitas are served as cooling accompaniments to balance spicy vegetable dishes and curries, and they provide moisture to counteract the dryness of breads and pilafs. For variation, a raita can be thinned with buttermilk to make a refreshing cold soup for a sweltering summer day.

Chaats are spicy and tangy snacks eaten in the midday or evening. A specialty of the northern state of Uttar Pradesh, chaat is part of a growing list of national favorites adopted by all. An assortment of fruits, vegetables, and crisp fritters (*pakoras*) or vegetable patties forms a rich mosaic of taste, texture, and tone, which is further enhanced by tantalizing hot and sweet chutneys and freshly squeezed juices. A hint of green chile, fresh mint, cilantro, or basil offers a perfect counterpoise, and a sprinkling of *chaat masala,* a tangy spice blend based on dried mango, provides the finishing touch. A recipe for homemade chaat masala appears on page 21, or you can use the Hi-Tech Foods brand available at Indian markets.

In India, chaats are mainly a snack food sold by beach and street vendors, and are less common at home. But to my mind they are close enough to salads that they can play the same role at the table, especially in combination with less spicy foods. My versions of chaat play down the importance of the pakoras and other fried foods, concentrating on combinations of fresh produce. Serve one of these chaats as a first course or alongside daily meals, or set them out on a party or cookout buffet table for guests to assemble to taste.

Another category of Indian salads, *kachumber,* uses a dressing based on oil rather than yogurt or juices. Most use one or two grated or shredded fresh vegetables, either raw or cooked, with a flavorful boost from the spice-infused oil and a touch of fresh herbs. Best of all, they are quick to fix. Take advantage of the seasonal bounty obtainable in the market and create these simple salads to add color, taste, and crunchy texture to your daily menus.

These categories of salads are not rigid divisions, and some dishes can cross over from one to the other. Fold yogurt into a potato chaat and it becomes a potato raita. Leftover carrot or daikon kachumber mixed with buttermilk makes a refreshing salad dressing for other vegetables. My aunt Vijaya in Bombay makes a soothing asparagus raita that is basically the asparagus chaat on page 184 without the oil and with yogurt added. You can even delete the onion and chaat masala from the Mughal Chaat on page 184 and stir in a scoop of vanilla ice cream for a luscious fruit salad.

# TOMATO AND CUCUMBER RAITA
## (Sautekai Pachadi)

Serves 4 to 6
Preparation time:
    10 minutes

1 large tomato (6 ounces),
    finely chopped
1 medium cucumber
    (10 ounces), peeled,
    seeded, and cut into
    ½-inch cubes
1 small white or red
    onion
1 tablespoon chopped
    fresh cilantro
½ cup plain nonfat or
    low-fat yogurt
½ cup sour cream
½ teaspoon salt
½ teaspoon sugar
1 tablespoon crushed
    roasted peanuts (page
    239)
5 butter lettuce leaves,
    washed and crisped
2 red and 2 green fresh
    chiles, stemmed and
    slivered

In India, cucumbers and tomatoes are available all year, and they are frequently used to make raitas. Either the regular waxy-skinned cucumbers or the thinner English or hothouse variety is appropriate. Crushed roasted peanuts, a traditional Maharashtrian touch, add flavor and texture. This raita goes well with flatbread and pilaf, and is a natural partner to many vegetarian and non-vegetarian dishes.

1. Combine the tomato and cucumber in a medium bowl. Peel and cut the onion into quarters, slice thinly lengthwise, and add to the bowl. Sprinkle in the cilantro. If made ahead, cover and chill for up to 4 hours.

2. Just before serving, combine the yogurt, sour cream, salt, sugar, and peanuts in a bowl. Beat with a fork or whisk until smooth. Fold into the vegetables.

3. To serve, line a shallow dish with lettuce leaves. Mound the salad in the center. Garnish with red and green chile slivers in petal fashion and serve.

**Note:** For convenience, the raita can be made 2 hours ahead and kept, covered, in the refrigerator.

As in many of the raita recipes, I recommend adding some sour cream to low-fat or nonfat yogurt to approximate the creamy texture of Indian yogurt. This is especially important in raitas made from high-moisture vegetables like cucumber and tomato; the extra butterfat keeps the raita from getting thin and watery as it stands. If you make your own yogurt with whole milk (see page 241), the sour cream is not necessary. If you are watching calories, you can use all low-fat yogurt; in that case, it's better to assemble the raita just before serving so it will maintain its body.

# COOL ONION AND TOMATO RAITA
## (Pyaz Tamatar Raita)

Serves 3
Preparation time:
    10 minutes

Use only vine-ripened tomatoes for this luscious raita, in which the tomatoes and onions are folded into creamy yogurt dressing. This raita is very tasty all by itself; pair it with a stir-fried vegetable side dish and serve with bread and a pilaf, or as a filling for a side dish of crepes.

1 teaspoon mild
    vegetable oil
¼ teaspoon mustard seeds
¼ teaspoon cumin seeds
Pinch asafetida *or* ½ tea-
    spoon minced garlic
1 small white onion
    (2 ounces)
1 medium tomato
    (4 ounces), chopped
1 fresh hot green chile,
    stemmed and minced
¼ cup plain nonfat or
    low-fat yogurt
2 tablespoons sour cream
    (optional; see Note,
    opposite)
½ teaspoon salt
1 teaspoon sugar
Chopped fresh cilantro,
    for garnish

1. Heat the oil in a small pan over medium-high heat until it ripples when the pan is tilted. Add the mustard and cumin seeds. When the seeds sizzle and splutter, add the asafetida. Turn off the heat and reserve. If using garlic, let it cook until lightly browned and aromatic.

2. Peel and halve the onion, slice thinly lengthwise, and place in a shallow serving bowl. Add the tomato and chile. Toss to mix.

3. Combine the yogurt, sour cream, salt, and sugar in a small bowl. Whisk to blend well and fold into the tomato-onion mixture. Pour the oil seasoning on top. Just before serving, stir once or twice. Garnish with cilantro.

**Note:** This raita can be made several hours ahead and refrigerated. The oil seasoning is optional but adds an exotic touch.

# WHOLE KERNEL CORN RAITA
## *(Punjabi Makkai Raita)*

Serves 3 to 4
Preparation time:
    10 minutes

1 cup whole kernel corn,
    fresh, canned, or
    thawed
½ cup plain nonfat or
    low-fat yogurt
1 tablespoon sour cream
    (optional; see Note,
    opposite)
¼ teaspoon salt
⅛ teaspoon freshly
    ground black pepper
1½ teaspoons mild
    peanut or sesame oil
⅛ teaspoon mustard seeds
⅛ teaspoon cumin seeds
1 green and 1 red fresh
    chile, stemmed and
    slivered
2 teaspoons minced
    fresh cilantro

Northern Indians use corn in many ways. This is one of the simplest and quickest, yet it makes a colorful and healthful addition to a meal. For a hotter version, add the chiles to the seasoning oil along with the spices to fry for a few seconds. This yogurt-based salad makes a nice addition to smooth soup and bread combinations such as Aromatic Lentil Soup (page 46) and Rustic Kidney Bean Flatbread (page 81).

1. Place the corn in a steamer basket over boiling water. Steam until tender, about 4 minutes. Set aside to cool. (If using canned corn, just drain but do not cook).

2. Combine the yogurt and sour cream in a shallow serving dish and whisk until smooth. Fold in the corn and season with salt and pepper.

3. Heat the oil in a small frying pan over medium-high heat until it ripples when the pan is tilted. Add the mustard and cumin. When the seeds sizzle and splutter, remove from the heat. Let cool slightly and pour over the corn mixture, scraping the pan with a rubber spatula.

4. To serve, garnish with red and green chile slivers alternating in a petal fashion. Sprinkle with minced cilantro.

# SPINACH RAITA WITH SESAME OIL SEASONING
## *(Palak Raita)*

Serves 4
Preparation time:
 10 minutes

2 cups packed chopped
 fresh or thawed
 spinach
¾ cup plain nonfat or
 low-fat yogurt, stirred
½ teaspoon salt, or to taste
1 tablespoon mild peanut
 or vegetable oil
½ teaspoon mustard
 seeds
¼ teaspoon cumin seeds
⅓ teaspoon black or
 white sesame seeds
2 dried red chiles,
 stemmed and broken

Nutritious and flavorful, this raita is made lively with a typical Indian oil seasoning of mustard, cumin, sesame seeds, and red chiles. The seeds add crunch and nutty flavor to the smooth yogurt-based salad. Serve with flatbreads, legume dishes, and pilafs. The spinach may be replaced with amaranth, watercress, Swiss chard, kale, or collard greens. Toss leftovers into the food processor with whole wheat flour to make easy spinach parathas (see page 77).

1. Place the spinach in a steamer basket over boiling water. Steam until tender, about 4 minutes. Plunge the spinach into cold water to stop the cooking.

2. When the spinach is cool enough to handle, drain and gently squeeze out the excess water. Place in a serving dish, fold in the yogurt, and stir in the salt.

3. Heat the oil in a small skillet over medium-high heat until it ripples when the pan is tilted. Add the mustard, cumin, and sesame. When the seeds sizzle and splutter, toss in the chiles and cook for a few seconds, until the chiles are crisp and lightly browned. Turn off the heat, let the oil cool, then pour it over the spinach-yogurt mixture, scraping the pan with a rubber spatula. Just before serving, stir once or twice to create swirls of oil.

**Microwave:** In step 1, place the spinach in a 1-quart microwavable bowl. Cover and cook at full power until it wilts, about 3 minutes. Remove from the oven and let stand covered for 5 minutes, then transfer to cold water.

# CRISP OKRA RAITA
## *(Bhendi Raita)*

Serves 4 to 6
Preparation time:
 20 minutes

3 tablespoons mild
 vegetable oil
½ teaspoon cumin seeds

In this preparation, okra is sparked with garlic and chiles and stir-fried crisp, then tossed in creamy yogurt dressing to mellow the flavors. With Whole Wheat Puffy Bread (page 87) or Whole Wheat Flatbread (page 79), it makes a nice accompaniment to legume dishes.

1. Heat the oil in a heavy medium skillet over medium-high heat. Add the cumin, okra, onion, garlic, and chile. Stir-fry until the edges of the okra are slightly browned, about 12 minutes. Reduce the heat to medium, add the

176

1 pound tender okra,
   trimmed and cut into
   ½-inch pieces
½ cup finely chopped
   onion
1 teaspoon crushed garlic
1 fresh hot green chile,
   stemmed and chopped
½ teaspoon curry
   powder, homemade
   (page 22) or bought
½ teaspoon salt
1 cup plain nonfat or
   low-fat yogurt
½ teaspoon sugar
1 tablespoon chopped
   fresh cilantro
Tomato wedges, for
   garnish

curry powder and salt, cover, and cook, stirring occasionally, until the okra is tender, about 5 minutes. Remove from the heat. Cool completely.

2. Meanwhile, combine the yogurt and sugar in a serving bowl and whisk to mix. Fold in the cooked okra. Serve with a sprinkling of cilantro and garnish with tomato wedges.

**Note:** The okra raita can be made 1 day ahead and kept, covered, in the refrigerator.

# BAKED POTATO RAITA WITH WALNUTS
## (Akhrot Alu Raita)

Serves 4
Preparation time:
    4 minutes

¾ cup plain nonfat or
    low-fat yogurt
¼ teaspoon ground
    toasted cumin
⅛ teaspoon cayenne
    pepper
¼ teaspoon salt
⅛ teaspoon freshly
    ground pepper
1 large russet potato
    (6 ounces), baked,
    peeled, and cut into
    1-inch dice
1 tablespoon coarsely
    chopped toasted wal-
    nuts
Lettuce leaves, washed
    and crisped
1 large ripe papaya (1
    pound), peeled and
    seeded
Sweet or hot paprika
1 tablespoon minced
    fresh cilantro or mint
    leaves

Traditionally this raita is made with boiled or steamed potatoes, but I prefer to bake them for a characteristic smoky flavor. This yogurt-based potato salad is gently tinted with cayenne, cumin, and pepper. Weight watchers will enjoy it as a lighter form of potato salad without the mayonnaise or sour cream of Western versions. For a tropical presentation, I mound the raita on lettuce leaves and surround it with rich papaya slices. If you prefer, you may use any seasonal fruit.

1. Combine the yogurt, cumin, cayenne, salt, and pepper in a mixing bowl and whisk to mix. Fold in the potato and walnuts.

2. Arrange the lettuce leaves on a serving platter. Slice the papaya thinly and arrange the slices neatly on the leaves. Mound the raita in the center and garnish with a sprinkling of paprika and cilantro.

**Variation:** A combination of potatoes of different colors — yellow-fleshed Yukon Gold, orange yams, or even blue or purple varieties — makes a dazzling raita.

# WARM CABBAGE SALAD WITH CRACKED PEPPER
## (Patta Gobi Salat)

Serves 3
Preparation time:
    10 minutes

Warm salads are not a common category in Indian cooking; most vegetable dishes are either raw or fully cooked. However, by now you will have realized that I prefer crunchy vegetables to the more conventional Indian style. Here I recommend cooking the cabbage only momentarily so that it is crisp and retains its color, nutritive value, and sweetness. The traditional Indian oil seasoning lends an exotic touch. For variety, use a combination of red and green shredded cabbage. Serve the salad on buttered toasts for a quick lunch.

1 tablespoon mild peanut
   or vegetable oil
⅛ teaspoon mustard seeds
¼ teaspoon cumin seeds
1 fresh hot green chile,
   stemmed and slit
   lengthwise
2 cups finely shredded
   green cabbage
¾ teaspoon salt
¼ teaspoon cracked pepper
1½ teaspoons lemon juice
1 tablespoon chopped
   roasted hazelnuts

1. Heat the oil in a wok or skillet over medium-high heat until it ripples when the pan is tilted. Add the mustard and cumin; when the seeds sizzle and splutter, immediately add the chile. Stir and cook 1 minute. Add the cabbage and stir-fry until it is well coated and begins to glisten with the oil, about 3 minutes. Remove from the heat, season to taste with salt and pepper, and sprinkle with lemon juice.

2. Transfer to a shallow serving dish. Fold in the hazelnuts. Serve immediately, with an additional sprinkle of cracked pepper if desired.

# Smoky Eggplant Raita
## (Badnekai Pachadi)

Serves 5
Preparation time:
   30 minutes

1 medium eggplant
   (1 pound)
2½ teaspoons mild
   vegetable or corn oil
½ cup plain nonfat or
   low-fat yogurt
⅓ teaspoon salt
½ teaspoon sugar
¼ teaspoon mustard
   seeds
½ cup chopped onion
1 fresh hot green chile,
   stemmed and chopped
½ pound large spinach
   leaves, stemmed,
   washed, and drained
1 tablespoon chopped
   fresh cilantro
Julienned red bell
   pepper, for garnish

Roasted eggplant is popular throughout India, but it appears in radically different styles from north to south. In the north, it is cooked briefly with onions, tomatoes, and spices as a side dish (see Roasted Eggplant Smothered with Tomatoes, page 96). In the following southern rendition, the same vegetable becomes a cooling yogurt salad to serve as a dip or to spread on cocktail toast rounds. Try zucchini in place of eggplant for equally outstanding results.

1. Rub the eggplant on all sides with ½ teaspoon oil. Prepare a broiler, charcoal grill, or stovetop burner for roasting whole vegetables as directed on page 95. Roast the eggplant, turning occasionally, until the outside is completely charred and the pulp is soft, about 20 to 25 minutes. Let the eggplant cool briefly, peel, then chop coarsely.

2. Combine the yogurt, salt, and sugar in a bowl and whisk until smoothly blended. Fold in the eggplant.

3. Heat the remaining 2 teaspoons oil in a small skillet on medium-high heat. Add the mustard seeds; when they sizzle and splutter, add the onion and chile. Cook until the onion is lightly brown, about 4 minutes. Remove from the heat and let cool slightly. Pour the oil over the eggplant mixture and mix gently.

4. Arrange the spinach leaves on a platter. Mound the eggplant raita in the center and garnish with cilantro and red pepper strips.

Note: The raita can be made several hours ahead, covered, and refrigerated.

# LENTIL SPROUTS SALAD WITH TOMATILLO DRESSING
## (Matki Kachumber)

Serves 6
Preparation time:
25 minutes

½ cup brown lentil
sprouts
½ cup mung bean
sprouts
5 cherry tomatoes,
quartered
½ cup shredded
green cabbage
¼ cup chopped green
onions, green and
white parts

*Tomatillo Dressing*
3 medium tomatillos
(¼ pound)
2 tablespoons coarsely
chopped cilantro
1 tablespoon coarsely
chopped mint
2 tablespoons roasted
peanuts
½ teaspoon crushed
fresh ginger
1 teaspoon lemon juice
1 fresh hot green chile,
chopped
1 teaspoon sugar
¼ teaspoon salt
❦
1 lime, thinly sliced
Cilantro sprigs

When I first came to America, I wasn't familiar with tomatillos, a Mexican vegetable that looks like a green tomato but is not related. When I wanted to make a green tomato dish and didn't have any in my garden, I tried substituting tomatillos and found the results rewarding. Now they are just one more vegetable in my cooking repertoire.

This salad keeps exceptionally well for many hours at room temperature, making it a good choice for picnics or buffets. I keep some Whole Wheat Flatbreads (page 79) and Yogurt Balloon Breads (page 90) handy. Spoon the salad into cones made of flatbreads or in balloon bread halves and serve them topped with dressing. A healthful and filling entree, this salad partners well with a cold, thirst-quenching soup such as Zippy Cucumber and Mint Soup (page 53).

If your local market or health food store sells lentil sprouts as well as the more common mung bean sprouts, you can prepare this salad on short notice. Otherwise, you will need to plan several days ahead and grow your own sprouts as directed on page 240.

1. Combine the sprouts, tomatoes, cabbage, and onions in a serving bowl. Set aside.

2. Preheat the oven to 500°F. Remove the papery husks from the tomatillos and rinse to remove the sticky film. Place in a pie pan or other shallow baking dish and bake for 15 minutes. Let cool, peel off the wrinkled outer skins, then chop the tomatillos coarsely and combine with the remaining dressing ingredients in a blender or food processor. Process until smooth.

3. Pour the dressing over the sprouts mixture. Toss well. Garnish with lime slices and cilantro sprigs.

**Note:** The salad keeps well for several hours at room temperature. Do not refrigerate before serving, as the cold will harden the beans.

# SWEET ONION SALAD IN TOMATO BASKETS
## (Tamatar Tokri)

Serves 6 to 8
Preparation time:
   12 minutes

4 medium tomatoes,
   ripe but firm
1 medium white onion
   (4 ounces)
2 cups water
½ teaspoon salt
2 teaspoons mild olive oil
   or walnut oil
¼ teaspoon cayenne
1 tablespoon chopped
   fresh or ½ teaspoon
   dried crushed thyme
1 tablespoon toasted
   sunflower seeds or
   pine nuts, lightly
   crushed

This simple dish needs only minutes to assemble. Soaking the onion in cold salted water removes the intense odor and sweetens the flavor. The salad goes very well with koftas and paneer dishes, accompanied by Calcutta Plain Flakybread (page 82). It tastes fine by itself, but it's more attractive when spooned into vegetable "baskets" made from firm, red tomatoes or green or red peppers.

1. With a sharp paring knife, cut two triangles out of the top half of each tomato, leaving a ½-inch-wide strip in the center intact as the "handle." Scoop the pulp out and reserve for another use. If made ahead, cover loosely and refrigerate up to 2 hours.

2. Peel and halve the onion, chop finely, and place in a bowl. Add the water and salt, cover, and set aside for 10 minutes.

3. Drain the onion and refresh it in cold running water. Place in a mixing bowl. Add all the remaining ingredients and toss to mix. Spoon into the prepared tomato baskets, or simply serve in a shallow bowl.

# YELLOW MUNG BEAN SALAD WITH WALNUTS
## (Kosambri)

Serves 4 to 6
Preparation time: 10
   minutes, plus 4 hours
   soaking

*Kosambri* is one of the most popular salads in southern India. Accompanied by a rice dish, it is traditionally featured at wedding banquets. Splashed with lime juice and studded with walnuts, this salad makes a delightful accompaniment to flatbreads, rice dishes, and even pastas. For interesting textural contrast, I like to serve it on a bed of shredded carrots. Dried red chiles may be added to the oil seasoning if desired.

¼ cup yellow mung
  beans (mung dal),
  picked clean
1 cup peeled and finely
  chopped cucumber
¼ cup fresh grated
  coconut (optional)
½ teaspoon salt
½ tablespoon lime juice
2 tablespoons chopped
  walnuts
2 teaspoons mild peanut
  or vegetable oil
½ teaspoon mustard
  seeds
Pinch of asafetida
  (optional)
½ cup grated carrot
2 tablespoons chopped
  fresh cilantro

1. Wash the mung dal in several changes of water. Add enough water to cover by at least 2 inches. Soak 4 to 6 hours. Drain well.

2. Place the mung dal, cucumber, and coconut in a mixing bowl. Toss to mix. Sprinkle with salt and lime juice and mix gently with a fork. Fold in the nuts.

3. Heat the oil in a small pan over medium-high heat until it ripples when the pan is tilted. Add the mustard; when the seeds sizzle and splutter, add the asafetida. Turn off the heat. Pour the oil over the salad and mix gently. Mound the salad in the center of a large serving platter, surround with grated carrot, and serve immediately with a sprinkle of cilantro.

**Variation:** Use ½ cup grated green mango (see page 238) in place of the cucumber and omit the lime juice.

# RAW PAPAYA SALAD WITH PINE NUTS
## (Papita Kachumber)

Serves 3 to 4
Preparation time:
  8 minutes

1 small raw papaya
  (1¼ pounds)
½ teaspoon ground
  toasted cumin
¼ teaspoon cracked
  black pepper
½ teaspoon salt
1 teaspoon lime or lemon
  juice, preferably fresh
2 tablespoons coarsely
  chopped toasted pine
  nuts or walnuts
1 tablespoon raisins
Watercress sprigs

I like to include papaya in my diet because it is low in calories and high in vitamin A. In this light preparation, papaya is flecked with cumin and pepper and garnished with a bouquet of watercress. Try it with Spicy Sesame Flatbread (page 81) and Fragrant Baby Dill with Garlic and Mung Beans (page 152). For a more elaborate meal, precede it with Hearty Vegetable Soup (page 45).

1. Peel the papaya and rinse thoroughly. Cut in half, remove the seeds, and chop the flesh finely. Measure 1½ cups into a serving bowl. If not serving right away, cover and chill up to 24 hours.

2. Sprinkle the cumin, pepper, salt, and lime juice onto the papaya. Toss to mix. Fold in the nuts and raisins. Arrange watercress sprigs neatly on top.

# MUGHAL CHAAT WITH PISTACHIOS
## (Phalon ka Chaat)

Serves 4
Preparation time:
    10 minutes

½ honeydew melon *or*
    ½ large cantaloupe
1 cup diced ripe papaya
½ cup chopped white
    onion
2 tablespoons fresh lime
    juice
1½ to 2 fresh hot red
    chiles, stemmed and
    slivered
¼ cup chopped fresh
    cilantro
2 tablespoons Roasted
    Honey Pistachios
    (page 28)
1 teaspoon chaat masala,
    homemade (page 21)
    or store-bought

This potpourri of fruits, onions, and fresh chiles intrigues the palate with contrasting flavors. Pass cayenne, chaat masala, and fresh lime juice for those who prefer their salads with extra tang.

1. With a melon baller, scoop out balls of melon flesh to make 1 cup. Scoop out the rest of the flesh and reserve for another use, leaving an even shell. (If you don't have a melon baller and want to serve the salad in a melon shell, scoop out the flesh in large pieces with a spoon and cut into even dice.) Combine the melon balls, papaya, onion, lime juice, chiles, and cilantro in a bowl. Mix well with a fork and let stand covered for the flavors to blend, about 15 minutes. If made ahead, cover and chill up to 2 hours.

2. Fold the nuts into the papaya-onion mixture. Sprinkle with chaat masala. Spoon the mixture into the melon shell.

**Variation:** Other spiced nuts (see pages 28-29) can be used in place of the pistachios. Peaches, mangoes, or nectarines may be substituted for papaya.

# ASPARAGUS CHAAT WITH CHILE OIL
## (Anokhi Chaat)

Serves 4
Preparation time:
    10 minutes

½ pound asparagus
½ cup chopped white
    or red onion
1½ tablespoons Hot
    Chile Oil (page 237)
4 teaspoons lemon juice
2 tablespoons chopped
    fresh cilantro
½ teaspoon salt
½ teaspoon chaat
    masala (page 21)
¼ cup cooked garbanzos
    drained and rinsed
2 tablespoons roasted
    peanuts

Asparagus is new to India, though it is available in big cities at springtime. I love asparagus because it takes very little cooking time and adapts itself exceptionally well to an appealing crunchy chaat. Serve with an entree of koftas, any of the paneer cheese dishes, or your favorite barbecued foods.

1. Trim off and discard the tough ends of the asparagus. Cut the spears diagonally into 1-inch pieces. Fill a large skillet with 1 inch of water and bring to a boil on high heat. Cook the asparagus until tender-crisp, about 3 minutes.

2. Transfer the cooked asparagus with a slotted spoon to a bowl of ice water. Drain and place in a serving bowl. Add the onion, oil, lemon juice, and cilantro. Mix lightly, cover, and let stand for the flavors to blend, about 15 minutes. If made ahead, cover and chill up to 2 hours. Just before serving, season with salt and chaat masala and toss in the garbanzos and nuts.

**Microwave:** In step 1, place the trimmed and cut asparagus in a shallow microwave-safe plate with the tips toward the center. Add 4 to 5 tablespoons water. Cover and cook at full power for 5 minutes. Let stand covered a few minutes more to complete the cooking. Drain off any remaining water.

# BOMBAY CHOWPATTY BEACH CHAAT
## (*Mumbai Bhelpuri*)

Serves 8 to 10
Preparation time:
  15 minutes

1 recipe Acorn Squash
  Wadas in Garlicky
  Peanut Oil (page 126),
  without the oil sea-
  soning
2 cups chopped ripe
  tomatoes
1½ cups finely chopped
  onion
¼ cup chopped fresh
  cilantro
6 fresh hot green chiles,
  stemmed and chopped
  (optional)
2 cups crushed tortilla
  chips
4 cups Rice Krispies
  cereal
2 tablespoons lemon
  juice, preferably fresh
1½ cups (triple recipe)
  Sweet Date and
  Tamarind Chutney
  (page 193)
2 cups (double recipe)
  Fresh Mint Chutney
  (page 192)
Sliced strawberries,
  mangoes, or peaches
Cayenne (optional)

All over Bombay — on street corners, in the bazaars, and at Chowpatty and Juhu beaches — you will see stands selling *bhelpuri,* a favorite palate-teaser. This delicious snack is a sweet-sour combination of puffed rice, vegetables, fresh herbs, and chutneys, sometimes with small crisp-fried pooris to use as a spoon. When we visited Bombay, I remember being strictly forbidden to eat at these stalls. The elders did not think highly of them. To tell you the truth, the temptation was too hard to resist!

I like to serve a version of this chaat buffet style for a spring or summer picnic, setting out a "salad bar" of assorted garnishes and seasonings for guests to assemble their own combinations. Tortilla chips take the place of the fried pooris, and I add steamed dumplings, either leftover or freshly cooked, for variety. I have served this salad chaat at northern California cricket matches, and even when my husband's team played against an all-English team, it has been a hit with players and fans from both sides.

1. Cut the dumplings in half and place in a large bowl. Add the tomatoes, onion, cilantro, chiles, chips, and cereal to the bowl and toss to mix. Sprinkle with lemon juice and mix well.

2. To serve, spoon the dumpling mixture into deep dishes. Drizzle each serving with a tablespoon or two each of the tamarind and mint chutneys. Top with fruit slices. Sprinkle with cayenne, if desired.

**Variation:** Substitute cooked, peeled, and diced potatoes for the steamed dumplings. Finely chopped green mango in place of the lemon juice makes a marvelous inclusion.

# KASHMIR MIXED FRUIT CHAAT
## (*Kashmiri Chaat*)

Serves 10 to 12
Preparation time:
   15 minutes

2 cups strawberries,
   hulled, rinsed, and
   halved
4 firm red plums, pitted
   and sliced into ½-inch
   wedges
1 medium avocado,
   peeled, pitted, and
   diced
1 cup fresh pineapple
   chunks
½ cup finely chopped
   red onion (optional)
1 medium red bell
   pepper, diced
1 cup diced English
   (hothouse) cucumber
¼ cup chopped fresh
   basil
1 tablespoon finely
   chopped fresh mint
2 *each* fresh hot red and
   green chiles, stemmed
   and chopped
¼ cup fresh lime juice
½ cup fresh orange
   juice
1 tablespoon chaat
   masala, homemade
   (page 21) or bought
½ teaspoon salt
   (optional)
1 recipe Tamarind-Apple
   Dipping Sauce (page
   39) *or* Sweet Date and
   Tamarind Chutney
   (page 193)

The lush greenery, plethora of crop fields, and orchards full of juicy apples, plums, and almonds form an unforgettable view in the Kashmir Valley of northern India. With its ring of snow-capped ranges, Kashmir is often described as "an emerald set in pearls" and "the Asian Switzerland." Another cultural form that adds to the charm of Kashmir is its lavish cuisine. I have mixed and matched combinations of fruits grown in Kashmir with others from California and Hawaii in this refreshing chaat. For additional crunch, sprinkle with chopped Sweet-Spiced Royal Almonds (page 28).

1. Combine the fruits, vegetables, and herbs in a serving bowl. Add the lime and orange juices. Mix gently, cover, and let stand at cool room temperature for about 15 minutes for the flavors to blend. If made ahead, cover and chill up to 2 hours.

2. Sprinkle chaat masala over the fruit mixture. Spoon into individual goblets and top each serving with a teaspoon or two of sauce.

# TANDOORI SALAD CHAAT
## (Seekh Salat Chaat)

Serves 3 to 4
Preparation time:
  10 minutes

*Dressing*
1 cup plain nonfat or
  low-fat yogurt
½ cup sour cream
2 tablespoons honey
2 tablespoons orange
  juice
1½ teaspoons chaat
  masala, homemade
  (page 21) or store-
  bought

3 small tender zucchini,
  sliced 1 inch thick
1 sweet red pepper, cut
  into 1-inch pieces
1 recipe paneer cheese
  (page 165), cut into 2-
  inch pieces
6 to 8 cherry tomatoes
2 tablespoons mild
  olive oil
½ cup corn kernels
  (2 small ears or ½ cup
  frozen), steamed until
  tender
½ cup chopped red onion

Here is a way to make great use of garden profusion. This smoky chaat combines seasonal vegetables and paneer cheese, which are grilled and cloaked in a yogurt-orange dressing. While roasting, drop some chaat masala onto the hot coals to create an aromatic smoke. Accompany the chaat with Fresh Cilantro Pilaf (page 134) for a light luncheon. Serve with Grilled Green Mango Thirst Quencher (page 228).

1. Combine all of the dressing ingredients in a small bowl. Whisk to blend. If made ahead, cover and chill up to 2 hours.

2. Prepare a medium-hot fire in a barbecue grill or preheat the broiler. Distribute the zucchini, pepper, paneer, and tomatoes on 6 thin skewers. Brush lightly with oil and grill until lightly brown and tender, turning occasionally, 4 to 5 minutes.

3. Place the corn kernels and onion in a serving bowl. Slide the grilled vegetables off the skewers into the bowl. Pour the dressing over all and toss well to coat the vegetables. Serve immediately.

# DAIKON SALAD WITH AROMATIC OIL
## (Muli ka Kachumber)

Serves 4
Preparation time:
  10 minutes

After cucumber, white radish is one of the favorite vegetables for salads in India. Every kitchen garden in the subcontinent will grow white radishes, and one can see the roots pushing up halfway out of the soil in home vegetable patches and commercial fields alike. Daikon, a large Japanese white radish available in America, makes an excellent substitute for the Indian variety. Here the shredded vegetable is glamorized with fragrant dill, sweet walnuts, and a final spritz of oil seasoning.

1 small tender daikon
    (½ pound)
¼ cup chopped fresh
    dill *or* 2 tablespoons
    fresh fenugreek leaves
¼ cup coarsely chopped
    toasted walnuts
½ teaspoon salt
1 tablespoon mild
    vegetable oil
½ teaspoon mustard
    seeds
½ teaspoon cumin seeds
3 or 4 dried red chiles,
    stemmed and broken
2 radicchio or red
    cabbage leaves,
    washed and cut in half

1. Peel the daikon and grate it with a hand grater or in a food processor. Transfer to a serving bowl. If made ahead, cover and chill up to 4 hours.

2. Add the dill, walnuts, and salt to the daikon and mix well.

3. Heat the oil in a small pan over medium-high heat until it ripples when the pan is tilted. Add the mustard and cumin; when the seeds sizzle and splutter, add the chiles. Cook until the chiles darken one or two shades, about 1 minute.

4. Line a serving platter with radicchio leaves. Pile the daikon salad in the center of the leaves and pour the oil seasoning on top. Serve immediately.

# LUCKNOW-STYLE POTATO CHAAT
## (*Lucknowi Chaat*)

Serves 4
Preparation time:
    30 minutes

1 pound red wax
    potatoes (3 medium
    or 6 to 8 small)
½ teaspoon ground
    toasted cumin
¾ teaspoon chaat
    masala, homemade
    (page 21) or bought
¼ teaspoon cayenne
½ teaspoon mustard
    seeds, lightly crushed
¼ cup thinly sliced
    green onion
¼ cup chopped fresh
    cilantro
2 tablespoons lemon
    juice
½ teaspoon salt
3 iceberg lettuce leaves,
    washed and crisped

New potatoes and green onions are dusted with cumin, chaat masala, and cayenne for a delectable first course. In India, this chaat is dressed with plain yogurt and served on crisp-fried pooris topped with fiery and sweet chutney. Chaat parties are fun for afternoon snacks for my children and their American friends, and have been vary popular with the students in my cooking classes. I serve this chaat on toasted mini-bagels, with Fresh Mint Chutney (page 192) and Tamarind-Apple Dipping Sauce (page 39) offered on the side.

1. Bring 2 quarts of water to a boil in a saucepan. Add the potatoes and simmer, covered, until tender, 15 to 20 minutes. Drain. Let the potatoes cool enough to handle, then cut them into 1-inch cubes.

2. Combine the cumin, chaat masala, cayenne, and mustard and sprinkle over the potatoes. Mix gently and let stand covered for 10 minutes.

3. Add the onion, cilantro, lemon juice, and salt to the potatoes. Toss lightly. Spoon onto a platter lined with lettuce leaves.

**Microwave:** In step 1, cut the potatoes into ½-inch cubes. Combine with ¼ cup water in a 3-quart microwavable casserole. Cover and cook at full power until the potatoes are tender, 10 to 12 minutes.

# Chutneys and Pickles

Fresh Mint Chutney or Dip

Fresh Cilantro Chutney with Cashews

Sweet Date and Tamarind Chutney

Flaked Coconut Chutney

Warm Tomato Relish

Fiery Pepper-Garlic Relish

Fresh Ginger Chutney with Cinnamon and Pistachios

Quick Tomato-Cinnamon Chutney

Tropical Pineapple Chutney

Nectarine and Currant Chutney with Pecans

Tangerine and Apricot Chutney

Dry Coconut Chutney

Powdered Peanut Chutney

Sweet Lime Pickles in Peppercorn Syrup

No-Cook Spicy Lime Pickles

End-of-the-Garden Mixed Veggie Pickles

Green Mango Pickles

Spicy-Sweet Pickled Dates

Pickled Baby Carrots

When an Indian meal is served, grace notes are added to please the eye and contrast the varying tastes and textures. These charming companions are chutneys and pickles.

The word "chutney" entered English dictionaries in the early 19th century as the anglicized version of the Hindi word *chatni,* meaning "to lick." Chutney is a generic term for a sauce, relish, or condiment made with herbs or fruits and usually flavored with spices and chiles. There is an astonishing range of chutneys, as diverse as the languages and cultures of India. But they all add the same special zest to any Indian meal, from a humble roti on a banana leaf to a banquet served on a silver plate to a dinner at a maharajah's palace.

Three main varieties of chutney are represented here. The first is a smooth uncooked puree of fresh herbs or coconut. Mild to very hot depending on the number of chiles used, a fresh chutney makes a cool, contrasting dip for pakoras, papads, and other spicy finger foods. They are best freshly made, though they will keep for several days in the refrigerator.

The type of chutney most familiar in the West (thanks to an 18th century British colonial officer named Major Grey) is a soft and pulpy mixture of cooked fruit with spices, sugar, and vinegar. Besides Major Grey's mango, you can make delicious chutneys from all sorts of fruits, including pineapple, plums, apricots, peaches, nectarines, and currants. These chutneys are a natural with Indian curries, koftas, and flatbreads, but go just as well in a Western menu; you can even serve them on pancakes or as sundae toppings or pie fillings.

A third type, dry chutney, is not well known outside India, but is extremely popular in my native southwestern region. Toasted nuts, coconut, or dals are ground to a powder with spices to make a dry seasoning to sprinkle over rice, dosas, or roasted or grilled vegetables. Or it may be mixed with plain yogurt or melted desi ghee as a dip or spread for bread. Dry chutneys remain fresh for a month or two at cool room temperature.

In addition to chutneys, certain fruits and vegetables are turned into flavorful accents to an Indian meal in the form of pickles. Pickles (discussed in more detail on page 202) are distinguished from chutneys by the use of oil and spices such as asafetida and fenugreek, which do not appear in chutneys.

## STORING CHUTNEYS AND PICKLES

Most of the chutneys and pickles in this chapter will keep for weeks or even months in the refrigerator, and a year or more in the freezer. For long-term storage at room temperature, fruit chutneys can be sealed in canning jars by standard home canning methods. A few hours of work can turn the seasonal bounty at your produce market or farmers' market into a year-round supply of delicious chutney, with some to spare for gifts. A chutney made with summer fruits is an especially nice addition to a Thanksgiving table.

The basic procedure is the same as for other high-acid foods: Fill hot sterilized jars with chutney, leaving ¼ inch of head space. Immediately wipe the rims clean with a towel dipped in hot water. Place the scalded lids on the jars and seal tightly. Arrange the jars slightly apart on a rack in a large pot half full of water. Add more hot water to cover the jars by at least 1 inch. Bring the water to a simmer, cover, and boil for 15 minutes. (If you have a pressure canner or other specialized canning equipment, follow the manufacturer's instructions.) Remove the jars from the water bath with tongs and place them on a towel or wooden board away from drafts to cool to room temperature. Test the seal of each jar by pressing the center of the lid; if it pops when pressed, there is no seal. Store any unsealed jars in the refrigerator and use within 1 to 2 months. Store the sealed jars in a pantry or other dark, cool place and use within a year or two.

# FRESH MINT CHUTNEY OR DIP
## (Pudina Chatni)

Makes 1 cup
Preparation time:
    6 minutes

1 fresh hot green chile,
    stemmed
1 tablespoon roasted
    peanuts (salted or
    unsalted)
2 tablespoons sweetened
    flaked coconut or
    grated fresh coconut
½ teaspoon salt (or less
    if using salted
    peanuts)
½ teaspoon ground
    cumin
⅓ cup plain nonfat or
    low-fat yogurt
1½ cups lightly packed
    fresh mint leaves with
    tender stems
½ cup lightly packed
    fresh cilantro leaves
    with tender stems

Mint chutney is popular throughout India as an aid to digestion, and also because it is delicious and easy to make. An Indian cook's grocery list will always include a bunch of fresh mint and cilantro. There are numerous ways of making this exhilarating chutney; with lemon juice in place of yogurt, with the addition of ginger, or as given here, with a combination of mint and cilantro. You can make it as hot as you like with the addition of more chiles. Serve it as a spread, or add a little water to make a dip, or thin it with buttermilk for an invigorating salad dressing. Also, it makes a terrific marinade for roasts.

1. Combine the ingredients in a blender or food processor. Process until smoothly pureed, stopping to scrape down the sides of the container with a rubber spatula. Transfer into a small ceramic bowl. Serve or cover and store.

Note: The chutney keeps well in a covered container for 5 days in the refrigerator or up to 1 month in the freezer. The color will darken in the refrigerator, but the flavor is not affected. Freezing maintains the original color.

# FRESH CILANTRO CHUTNEY WITH CASHEWS
## (Hara Dhania Chatni)

Makes 1 cup
Preparation time:
    6 minutes

Cilantro — the small, fragile green leaves of the coriander plant — is enjoyed all over India for its robust herbal taste, which is both refreshing and palate-stimulating. Here the herb is pureed with tomato and cashews to make a zesty chutney. Try it with flatbreads, or for variety, spread on warm toasts or in sandwiches, or use as a topping for mashed or baked potatoes, or serve as a dip for finger foods. Herb condiments like this are a special boon for people watching their weight because they offer a low-calorie alternative to mayonnaise in sandwiches and snacks.

2 cups lightly packed
fresh cilantro leaves
with tender stems
2 medium ripe Roma
tomatoes, coarsely
chopped
2 fresh hot green chiles,
stemmed and chopped
1-inch piece fresh ginger
½ cup toasted cashews
or peanuts
1 teaspoon cumin seeds
½ teaspoon honey
1 teaspoon salt

1. Combine all the ingredients in a blender or food processor. Process to a smooth puree, stopping to scrape down the sides of the container as necessary with a rubber spatula. Transfer into a small ceramic bowl.

Note: This chutney keeps well in a covered container for 6 days in the refrigerator or up to 1 month in the freezer.

Variation: CILANTRO-ONION CHUTNEY (*Pyaz Aur Dhania Chatni*)
In place of the tomatoes, add 1 small onion, peeled and coarsely chopped, and lemon juice to taste.

# SWEET DATE AND TAMARIND CHUTNEY
## (*Mathurewali Khajoor Chatni*)

Makes ½ cup
Preparation time:
    4 minutes

¼ teaspoon hot pepper
flakes
¼ teaspoon ground
coriander
¼ teaspoon ground
cumin
⅓ to ½ teaspoon
tamarind concentrate
dissolved in 2 table-
spoons water
1 teaspoon brown sugar
¼ teaspoon salt
¼ cup water
10 whole dates, pitted
and coarsely chopped
*or* ½ cup chopped
dates

This is a popular sweet condiment in India. It is almost always paired with a hot herb chutney and spread on chaats to create mouth-watering snacks. It partners well with spicy finger foods, or spice-flavored Toasted Lentil Wafers (page 30). For more sour tang, add the greater amount of tamarind mentioned in the recipe.

1. Combine all the ingredients in a blender or food processor. Process to a smooth puree, stopping the machine as necessary to scrape down the sides of the container. Transfer to a small ceramic bowl.

Note: Dates sometimes get quite hard and dry when stored; if so, soak them in a little water first to plump them up.
    The chutney keeps well in a covered container for 5 days in the refrigerator or up to 1 month in the freezer.

# FLAKED COCONUT CHUTNEY
## (Tengankai Chatni)

Makes 1¼ cups
Preparation time:
    6 minutes

2 large garlic cloves
1 or 2 fresh hot green
    chiles, stemmed and
    chopped
¼ cup packed fresh
    cilantro with sprigs
½ teaspoon cumin seeds
2 tablespoons roasted
    unsalted peanuts
½ cup plain yogurt
½ cup water
1½ cups lightly packed
    sweetened flaked
    coconut or grated
    fresh coconut
1 teaspoon salt

Here readily available coconut flakes take on a wonderfully varied flavor from the assertive seasonings, garlic and onion; yogurt and nuts add nutrition, and cilantro gives a delicate herbal overtone. Freshly grated coconut is even better, if you can find it. My sons love this chutney with their favorite southern Indian specialties, idlis and dosas (page 63). If a hotter flavor is desired, add another chile or two. For another variation in flavor and appearance, I sometimes top the chutney with mustard-cumin infused oil (see page 13).

1. Combine all the ingredients in a blender or food processor. Process to a smooth puree, stopping to scrape down the sides of the container as necessary with a rubber spatula.

Note: The chutney can be kept up to 5 days covered in the refrigerator or frozen up to 1 month. Bring to room temperature before serving.

# WARM TOMATO RELISH
## (Gujrati Kasundi)

Makes ⅔ cup
Preparation time:
    30 minutes

1 tablespoon mild
    vegetable oil
½ teaspoon mustard seeds
1½ tablespoons sliced
    garlic
½ teaspoon turmeric
1 teaspoon cayenne
½ teaspoon salt
1 teaspoon sugar
2 large ripe tomatoes
    (10 ounces total),
    peeled and chopped
    (see Note)
¼ cup distilled white
    vinegar

Kasundi is a specialty of Gujarat state in western India where 90 percent of the population is vegetarian. Creative Gujrati cooks have developed many stimulating relishes like this to complement their entrees. If you are not a garlic lover, you will want to reduce the amount here to suit your taste, but do not eliminate it totally, since it is essential to mellow and bind the taste. Try this relish warm, cold, or at room temperature with any of the puffy breads and stir-fried vegetables.

1. Heat the oil in a heavy skillet over medium heat. Add the mustard seeds; when they begin to sizzle and splutter, stir in the garlic. Cook, stirring occasionally, until the garlic starts to brown, about 4 minutes. Add the turmeric, cayenne, salt, and sugar and cook, stirring, for 1 minute. Add the tomatoes, stir, and cook for 2 minutes. Add the vinegar and bring to a boil. Reduce the heat, cover, and simmer until thick, about 15 minutes.

Note: The relish keeps well, covered, in the refrigerator for several weeks.
    To peel tomatoes, blanch them in boiling water for 4 or 5 minutes, then immerse in cold water. The skins will peel off easily.

194

# FIERY PEPPER-GARLIC RELISH
## (Belluli Chatni)

Makes ½ cup
Preparation time:
    10 minutes, plus 30
    minutes soaking

½ ounce small dried red
    chiles (about 40 to 50)
6 large garlic cloves
12 fresh kari leaves *or*
    1 teaspoon crushed
    dried kari leaves
1 teaspoon tamarind
    concentrate, dissolved
    in 4 tablespoons water
3 tablespoons brown
    sugar
½ teaspoon salt

This medium-hot relish from southwest India makes a perfect accompaniment to mellow dishes containing yogurt or cream. Traditionally it is very hot, but it varies from one family to the next; my grandmother's version, for example, used a much higher proportion of garlic to chile. I have incorporated brown sugar to balance the heat and round off the flavors. Even so, I would recommend you serve this chutney in moderation — a quarter to half a teaspoon may be plenty. In India it is mixed with plain yogurt or desi ghee and served with flatbreads, or used as a quick "wet masala" for curries and vegetable dishes. You may mix it with softened butter or cheese for a peppery vegetable dip or to spread on breads. To add excitement, serve it alongside barbecued foods as a condiment. Some of our Indian friends love it on homemade pizza and Uppama (page 58).

1. Remove the stems from the chiles and rinse in 2 or 3 changes of water. Add enough water to cover by at least 2 inches. Soak for 30 minutes. Drain, reserving some of the soaking water.

2. Combine the drained chiles and the remaining ingredients in a blender (a blender works better than a food processor in this case). Process to a fine puree, scraping down the sides of the container as necessary with a rubber spatula. Thin with a little of the chile soaking water, if desired. Transfer the relish into a small jar. Serve or store in a cool place.

**Note:** The relish will keep well for a week at cool room temperature, up to 2 months in the refrigerator, or 1 year in the freezer.

**Variation:** As with the other chutneys, you can adjust the number of chiles to suit your liking. If you want to try something volcanic, add the vibrant orange fresh habanero chiles (there is no need to soak them). In my opinion the habanero has a hot bite at first but its intense fire is felt even more when it reaches the stomach.

# FRESH GINGER CHUTNEY WITH CINNAMON AND PISTACHIOS
## (Adrak Chatni)

Makes 1 cup
Preparation time:
    45 minutes

2 cups lemon juice
½ cup plus 1 tablespoon
    sugar
4 ounces fresh ginger
⅛ teaspoon cinnamon
¼ cup shelled toasted
    pistachios
¼ teaspoon salt

In the tropics, ginger is the most effective digestive aid of all. This fragrant chutney of julienne strips of fresh ginger steeped in a cinnamon-perfumed lemony syrup not only complements Indian dishes, it is marvelous with any Western cuisine as well. My cousins Parvati and Dhanashri serve it along with large idlis and on salads too.

1. Combine the lemon juice and sugar in a heavy non-aluminum saucepan. Cook over medium-high heat, stirring, until the sugar dissolves. Reduce the heat to medium and cook uncovered until the syrup is slightly thick and the sugar at the bottom of the pan turns golden, 18 to 20 minutes.

2. Meanwhile, lightly peel the ginger. Cut into 1-inch segments and slice lengthwise (with the grain). Stack the slices 3 or 4 at a time and cut them lengthwise into julienne strips. Measure 1 heaping cup.

3. Add the ginger and cinnamon to the lemon syrup. Reduce the heat to low, cover, and simmer until the ginger is glazed, 20 to 25 minutes. Stir in the nuts and salt. Remove from heat.

4. Spoon the chutney into sterilized jars to within ¼ inch of the top. When completely cool, cover with lids. Store in a cool dry place away from direct light.

# QUICK TOMATO-CINNAMON CHUTNEY
## (Lal Tomatar Chatni)

Makes 1 cup
Preparation time:
   30 minutes

3 medium-size tomatoes
   (¾ pound), peeled and
   finely chopped (see
   Note, page 194)
1 teaspoon minced fresh
   ginger
1 tablespoon minced
   garlic
1 tablespoon dark raisins
   or currants
½ teaspoon cayenne
⅛ teaspoon cinnamon
2 tablespoons white or
   cider vinegar
½ teaspoon salt
2 tablespoons sugar
1 tablespoon slivered
   toasted pistachios

This is one my favorite chutneys, simple and quick. Tomatoes are simmered in their own juices with flavorful ingredients until thick. Toasted pistachios add a chunky texture to the otherwise velvety smooth chutney. You can easily double or triple the recipe in summer, when tomatoes are plentiful, and freeze or can it for later use. Serve this delicate chutney with any of the flatbreads, or with savory puff pastries, or spread on grilled garlic bread.

1. Combine the tomatoes, ginger, garlic, raisins, cayenne, and cinnamon in a heavy skillet. Cook uncovered on medium-high heat, stirring occasionally, until most of the liquid is evaporated, about 12 minutes.

2. Add the vinegar, salt, and sugar and bring to a boil. Reduce the heat, cover, and simmer until thick, about 10 minutes. Add the pistachios. Spoon into clean jars and seal or refrigerate.

**Microwave:** Combine the step 1 ingredients in a 1-quart microwave-safe dish. Cook uncovered at full power, stirring once, until the tomatoes are soft, about 8 minutes. Add the remaining ingredients except the nuts and mix well. Cook uncovered, stirring twice, 8 minutes. Add the pistachios and store as described above.

# TROPICAL PINEAPPLE CHUTNEY
## (Ananas Chatni)

Makes 1¾ cups
Preparation time:
   30 minutes

2 dried red chiles,
   stemmed
1½ teaspoons mustard
   seeds
1-inch piece fresh ginger,
   minced
6 cloves garlic, minced
1 20-ounce can pineapple
   chunks in unsweet-
   ened juice

I like this chutney because it is such a breeze to make with canned pineapple. Of course, you can also use fresh pineapple, with all the juice you can squeeze from the rind and trimmings. Two small red chiles are enough to add contrast to the sweetish-sour fruit; if you like it really hot, add another one or two. The sweet and sour chutney makes an excellent accompaniment to savory breakfast or brunch dishes such as Braised Bread Morning Special (page 60) or Warm Cream of Wheat Pilaf (page 59).

1. Lightly crush the chiles and mustard seeds in a mortar or spice grinder, or on a board with a rolling pin. Combine with the remaining ingredients except the walnuts in a medium saucepan and bring to a boil. Reduce the heat, cover,

⅓ cup distilled white
   vinegar
½ cup sugar
1 teaspoon salt
1 cup coarsely chopped
   walnuts

and simmer, stirring occasionally, until the chutney is slightly thick and glazed, about 25 minutes.

2. Fold in the walnuts. Spoon the chutney into clean jars. Seal or refrigerate.

**Microwave:** Place the step 1 ingredients in a microwave-safe bowl. Cook uncovered at full power for 10 minutes. Remove from the oven, stir once, cover, and continue cooking at full power for another 10 minutes. Continue with step 2.

# NECTARINE AND CURRANT CHUTNEY WITH PECANS
## (Kishmis Chatni)

Makes 1½ cups
Preparation time:
   25 minutes

4 medium-size firm,
   ripe nectarines
   (1 pound total)
10 whole cloves
½ teaspoon cinnamon
¼ teaspoon hot pepper
   flakes
1 teaspoon ground
   coriander
1 teaspoon grated fresh
   ginger
¾ cup fresh red
   currants, stemmed, *or*
   1 tablespoon dried red
   or black currants
½ teaspoon salt
¾ cup sugar
½ cup plus 2 table-
   spoons distilled white
   vinegar
¼ cup chopped toasted
   pecans

Sweet nectarines and sour red currants make a happy marriage of flavors when simmered with "warm" northern Indian seasonings. Although not widely available, fresh currants can be found in specialty stores and farmers' markets from June through August. If fresh are unavailable, dried red or black currants make an excellent substitute. This chutney achieves a very beautiful rosy-pink hue with a glossy finish. Spoon it in a jar and tie a piece of plaid fabric around the neck for a gorgeous homemade gift. Serve with kofta kababs, or paneer cheese dishes accompanied by flatbreads.

1. Halve the nectarines and remove the pits. Cut each half into ½-inch thick wedges. Combine with the remaining ingredients except the pecans in a heavy non-aluminum saucepan. Bring to a boil, reduce the heat, and cook uncovered, stirring occasionally, until the chutney is thick and glossy, about 15 minutes.

2. Remove from the heat and stir in the pecans. Spoon the chutney into sterilized jars. Seal or refrigerate. Let the chutney ripen for a day before serving.

**Microwave:** Place the step 1 ingredients in a 2-quart microwave-safe bowl. Cook uncovered at full power for 6 minutes. Remove from the oven and stir. Continue cooking uncovered at full power until the chutney is thick and glossy, 6 to 8 minutes. Continue with step 2.

# TANGERINE AND APRICOT CHUTNEY
## (Mausambi-Khubani Chatni)

Makes 2 cups
Preparation time:
    30 minutes

2 medium-size tangerines
    (10 ounces total)
½ cup plus 3 table
    spoons light brown
    sugar
¼ teaspoon cinnamon
4 tablespoons distilled
    white vinegar or
    lemon juice
6 cloves garlic, sliced
½ teaspoon whole
    cloves
1 cup dried apricots,
    chopped
¼ teaspoon cayenne
¼ teaspoon salt

Traditionally this chutney is made with *mausambi,* a sweet lime similar to a tangerine that I have never seen in this country. (The citrus variety known here as Rangpur lime, though it sounds similar, is not the same thing.) However, two fruits more readily available here, tangerine and apricot, marry well to make a similar fruit chutney that adds a bold accent to any stew or curry.

1. Grate the orange zest from the tangerines and measure 2 teaspoons. Peel and section the tangerines, removing any stringy white membranes. Cut each section in half and discard any seeds.

2. Combine the sugar, cinnamon, and vinegar in a heavy non-aluminum saucepan and bring to a boil. Add the tangerine pieces and zest and the remaining ingredients. Reduce the heat, cover, and cook until the mixture resembles thick jam, 15 to 20 minutes.

3. Spoon the chutney into a clean jar. Seal or refrigerate. Let the chutney ripen for a day before serving.

**Note:** Cooking the dried apricots without soaking them in water helps retain their flavor and character; if you prefer them butter-soft, then soften them for several hours in water before making the chutney.

# DRY COCONUT CHUTNEY
## (*Khobri Chatni*)

Makes 1 cup
Preparation time:
   3 minutes

1 cup loosely packed
   sweetened flaked
   coconut
Scant ½ teaspoon cayenne
2 teaspoons minced
   garlic
½ teaspoon ground cumin
¼ teaspoon salt
1 tablespoon dried
   cilantro leaves

Packaged coconut makes it a snap to create this delectable dry condiment, spiced with cayenne, garlic, and cumin. Try it scattered over plain rice, or mixed with yogurt or desi ghee as a spread for flatbreads; or in a Western context, sprinkled on a mixed green salad or on warm buttered toast.

1. Combine the ingredients in a food processor or blender. Process until thoroughly mixed and the coconut is chopped into pieces about the size of plump bulgur wheat grains, about 2 minutes. Transfer to a small jar and store in a cool place or the refrigerator. Use within a week.

# POWDERED PEANUT CHUTNEY
## (*Shenga Chatni*)

Makes 1 cup
Preparation time:
   3 minutes

3 large cloves garlic,
   peeled
2 tablespoons dried
   cilantro (optional)
½ teaspoon cayenne
1 cup roasted peanuts,
   unsalted or salted
½ teaspoon ground
   cumin
¼ teaspoon salt (omit if
   using salted peanuts)
½ teaspoon sugar

This dry chutney is an old favorite that has always graced our dinner table. Sometimes the maid would prepare it, but I am sure my brother and cousins would agree that our great-aunt made the best *shenga chatni* of all. She lived for 103 years, and every year she would lovingly fill large packages of this cherished chutney with her fragile hands and send them to us.

Mixed with melted desi ghee as a spread for hot Whole Wheat Flatbreads, peanut chutney is a favorite with my sons as well as their peanut butter-loving American friends. Served in moderation, it makes a healthful accompaniment to vegetarian diet.

1. Mince the garlic in a mini-blender, blender, or food processor. Add all the remaining ingredients and process until peanuts are powdered. Transfer into a screw-top jar. Store in a cool place up to 1 month.

**Note:** To dry cilantro, place leaves and tender stems on a baking sheet and pat dry with a kitchen towel. Toast in a 350°F oven for 12 to 15 minutes or until crisp, or air-dry on the table (see page 15). Cool and store in a covered jar at cool room temperature up to 1 month. You can also use the dried variety sold in spice jars.

S

...mpany most Indian meals, along with
or instead of chutney. A small piece of one of these
highly seasoned preserves is just enough to tease
the palate and add extra zip to a meal.

Traditional Indian pickling is a large-scale
process, typically done in the summer when the
intense heat of the sun is used to "cook" the pickles. Over a couple of weeks, the crocks are left to
bake in the sun all day and brought indoors at
night. The sun heats the mixture enough to kill

any bacteria, making pickles that can last for years.

Fortunately for Western cooks, the same flavors
can be obtained on a smaller scale in the kitchen. A
variety of fresh fruits and vegetables can be steeped
in a spicy-sweet syrup of sugar, salt, ground spices,
and lime juice to make simple but delicious Indian-
style pickles. Here is a selection of easy-to-make
pickles with a range of flavors, from the piquant
Spicy-Sweet Pickled Dates to the refreshing bitter-
ness of Sweet Lime Pickles and the mouth-watering
tartness of Green Mango Pickles. Select your personal choice to add additional punch to any meal.

# SWEET LIME PICKLES IN PEPPERCORN SYRUP
### (Nimbu ka Meetha Achaar)

Makes 1 cup
Preparation time:
    25 minutes plus
    1 hour resting time

4 limes (¾ pound)
1 teaspoon salt
¼ teaspoon turmeric
¼ teaspoon fenugreek
    seeds
½ cup sugar
¼ cup water
½ teaspoon cayenne
½ teaspoon whole black
    peppercorns

In India, pickle recipes are passed from generation to generation like family
heirlooms. This lovely recipe was given to me by my mother-in-law.
Simmering the limes in a spicy syrup replaces the traditional week or more of
"cooking" in the sun, but the results are amazingly similar. The flavor
improves considerably with keeping, although they are so irresistible, they disappear in a few days. Since this sweetish pickle contains water, it is best made
in small quantities and refrigerated. The pickles make an excellent accompaniment for spicy dishes.

1. Wash the limes and pat them dry with a kitchen towel. Cut each lime in
half crosswise, then cut each half into about 1-inch wedges. Remove and discard any seeds. Place the lime wedges in a medium-size glass bowl. Sprinkle
with the salt and turmeric, toss with a fork, cover, and set aside for 1 hour.

2. Meanwhile, toast the fenugreek seeds in a small dry skillet over medium-
high heat until fragrant, about 5 minutes. Grind to a fine powder.

3. Combine the sugar and water in a heavy non-aluminum pan. Cook on medium-high heat, stirring occasionally, until the syrup reaches 200°F on a candy
thermometer, about 8 minutes. Reduce the heat to medium. Add the limes
with their juices, cayenne, fenugreek, and peppercorns and mix well. Cook

uncovered until the lime rind is a dull olive green and the mixture is thick and syrupy, about 10 minutes.

4. Spoon the limes and syrup into a sterilized jar. Cool, cover, and store in a dry place. Let the pickles cure for 3 days before serving. Refrigerate if storing longer than a week; the pickles keep well up to 2 months in the refrigerator.

# NO-COOK SPICY LIME PICKLES
## (Nimbu Achaar)

Makes 5 cups
Preparation time:
    20 minutes

10 medium limes
    (2 pounds)
½ tablespoon fenugreek
    seeds
½ tablespoon cumin
    seeds
1 tablespoon mustard
    seeds
¼ teaspoon asafetida
½ teaspoon turmeric
½ cup sugar
¼ cup cayenne
½ cup salt

This is my mother's 40-year-old pickle recipe, which she makes every year to present to numerous friends and relatives. Make these in late spring or early summer when limes are large and juicy. Lemons give a similar flavor, but for some reason they don't keep as well; my lime pickles stay fresh for a year or more, but lemons are good only for about a month. As these pickles are moderately hot and spicy, I like to serve them with a complete meal consisting of Whole Wheat Flatbread, a legume dish, a vegetable side dish, a yogurt-based raita, and plain basmati rice.

1. Wash the limes and wipe them dry with a kitchen towel. Cut each lime in half crosswise, then cut each half into 4 wedges. Remove and discard any seeds. Place the lime pieces in a glass mixing bowl.

2. Toast the fenugreek and cumin seeds in a small dry skillet over medium heat, shaking the pan frequently, until lightly brown and aromatic, about 5 minutes. Transfer to a spice grinder and grind to a fine powder. Turn into a small bowl. Toast the mustard seeds separately and grind coarsely. Add to the bowl. Stir in the asafetida, turmeric, sugar, cayenne, and salt. Mix well.

3. Sprinkle the spice mixture over the limes and mix thoroughly. Spoon into a crock or 3 pint-size jars. Cover with lid and store in a cool dry place. Let the pickles cure for 1 week before serving.

**Variation:** I sometimes slit some serrano chiles in half and toss them in in addition to the cayenne. The spices and lime juice permeate and tame the chiles, turning them into another kind of pickle to include with dinner.

# END-OF-THE-GARDEN MIXED VEGGIE PICKLES
## (Achaar Amritsari)

Makes 4 cups
Preparation time:
   30 minutes

1 cup carrots, cut into
   1½-inch sticks
1 cup cauliflower, cut
   into ½-inch florets
1 cup cucumber, peeled,
   seeded, and cut into 1-
   inch cubes
1 cup green beans,
   trimmed and cut into
   1-inch pieces
6 pearl onions, peeled
3 tablespoons mild
   mustard oil (see note,
   page 207) or sesame
   oil
2½ tablespoons sliced
   garlic
2½ tablespoons fresh
   ginger cut into juli-
   enne strips
4 to 6 dried red chiles,
   stemmed and broken
½ cup plus 2 table-
   spoons distilled white
   vinegar
¼ cup plus 1 tablespoon
   light brown sugar
1½ teaspoons mustard
   seeds, lightly crushed
1¼ teaspoons garam
   masala, homemade
   (page 21) or bought
1 teaspoon salt

This pickle preserves the seasonal bounty of the late summer garden in a simple but scrumptious preparation. The medley of vegetables is drenched in a cloud of sweetish-sour flavoring with a generous smattering of garlic and ginger. Blanching the vegetables ensures that they remain bright, colorful, and crunchy. They make a pleasant companion to a supper of smooth soup and flatbread on a cold evening.

1. Combine the vegetables in a large shallow dish. Bring 2 quarts of water to a rolling boil; pour it over the vegetables and let stand 5 minutes. Drain the blanched vegetables in a colander, spread on a cookie sheet lined with clean kitchen towels or paper towels, and pat dry thoroughly. Loosely pack the vegetables into a clean 2-quart crock or jar.

2. Heat the oil in a small skillet over medium heat. Add the garlic and ginger and cook until aromatic and the garlic starts to brown, about 4 minutes. Stir in the chiles and cook 1 minute. Remove from the heat and set aside.

3. Bring the vinegar and sugar to a boil in a small saucepan. Reduce the heat and simmer until slightly thick, about 10 minutes. Add the mustard, garam masala, and salt and remove from the heat. Stir in the ginger-garlic oil seasonings. Pour over the vegetables. Cool, cover, and set aside in a cool place. Let the pickles cure for 1 day before serving. Refrigerate for longer storage; use within 2 weeks.

**Microwave:** In step 1, combine the vegetables in a 3-quart microwavable dish with ⅓ cup water. Cover and cook at full power for 5 minutes. Remove from the oven, drain, and continue with the rest of step 1.

**Note:** This recipe works with any assortment of garden-fresh produce at the peak of its season; in winter, for example, add any combination of crunchy root vegetables such as beets, daikon, jicama, kohlrabi, rutabagas, and turnips to the mix.

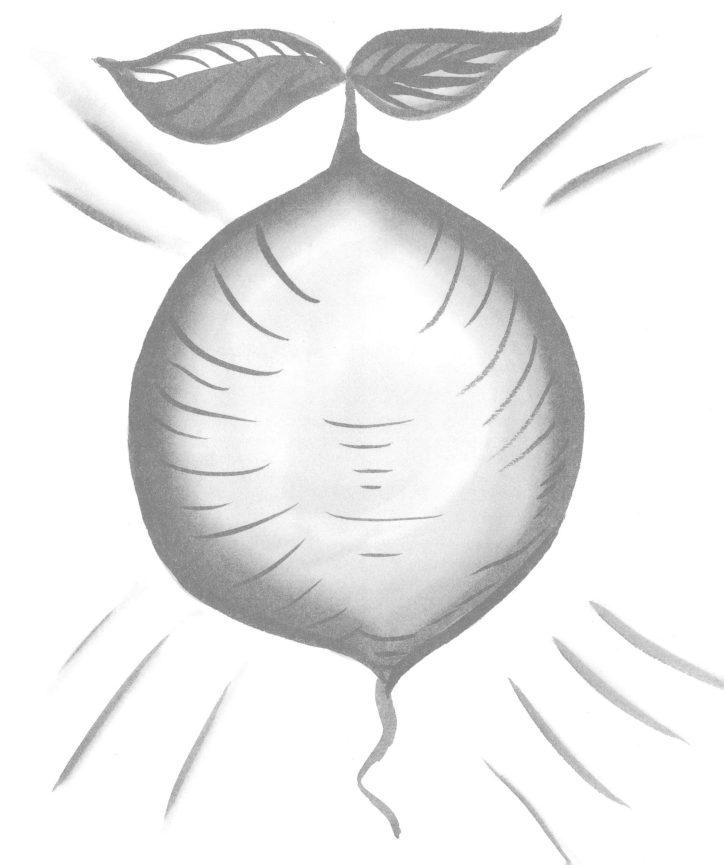

# GREEN MANGO PICKLES
## (Mavinkai Uppinkai)

Makes 1¼ cups
Preparation time:
    15 minutes

½ teaspoon fenugreek
    seeds
1½ tablespoons mild
    vegetable oil
2 teaspoons mustard
    seeds, lightly crushed
⅛ teaspoon asafetida
1 medium-size (½ pound)
    green mango
¼ cup brown sugar
1 teaspoon cayenne
1 teaspoon salt

My childhood memories come rushing back when I make this pickle. I remember plucking unripe mangoes from the garden, and our maid cutting them into thin slices. Before my mother would start the pickling process, we would eat some of the raw slices, dipping them first in a heap of salt. The taste of fresh mangoes was simply divine! What we didn't eat right away went into my mother's delectable pickles. Serve a teaspoon or two of these pickles with a meal of flatbread, dal, rice, and a vegetable side dish. Or add pizzazz to a pasta dish with a spoonful served alongside.

1. Toast the fenugreek seeds in a small dry skillet over medium heat until lightly brown, 4 to 5 minutes. Grind to a fine powder.

2. Heat the oil in a small saucepan over medium heat until it ripples when the pan is tilted. Add the mustard seeds; when the seeds sizzle, stir in the asafetida. Remove from the heat.

3. Peel and dice the mango as directed on page 238. Combine the cubes in a glass bowl with the sugar, cayenne, salt and fenugreek and mix well. Drizzle the mustard oil seasoning on top and mix gently. Cover and set aside in a cool dry place. Let the pickles ripen for a day or until the sugar is melted and syrupy. Refrigerate for longer storage, but use within about 5 days.

**Note:** Adjust the seasonings according to the tartness of the fruit and your taste. This pickle is not especially suitable for canning, as the pectin content of the typical half-ripe mangoes available here is not the same as the true green mangoes used for pickling in India.

# SPICY-SWEET PICKLED DATES
## (Khajoor Achaar)

Makes 2 cups
Preparation time:
    20 minutes

Dry roasted slivers of plump, sweet dates steeped in a syrup flavored with curry and cayenne turn delicately spicy and exceptionally succulent. I urge you to try these pickles with both Indian and Western cuisine. Spoon them on chaats or other salads for variation.

1 package (10 ounces)
   whole California dates
1 teaspoon curry powder,
   homemade (page 22)
   or bought
½ teaspoon cayenne
½ teaspoon salt
2 tablespoons sugar
½ teaspoon whole
   cloves
½ teaspoon black
   peppercorns
1 cup lime or lemon
   juice, preferably fresh

1. Preheat the oven to 300°F. Spread the dates on a cookie sheet and bake 10 minutes. Let the dates cool completely, then cut them in half, remove the seeds, and cut the dates into ¼-inch-thick slivers.

2. Combine the curry powder, cayenne, salt, and sugar in a small bowl. Sprinkle the dates with the spice mixture and toss well. Spoon into a clean jar. Add the cloves and peppercorns. Pour in the lime or lemon juice (don't worry if the juice does not cover the dates; they will absorb it evenly). Cover the jar with a lid and let stand at cool room temperature. Allow to cure for 3 days before serving. Store at cool room temperature for up to a week, or refrigerate up to 6 months.

## PICKLED BABY CARROTS
### (Gaajar Loncha)

Makes 1½ cups
Preparation time:
   45 minutes

¼ teaspoon fenugreek
   seeds
½ teaspoon sesame
   seeds
1 teaspoon cumin seeds
¼ teaspoon peppercorns
4 whole cloves
½ teaspoon crushed
   saffron threads
1 tablespoon mustard oil
   (see Note) or sesame
   oil
½ tablespoon finely
   chopped garlic
1 teaspoon finely
   chopped fresh ginger
½ pound ready-to-eat
   peeled baby carrots
¼ teaspoon cayenne
½ teaspoon salt
1½ tablespoons sugar
¼ cup distilled white
   vinegar

Each state in India has its own style of making carrot pickles. This spicy, sweet, and sour version, rounded with the essence of saffron, is from Maharashtra on the west coast. There it is made from full-grown carrots cut into 2-inch sticks. Lightly cooked baby carrots are a particularly appealing alternative. Try these pickles with mellow dishes such as koftas or creamed lentils, with plain whole wheat flatbread or puffy bread and a yogurt-based salad.

1. Combine the seeds, peppercorns, and cloves in a small dry skillet. Toast on medium heat, shaking the pan frequently, until fragrant, about 4 minutes. Add the saffron and toast another minute. Grind to a fine powder.

2. Heat the oil in a 2-quart saucepan over medium heat. Add the garlic and ginger. Stir and cook until aromatic, about 4 minutes. Add the carrots and cook, stirring occasionally, for 2 minutes. Add the cayenne, salt, ground spices, sugar, and vinegar. Raise the heat to medium-high and bring to a boil. Reduce the heat to low, cover, and simmer, stirring occasionally, until the carrots are tender, 20 to 25 minutes. Spoon into clean jars and seal or refrigerate. Let the pickles cure for at least 3 days before serving.

Note: Mustard oil, a slightly bitter oil with an intense mustardy aroma, is a common ingredient in Indian pickles for its preserving qualities. Heating the oil to the smoking point allows the volatile mustard gas to escape, leaving the oil docile and fragrant. Mustard oil is sold in Indian markets, both for cooking and as a home remedy for rheumatic pains and as a hair tonic in India.

# DESSERTS

## AND BAKED GOODIES

EASY FUDGE BARS

ALMOND FUDGE

FRAGRANT FRESH COCONUT BARS

CHAYOTE HALVAH

PUMPKIN CHEWS

CREAMY SAFFRON YOGURT WITH ALMONDS

FUDGE BALLS IN ROSE-PERFUMED SYRUP

BASMATI RICE PUDDING

GLAZED GARBANZO-MILK CONFECTION

ROSE-SCENTED RICOTTA PATTIES IN CREAM

FROZEN MANGO "PIE"

FRAGRANT CREAM OF WHEAT BARS WITH YOGURT

COCONUT-STUFFED MINI-CRESCENTS

BAKED CARROT HALVAH

In India desserts are not characteristic of every meal; they are eaten in moderation as Westerners eat cakes and candies, between meals and on special occasions. They are also made to give as gifts as one would give gift baskets filled with goodies in America.

Feasting is part of special occasions — festivals, weddings or engagements, births, and family get-togethers. Many kinds of sweets and other foods are prepared during religious festivals as *prasaadam*, food offerings to the gods. After first being offered to the gods, these sweets are distributed to one and all in the family in small portions, to be consumed with respect and reverence. Diwali, the brightest feast, forms the grand finale of all the festivals. I have pleasant memories as a child of the prefestival arrangements that would begin several days in advance. The professional cooks hired by my parents would bring their own enormous utensils and set up a wood-burning stove in the backyard to make *boondi laddu*. Observing them was quite an education. My sister and I would watch them steadily stirring the sugar syrup as they fried tiny droplets of chick-pea flour. With great expertise, they combined the still hot mixture with the syrup, rolling it in seemingly heat-resistant hands into plump, round balls. We would pack large quantities of these and other sweets and snacks in baskets or trays lined with napkins and distribute them to friends and neighbors to convey affection, appreciation, and joy.

This chapter covers the whole spectrum of Indian regional sweets. With a simple dairy base, some flavoring agent, and nuts, vegetables, or grains, you will be able to make delectable fudge-like *barfi*, chewy *halvah*, old-fashioned puddings (*kheer*), and other delights.

To most Americans "fudge" implies chocolate, but in most dictionary definitions it's a more general type of confection that can be made in various flavors. Somewhere along the line it became the translation for the Indian names *barfi* and *halvah*. Barfis are subtly flavored bars, made of nuts or dairy ingredients slowly cooked down to a fudge-like consistency. Serve in little portions after a light meal.

Indian halvah is unique and delicious, with a texture softer than barfi (and also much softer and moister than the Turkish ground sesame candy of the same name). Grated vegetables or mashed fruits are stir-fried in desi ghee until they exude a wonderful fragrance, then further cooked down to a fragile and moist but chewy texture. You can serve them warm straight from the pan, or chilled. Halvah is an all-occasion pleaser; serve anytime as you would offer cake. Both barfi and halvah can be stored at room temperature; however, since they contain dairy products, just to be safe I suggest refrigerating them.

Other sweet delights include *kheer,* thick and creamy puddings of grain simmered in milk that are delicious served warm on a cold night or chilled on warmer days; *gulab jamun,* fried fudge balls made with dry milk that are fluffier and moister than the traditional ones made with khawa milk; and *ras malai,* poached ricotta cheese patties with the fragrance of rose petals.

If these authentic Indian desserts seem a little too exotic, you might begin with the Frozen Mango "Pie" on page 220, or the recipes grouped together under "Baked Goodies" at the end of the chapter. Although baked desserts are not common in India, in my years in America I have developed several adaptations of traditional Indian desserts that can be baked in the oven. With additional flour or other grains, they are a little less sweet than the originals, more like Western-style coffee cake.

A few ingredients that recur in the recipes may be unfamiliar to Western cooks. Liquid essences and extracts, especially rose and kewra (screwpine), are found in every Indian cook's pantry just like vanilla in the West. Many traditional desserts are based on khawa milk, sweet milk cooked down to a fudge-like consistency. Indian cooks buy khawa milk regularly as we buy fresh milk, but it is not easy to find here. I have given a recipe for those who want to make their own, but I have also found that the dry milk sold in American supermarkets is a fine substitute.

As a finishing touch, many Indian sweets are topped or marbled with nuts, or royally adorned with silver or gold leaf (*varak,* page 239). Also, many of these desserts and goodies are designed to be cut into bars, diamonds, or other bite-size pieces that are perfect to give as gifts. Nestle the individual pieces in colorful paper candy cups and set them in a box for a gift that is sure to please family and friends.

# EASY FUDGE BARS
## (*Barfi*)

Makes 18 1½-inch bars
Preparation time:
    10 minutes

½ cup water
½ cup sugar
½ cup melted vegetable
    shortening
Scant 3 cups low-fat
    dry milk
Seeds from 4 green
    cardamom pods,
    crushed
Toasted sliced almonds
    or hazelnuts, for
    garnish
2 4-inch squares silver
    leaf (*varak,* optional)

As the name suggests, this popular fudge is simple to make. Here I have substituted commercially available dry milk for the traditional khawa milk (see page 238), with pleasant results. In India barfi is either made or purchased from local candy store called "halwais" and then distributed to friends and neighbors to celebrate good news such as a baby's birth, a wedding engagement, or a graduation.

1. Bring the water, sugar, and shortening to a boil in a medium saucepan, stirring constantly. Remove from the heat. Gradually stir in the dry milk, mixing well so that no lumps form. Add the cardamom and mix well. The mixture should resemble a very soft and sticky dough; if it is still too wet, add 1 or 2 tablespoons dry milk.

2. Spread the fudge evenly in a serving plate to a thickness of 1/4 inch. Sprinkle the nuts on top and press them in lightly so the fudge is neatly studded with nuts. Garnish with the silver leaf. Refrigerate 1 to 2 hours, then cut into 1½-inch bars. Serve at room temperature on an attractive silver platter; store any leftovers in a covered container.

**Microwave:** Place the step 1 ingredients in a 2-quart microwavable bowl. Stir to dissolve the sugar. Cook at full power for 3 to 4 minutes. Remove from the oven and continue with step 2.

**Note:** The fudge can be prepared 1 week ahead and kept, covered, in the refrigerator. Let it return to room temperature before serving.

**Variation:** PISTACHIO CANDIES *(Peda)*

Omit the almonds or hazelnuts and varak. When the fudge is still warm and easy to handle, pinch off about a tablespoonful and roll it between your palms into a smooth 1-inch ball. Press a sliver of pistachio into the center of the ball. Place on a cookie sheet and repeat with the remaining fudge. Serve in colorful paper cups or pack in pretty boxes to present as gifts. Makes about 2 dozen.

# ALMOND FUDGE
## *(Badaam Barfi)*

Makes 28 1½-inch
   diamonds
Preparation time: 1 hour

1 cup raw whole
   almonds
¾ cup water
1 cup whipping cream
1 cup plus 2 tablespoons
   sugar
¼ cup (½ stick)
   unsalted butter
4 4-inch squares silver
   leaf *(varak),* for
   garnish

One of the favorite holidays in India is Diwali, the festival of lights, which falls in winter. Like Christmas, Hanukkah, Chinese New Year, and other religious festivals of this time of year, it's a time when houses are lit up with flickering oil lamps or colored bulbs, and doorways are decorated to welcome guests. Neighborhoods come alive with sounds of firecrackers. Merchants celebrate by revamping their shops and offering prayers to the goddess of wealth, Laxmi. Special foods and entertainment are main ingredients of the festival, and visitors are always welcomed with something sweet. Barfi, a sweet fudge made of almonds, is the favorite of all.

This barfi is easy to prepare any time of year and well worth the time. Pistachios or cashews may be substituted for the almonds. Serve it in small portions for mid-afternoon snacks accompanied by a savory snack such as Garbanzo Bean Spiral Crunchies (page 40).

1. Blanch the almonds and remove the skins. Place the nuts in a blender or a food processor with the water and ½ cup of the cream. Process until smooth.

2. Pour the almond puree into a heavy skillet or wok. Add the remaining cream and the sugar and bring to a boil. Reduce the heat to medium and cook, stirring occasionally, until the mixture is reduced to a thick paste and most of the liquid is absorbed, about 25 minutes.

3. Cut the butter in chunks and add it to the skillet. Cook, stirring constantly, until the mixture forms a lumpy paste too thick to stir, about 25 minutes (reduce the heat to low in the last 10 minutes to prevent scorching). Transfer to a serving plate. Spread evenly with the back of a spoon to ¼ inch thick. Garnish with silver leaf. Cool completely. Cut into 1½-inch diamonds.

**Note:** The barfi can be made 1 week ahead and kept, covered, in the refrigerator.

# FRAGRANT FRESH COCONUT BARS
## (Khobri Meethai)

Makes 30 2-inch squares
Preparation time:
    40 minutes

4 cups fresh grated
    coconut (from 1
    medium coconut)
3 cups sugar
1 cup whole milk
Seeds from 8 green
    cardamom pods,
    ground
10 raw almonds, coarsely
    chopped
1 teaspoon vanilla extract
1 teaspoon melted butter,
    for brushing

Known as *nariyal burfi* in northern India and *khobri meethai* in the south, this delectable dessert is featured at festive occasions or at teatime, teamed with hot spicy snacks. These bars are traditionally made colorful with the addition of red, yellow, or green food color. To make them appealing to children, I sometimes borrow an American technique — I dip the barfi diagonally into chocolate for a fun look and taste.

1. Combine the coconut and sugar in a large heavy skillet or Dutch oven. Stir on medium-high heat until the sugar dissolves, 3 to 4 minutes. Add the milk and cook uncovered, stirring occasionally, for 15 minutes.

2. Reduce the heat to medium and continue cooking and stirring until all the liquid is absorbed, another 12 to 15 minutes. Stir in the cardamom, almonds, and vanilla, mix well, and remove from the heat.

3. Brush a large platter or 2 dinner plates with butter. Pour the coconut mixture in the center. Spread evenly into a ¼-inch-thick layer. Cool and cut into 2-inch squares. Cover tightly if not serving immediately.

# CHAYOTE HALVAH
## (Sime Badnekai Halwa)

Makes 20 1-inch squares
Preparation time:
    25 minutes, plus
    chilling time

1 chayote squash
    (8 ounces)
3 tablespoons desi ghee
    or unsalted butter
½ cup sugar
¼ cup half-and-half
Seeds from 4 green
    cardamom pods,
    ground
4-inch square gold leaf
    (*varak*), optional

Chayote, a pear-shaped tropical vegetable of the squash family, is relatively unknown and under-appreciated in this country. If you have seen it in your supermarket and not known what to do with it, try this delectable halvah. The delicate flavor of the vegetable combines with cream, sugar, and cardamom to make a classic dessert with a beautiful light green hue. If you prefer a little more embellishment, decorate the top with elegant gold leaf.

1. Wash and wipe the chayote. Using a hand grater, grate one side down to the large, soft seed. Carefully remove and discard the seed, then continue grating. Measure 1 cup.

2. Combine the desi ghee and the grated chayote in a heavy 12-inch skillet or wok. Cook over medium-high heat, stirring constantly, until all the liquid

evaporates and the mixture is fragrant but not browned, about 4 minutes. Add the sugar and half-and-half and reduce the heat to medium. Cook, stirring constantly, until the mixture is reduced to a thick paste that pulls away from the sides of the pan and no liquid seeps out, 12 to 15 minutes.

3. Remove the pan from the heat. Stir in the cardamom. Pour the halvah onto a dinner plate. Spread into a ¼-inch thick cake. Garnish with gold leaf, if desired. Chill for 4 hours. Cut into 1-inch squares to serve.

**Variation:** To serve the halvah warm, spoon it from the pan into individual custard cups, then invert the cups onto serving plates. Sprinkle with crushed sliced almonds or garnish with torn gold leaf pieces, if desired.

# PUMPKIN CHEWS
## (Lal Bhopla Halwa)

Makes 16 1-inch squares
Preparation time:
  25 minutes

1 teaspoon plus 1 table
  spoon desi ghee or
  unsalted butter
¼ cup khawa milk
  (page 238), crumbled
  *or* dry milk
1 cup (packed) peeled
  and grated fresh
  pumpkin
¼ cup sweetened flaked
  coconut
¼ cup sugar
Seeds from 2 or 3 green
  cardamom pods,
  crushed
2 tablespoons chopped
  cashews

The squash family presents a bewildering variety of choices in shape and color. Indian cooks use them very creatively, including transforming these humble vegetables into elegant desserts like these chewy squares. The vibrantly colored shreds of pumpkin are first stir-fried in desi ghee until aromatic, and then cooked with khawa milk (or dry milk) and sugar. The squares are lightly sweetened, the way I always prefer my desserts.

1. If using khawa milk, heat 1 teaspoon ghee in a nonstick medium saucepan over moderate heat. Add the khawa milk and cook, stirring, until soft, about 4 minutes. Remove from the pan and set aside until needed. (If using dry milk, omit this step.)

2. Add the remaining 1 tablespoon desi ghee to the same pan. Stir in the pumpkin and stir-fry until aromatic, 5 to 6 minutes. Reduce the heat to low, cover, and cook until the pumpkin is just tender, about 4 minutes.

3. Add the coconut and sugar to the pan. Cook uncovered, stirring occasionally, until the mixture is reduced to a thick paste that pulls away from the sides of the pan and no liquid seeps out, about 10 minutes. Stir in the khawa milk or dry milk and cardamom. Mix well. Remove from the heat and spoon the mixture onto a plate. Spread evenly with the back of a spoon to ¼ inch thick. Sprinkle with cashews and press them in lightly. Cool and cut into 1-inch squares. Serve at room temperature on a silver platter.

**Variation:** Substitute banana squash or spaghetti squash for the pumpkin.

# Creamy Saffron Yogurt with Almonds
## (Shrikhand)

Makes 1¼ cups
Preparation time:
    10 minutes, plus
    draining and chilling
    time

4 cups plain yogurt,
    low-fat or homemade
    (page 241)
⅓ teaspoon saffron
    threads
¼ cup sour cream
½ cup sugar
Seeds from 4 green
    cardamom pods,
    ground
1 cup fresh fruit —
    orange segments,
    sliced peaches, or
    strawberries (optional)
Toasted sliced almonds
    (optional)

This luscious dessert, with the consistency of whipped cream cheese and the flavor of spices and fruit, is one of my favorites. (Also of my sister-in-law in Pune, Anjali Hiremath, who serves it along with chapatis as part of a luncheon menu.) In the days before refrigeration, the ingenious cooks of the state of Maharashtra in southwest India wrapped their plentiful leftover yogurt in cloth before it soured any further and left it to drain overnight. The yogurt "cheese" was then combined with cardamom, saffron, and sugar and served with seasonal fresh fruits. I add sour cream to give a thicker, creamier texture, but the weight-conscious can eliminate it.

1. Line a colander with a double thickness of cheesecloth. Spoon the yogurt into the cloth, gather the four corners, and tie with a string. Hang it above the sink to drain for 12 to 15 hours. (In summer, place it in a strainer set over a bowl in the refrigerator.)

2. Toast the saffron threads in a dry skillet until brittle. Transfer to a cutting board and crush with the back of a spoon or a rolling pin. Place in a small bowl or cup and add 2 tablespoons boiling water.

3. Transfer the yogurt cheese to a mixing bowl. Add the sour cream, sugar, and dissolved saffron and beat with a fork until fluffy, about 2 minutes. Fold in the cardamom. Refrigerate until well chilled, about 4 hours.

4. To serve, scoop into goblets or sundae dishes. Top with fruit and sprinkle with almonds.

**Note:** The shrikhand can be made 4 days ahead and kept in a tightly covered container in the refrigerator.

# FUDGE BALLS IN ROSE-PERFUMED SYRUP
## (Gulab Jamun)

Makes 35 medium fudge
balls (10 to 12 serv-
ings)
Preparation time:
35 minutes, plus 3
hours soaking time

*Syrup*
1½ cups sugar
2½ cups water
Seeds from 4 green
cardamom pods,
crushed
1 teaspoon rose essence
*or* 2 teaspoons rose
water

*Fudge Balls*
2 cups nonfat Carnation
dry milk
½ cup unbleached
all-purpose flour
1 teaspoon baking
powder
½ cup melted vegetable
shortening
½ cup whole or low-fat
milk
1 tablespoon water
Mild vegetable oil, for
frying

The name of this dessert combines the words for rose *(gulab)* and an Indian berry *(jamun)* that is deep crimson in color and shaped more or less like a date. These dainty sweets look like the fruit, and have the fragrance of a rose.

The ability to make this dish is one of the hallmarks of a good Indian cook, and when I first came to America I naturally wanted to continue to make it for my family. But one of the key ingredients, khawa milk (see page 238), was hard to obtain, and making my own was too time-consuming. So I tried various recipes including cream and even instant baking mix, trying to recreate the texture and flavor I remembered. Carnation dry milk turned out to be the best substitute. And while I am usually not a fan of vegetable shortening, it makes fudge balls that are even fluffier and moister than the original. Serve them at room temperature with the syrup spooned over the balls as the perfect ending for a special family meal. Of late, for fun I soak half of the jamuns in pineapple juice instead of the sugar syrup; it's not authentic, but delicious.

1. For the syrup, combine the sugar and water in a Dutch oven. Bring to a boil, stirring until the sugar dissolves. Reduce the heat to low and simmer uncovered for 15 minutes to reduce the volume slightly. Turn off the heat and stir in the cardamom and rose essence.

2. Combine the dry milk, flour, and baking powder in a large mixing bowl. Gradually pour in the melted shortening. Mix until crumbly. Add the milk and water and knead into a smooth, pliable dough. *To make the dough in the food processor:* Combine the dry ingredients and shortening in the work bowl and process until crumbly, about 30 seconds. With the machine running, gradually add the milk and water in a steady stream through the feed tube. Process until the dough begins to clean the sides of the bowl. Form the dough into a smooth ball. Set aside.

3. Fill a wok or skillet with oil to a depth of 2 inches and heat to 225 to 250°F. Pinch off portions of dough and roll between your hands into smooth balls about 1 inch in diameter. Slip about 8 to 10 balls carefully into the hot oil; after about 30 seconds, stir them gently so they brown evenly (do not stir them immediately or they may break). Fry until golden brown all over, 4 to 5 minutes in all. Remove with a slotted spoon, drain briefly over the oil, and add to the sugar syrup. Repeat with the remaining dough. (If the dough starts to

crumble or develop cracks while you are making the balls, return it to the food processor or bowl and mix again with 1 tablespoon water to restore the consistency.) Cool completely, cover and let the fudge balls soak for at least 3 hours before serving. Serve at room temperature or chilled.

**Microwave:** Combine the sugar and water in a 2½-quart microwavable bowl and stir to dissolve the sugar. Cook at full power for 15 minutes, stirring once. Remove from the oven. Stir in the cardamom and rose essence. Cool and continue with step 2.

# BASMATI RICE PUDDING
## (Kheer)

Serves 4
Preparation time:
    40 minutes

¼ cup raw basmati, jasmine, or other long-grain rice
1 quart whole or low-fat milk
½ cup sugar
2 tablespoons chopped pistachios
1 tablespoon chopped dates (optional)
⅛ teaspoon kewra essence *or* ¼ teaspoon rose essence *or* ½ teaspoon rose water

Rice pudding is popular in many cuisines, in many versions. The type most familiar to Westerners starts with rice cooked in water, which is then simmered or baked in a milk and egg custard. In the Indian style, the uncooked rice (preferably basmati or another fragrant variety) is cooked in milk until it acquires a thick consistency. I prefer to slowly simmer this pudding as I cook other dishes. It is delicious served warm or chilled. Serve as a midday snack or a satisfying dessert.

1. Wash the rice in several changes of water; drain well. Place the rice and milk in a large heavy skillet or Dutch oven. Bring to a boil on medium-high heat, stirring constantly. Reduce the heat to medium and cook uncovered, stirring occasionally, until the rice is tender, about 15 minutes.

2. Stir in the sugar, pistachios, and dates. Continue to simmer, stirring occasionally, until the pudding is thick and reduced by half, 20 to 25 minutes.

3. Remove the pudding from the heat and stir in the essence. Serve warm or chilled, in stemmed glasses.

**Note:** The rice pudding can be made 5 days ahead and kept, covered, in the refrigerator.

# GLAZED GARBANZO-MILK CONFECTION
## (Kabuli Chana ki Barfi)

Makes 25 1-inch squares
Preparation time:
  5 minutes, plus
  baking and chilling
  time

1 cup cooked garbanzo
  beans (homemade or
  canned), drained
⅔ cup confectioners'
  sugar
½ cup (½ recipe)
  khawa milk (page
  238), crumbled *or*
  ½ cup dry milk
⅛ teaspoon nutmeg
2 tablespoons chopped
  cashews
3 tablespoons melted
  desi ghee or unsalted
  butter
¼ cup whole or low-fat
  milk

These tender treats, which have become a coffee-break favorite among my American friends, are based on *laddu,* a traditional but very rich sweet from Maharashtra. The original consists of equal quantities of mashed garbanzo beans and desi ghee, stir-fried and then mixed with sugar syrup. This baked version is a snap to assemble if you have a can of garbanzo beans. The khawa milk or dry milk binds the ingredients and makes the resulting mixture silky soft.

1. Position a rack in the center of the oven and preheat to 350°F. Blend the garbanzo beans in a food processor until completely mashed, about 30 seconds. Transfer to a mixing bowl. Add the sugar and beat well with a spoon. Add the khawa milk and nutmeg and beat again until thoroughly mixed, about 1 minute. Sprinkle in the nuts and stir in the desi ghee and milk. Mix well and pour into an 8-inch square (2-quart) baking dish.

2. Bake until the top is glazed and light golden, 35 to 40 minutes. Cool completely. Chill for 2 to 4 hours before cutting into 2-inch squares.

**Note:** The confection can be made 4 days ahead and stored in the refrigerator.

# ROSE-SCENTED RICOTTA PATTIES IN CREAM
## (Ras Malai)

Serves 8 to 10
Preparation time:
40 minutes

1 cup plus 1 tablespoon
  sugar
2 cups water
¼ cup unbleached
  all-purpose flour
2 tablespoons plus 1
  teaspoon quick-cook-
  ing cream of wheat
1 container (15 ounces)
  ricotta cheese, whole
  milk or part skim
Seeds from 4 green
  cardamom pods
¼ tablespoon rose
  essence or ½ table-
  spoon rose water
½ cup whipping cream
Finely crushed toasted
  pistachios

No other state in India can pride itself on such a variety of sweets as West Bengal. *Ras malai,* which translates literally into "creamed syrup," consists of patties of paneer cheese slowly poached in sugar syrup and then soaked in cream sauce. I have had favorable results substituting ricotta cheese with a trace of cream of wheat added as a binder.

1. Combine 1 cup sugar and 2 cups water in a large skillet or Dutch oven. Bring to a boil, stirring constantly until the sugar is dissolved. Reduce the heat to low, cover, and simmer for 10 minutes.

2. Meanwhile, combine the flour, cream of wheat, and ricotta in a medium bowl. Mix thoroughly and knead for 8 to 10 minutes. Form the cheese mixture into 24 walnut-size (about 1 tablespoon) balls. Press 1 cardamom seed in the center of each ball and flatten into ¼-inch-thick patties.

3. Add 8 to 10 patties (or as many as will fit in a single layer) to the sugar syrup and raise the heat to medium-high. Simmer for 5 minutes, turn with a slotted spoon, and simmer the other side until firm, 3 to 4 minutes longer. Transfer the patties to a 3-quart serving casserole. Repeat with the remaining patties.

4. Boil the syrup until reduced to 1 cup. Stir in the rose water and pour the syrup over the patties.

5. Stir the remaining 1 tablespoon sugar into the whipping cream and bring to a boil. Remove from the heat and cool completely. Pour the cream sauce over the patties. Turn them gently with a slotted spoon so that cream incorporates with the syrup. Cover and chill overnight.

6. Place 2 ricotta patties per serving in custard cups or deep plates. Spoon cream sauce over the top. Sprinkle with pistachios and serve.

**Note:** The ras malai can be made 3 days ahead and kept, covered, in the refrigerator.

Be sure to knead the mixture thoroughly; the more you knead, the lighter and fluffier the patties will be. A whole cardamom seed in the center of each ball gives an intense burst of flavor; if you prefer a milder effect, grind the seeds and mix them with the ricotta.

219

# Frozen Mango "Pie"
## (Aam Ice Cream)

Serves 20
Preparation time:
    10 minutes, plus
    freezing time

1 package (8 ounces)
    cream cheese, soft-
    ened
1 container (8 ounces)
    whipped topping,
    thawed
¾ cup sugar
1 can (30 ounces)
    alphonso mango pulp
    (see page 239) or
    3¾ cups puree from
    5 ripe mangoes
    (3½ pounds)
Mango or peach slices,
    preferably fresh

I call this a "pie" rather than a frozen mousse or some other name because of the way it first came about. One of the first new recipes I learned after coming to America was apple pie. When that came out well, I started exploring other American pies. One was a cherry cheese pie. I baked a pastry shell, beat the cream cheese until fluffy, thawed the whipped topping, folded in the sugar, and only then discovered that I did not have enough cherry pie filling. Looking for a substitute, I stirred in a can of mango pulp. The result, I think, was magical. Now I skip the crust and simply freeze the filling as a sort of rich ice cream.

1. In a large mixing bowl, beat the cheese with an electric mixer until fluffy. Gradually beat in the whipped topping and sugar, then fold in the mango pulp. Pour the mixture into 10½ x 15-inch casserole. Freeze until set, 8 hours to overnight. To serve, slice into 2 x 3-inch pieces and place on a small plate. Serve with fresh mango slices on top.

**Note:** This dish can be freezer wrapped and frozen up to 3 months. If you prefer, you may soften it in the refrigerator for 15 minutes before serving.

# Baked Goodies

The following recipes represent a new twist on some old favorites. Oven baking is not traditional in India, but I have found that many Indian sweets like barfi and halvah are easily adapted to the convenience of baking. With the addition of flour or other grains, these baked versions come out with a texture and a level of sweetness more like coffee cake than candies or desserts. They are generally lower in fat as well, and they are quick and easy to assemble; all it takes is a few minutes to stir together the batter and pop it in the oven.

Serve these delicate, healthful sweet treats with afternoon tea or coffee. I can't think of a better accompaniment than one of the Indian-style spiced teas on page 226. Get out your best china, sit down, and enjoy a leisurely tea with family or friends.

# Fragrant Cream of Wheat Bars with Yogurt
## (Suji Halwa)

Makes 9 2-inch bars
Preparation time:
    10 minutes, plus 30
    minutes baking

¼ cup plain nonfat or
    low-fat yogurt
⅓ cup sugar
1 tablespoon melted
    desi ghee or unsalted
    butter
¼ cup whole or low-fat
    milk
½ cup quick-cooking
    cream of wheat
¼ cup water
Seeds from 2 green
    cardamom pods,
    crushed
½ teaspoon rose essence
    *or* 1 teaspoon rose
    water
¼ cup whipped cream
A few insecticide-free
    garden-fresh rose
    petals, for garnish
    (optional)

This recipe is based on a pudding, but baked to a different texture. A touch of yogurt adds a subtle flavor, and rose water provides a delicate fragrance. These moist and delicious bars are good by themselves either warm or at room temperature. For a palate-pleasing finale, dress up these bars with vanilla ice cream or whipped cream and rose petals or sliced banana.

1. Position a rack in the center of the oven and preheat to 350°F. Beat the yogurt until smooth with the back of a large spoon. Add the sugar and beat again until dissolved, about 2 minutes. Stir in the melted desi ghee, milk, cream of wheat, and water. Mix well until smooth. Stir in the cardamom and rose essence.

2. Pour the batter into an ungreased 6½-inch square glass baking dish. Bake until the top is light brown and a toothpick inserted in the middle comes out clean, about 30 minutes. Cool slightly, then cut into 2-inch bars. To serve, place 1 yogurt bar in a glass dessert bowl. Top with whipped cream and garnish with rose petals.

**Note:** The *halwa* can be prepared 5 days ahead and kept, uncut and covered, in the refrigerator. Let it return to room temperature and cut into bars just before serving.

# COCONUT-STUFFED MINI-CRESCENTS
## (*Karanji*)

Makes 10 crescents
Preparation time:
   10 minutes, plus 30
   minutes baking

½ cup quick cooking
   cream of wheat or fine
   semolina
¼ cup plus 1 tablespoon
   water
2 tablespoons mild
   vegetable oil
¼ teaspoon salt
½ cup unbleached
   all-purpose flour
Rice flour for dusting
Melted desi ghee or
   unsalted butter, for
   brushing

*Filling*
1 cup sweetened flaked
   coconut or fresh
   grated coconut
2 tablespoons sugar
   (if using fresh
   coconut)
1 tablespoon toasted
   sesame seeds
½ teaspoon ground
   cardamom
½ teaspoon ground
   nutmeg
❀
1 tablespoon milk,
   for sealing

I have reworked a traditionally rich recipe into a light version. Karanji is a popular snack from southwest India, crisp deep-fried pastries stuffed with coconut and infused with sweet spices. In India, this is served as an after-school snack for children, and during festivals. In the southwest, people gather on the beaches on Narli Purnima or "Coconut Day" and offer coconuts to the god of waters. Those residing away from the coast break coconuts to invoke the blessings of God. These crescents, made from the grated coconut meat, are part of the celebration. If you are looking for something different to serve at coffee, try this baked rendition. They will make a delightful Christmas gift when presented in an attractive napkin-lined basket. Type the recipe on a card and present it along with the freshly baked crescents.

1. Mix the cream of wheat and water in a medium bowl. Let stand for 10 minutes. Meanwhile, heat the oil on high heat until it ripples when pan is tilted, 2 minutes. Add to the cream of wheat mixture. Add the salt and flour. Knead into a smooth dough. Divide into 3 equal portions and roll each portion between your hands to form a smooth ball. Put on a plate.

2. Place a ball of dough on a work surface and roll it out to an 8-inch square, dusting with rice flour as necessary to keep it from sticking. Brush the top lightly with melted ghee using a pastry brush, and sprinkle a teaspoon of rice flour evenly over the surface. Roll out, brush, and flour the second portion of dough and lay it on top of the first. Repeat with the third piece of dough. Roll up the stack jelly roll fashion and cut crosswise with a sharp knife into 10 equal portions. Cover with a kitchen towel and set aside.

3. Combine the filling ingredients in a bowl and set aside. Position a rack in the center of the oven and preheat to 400°F.

4. Place a portion of the dough cut side up on a surface lightly dusted with rice flour. Flatten and roll into a 3-inch circle, dusting with rice flour as needed to keep it from sticking. Place 1 tablespoon of the filling mixture in the center. Brush half of the edge of the circle with milk. Fold the other side of the dough over the filling, forming a semicircle, and pinch the edges together. Trim the edge with a pastry wheel and repeat with the remaining dough and filling (dough trimmings can be re-rolled once into additional 3-inch circles). Place the filled pastries on a cookie sheet and cover with a kitchen towel as you work.

5. Brush all the crescents lightly with melted desi ghee or butter and bake until golden brown, about 30 minutes. Let cool before serving.

Note: The karanji can be stored in an airtight container up to 1 month.

# BAKED CARROT HALVAH
## (Gaajar Halwa)

Makes 15 1½-inch bars
Preparation time:
    15 minutes, plus 30
    minutes baking

¼ cup plus ½ table
    spoon melted unsalted
    butter or desi ghee
1 cup peeled and grated
    carrot (about 2 medi-
    um-size carrots)
¼ cup quick-cooking
    cream of wheat
¼ cup unbleached
    all-purpose flour
½ cup milk
1 tablespoon chopped
    raw cashews
½ cup sugar
¼ teaspoon vanilla
    extract
¼ teaspoon rose essence
    or ½ teaspoon rose
    water
Pinch of salt
⅛ teaspoon baking soda
2 4-inch squares silver
    leaf (varak), for gar-
    nish (optional)

In the classic tradition, carrot halvah would be cooked in milk until thickened; but try this simple new baked version. Carrot shreds are first stir-fried until aromatic, then mixed with the remaining ingredients and baked. The result is a brilliant, exotic cake. Serve at children's birthday parties. Adorn with silver leaf for an elegant yet easy garnish.

1. Position a rack in the center of the oven and preheat to 350°F. Heat ½ tablespoon butter in a heavy medium skillet on medium heat. Stir-fry the carrots until fragrant, 5 minutes.

2. Transfer the carrots to a medium mixing bowl. Add the remaining butter, cream of wheat, flour, milk, cashews, sugar, vanilla, rose water, salt, and soda and mix well. Pat the mixture into a 9-inch pie pan. Bake uncovered until the top is lightly brown, about 30 minutes. Let cool 10 minutes.

3. Garnish the top of the halvah with silver leaf, if desired. Cut into 1½-inch diamonds. Serve warm or at room temperature.

Note: The halvah can be made 1 week ahead and kept, covered, in the refrigerator. To rewarm, place in a cold oven, turn it to 200°F, and bake for 12 to 15 minutes.

# BEVERAGES

Fragrant Cardamom Tea (Masala Chah)

Kashmir Spiced Tea

Roasted Green Mango Thirst Quencher

Mango Nectar

Yogurt Mango Cooler

Sweetened Buttermilk Shake (Lassi)

Spicy Buttermilk Refresher

Fresh Mint Lemonade

Cranberry Cocktail

Mughal Milkshake on Sparkling Rocks

Bombay Juhu Cooler

Papaya Cooler

Pineapple Pistachio Cooler

In this chapter you will find an array of beverages to sip along with or after meals, as well as refreshing drinks for the "refrigerator raiders" between meals. Ranging from classics to new creations, they include milk-based and fruit drinks, and of course, the tea for which India is famous.

Some of the world's finest tea is grown in the Indian subcontinent, and varieties like Assam and Darjeeling are available in most supermarkets. A cup of strongly brewed tea made with milk is a morning ritual in India as cafe au lait is in France. This and other Indian teas are made by actually simmering the tea leaves in a pan with the water and milk, a very distinct method unlike the English and Chinese style of simply pouring boiling water over the leaves in a teapot and letting them steep. Cardamom and other sweet spices, fragrant herbs, and even almonds are added to tea in various regional specialties.

Assam tea, from the valley of the same name in the northeast of India, makes a bright reddish-brown brew, full-bodied with a malty taste. Darjeeling tea from the foothills of the majestic Himalaya mountains, has a delicate flavor of sweet muscatel wine and black currant. For a characteristically rich taste, use equal parts of each.

A common sight in Kashmir, the part of India closest to the ancient trade routes of central Asia, is the Russian-style metal teapot called a samovar. Red-cheeked children carry steaming samovars to their parents working in the fields. Boat owners balance them in their slender houseboats that cross the canals. Shopkeepers can be seen huddling around a samovar set on a charcoal fire, puffing on a *hookah* (water pipe) full of musky tobacco. Inside the samovar is one kind or another of strongly brewed and flavored tea, either a salty variety made with cream or a delicately flavored sweet tea called *kahava.* The latter is made with green tea and enriched with honey, spices, almonds, and saffron.

South Indians have a penchant for coffee. Coffee beans from the lush hills of Karnataka, my home state in India, are freshly roasted and ground to make filtered coffee. If you travel by train down south, you will find vendors who pour hot coffee from one cup into another from a height of 2 to 3 feet, creating a creamy froth without spilling a drop and with the coffee still steaming. Unbelievable as it may seem, they do as fine a job as any expensive espresso machine.

Crystal clear water and buttermilk top the list of cold beverages in India. Lassi is a buttermilk or yogurt drink that can be sweet or salty, enriched with mango puree or flavored with rose flower water. Try lassi or the Spicy Buttermilk Refresher before or during a meal to stimulate the appetite. Pistachio Cooler is an elegant variation suitable for a formal dinner party.

In the sun-drenched subcontinent, juice bars are popular. Fruit juices, punches and slushy shakes are consumed anytime. One style, the Mughal *sharbat,* is a mixed fruit drink that shares a root meaning with the English word sherbet. I have adapted it to American cranberries for a delicious drink that also blends well with gin or vodka as a cocktail. Sweet, ripe mango forms the base of a number of popular drinks; even the unripe green version, grilled, baked, or boiled until tender and mixed with water and cardamom, makes a refreshing thirst quencher. Keep some concentrate for Fresh Mint Lemonade on hand in the refrigerator for an instant drink to enjoy after games or workouts.

# FRAGRANT CARDAMOM TEA
## (Masala Chah)

Serves 4
Preparation time:
    8 minutes

2 cups whole milk
2 cups water
8 teaspoons sugar
Seeds from 4 green
    cardamom pods,
    ground
4 Assam or orange pekoe
    tea bags *or* 4 heaping
    teaspoons leaf tea

Hospitality has been a salient virtue of the Indians from ancient times. A guest is always offered at least a cup of tea, and the host will always make it special by adding a few pods of cardamom. For a change, a slice of fresh ginger will provide extra zip. Indian spiced coffee is prepared in a similar fashion by substituting coffee crystals for tea leaves.

1. Combine the milk, water, sugar, and cardamom in a medium saucepan. Bring to a boil on medium-high heat, stirring occasionally. Add the tea bags and boil, stirring gently, 1 to 2 minutes longer. Turn off the heat, cover, and let steep to a strong reddish-brown color, about 1 minute. Strain into a heated teapot. Pour into cups (I like to serve it in old-fashioned metal cups) and serve.

**Variation:** Use all Darjeeling tea, and leave out the milk. The lighter, more mellow taste of this tea comes through better without milk.

# KASHMIR SPICED TEA
## (Kahava)

Serves 3
Preparation time:
    9 minutes

3 cups water
3 teaspoons Chinese
    green leaf tea *or* 3 bags
    orange pekoe tea
2-inch stick cinnamon
4 whole cloves
Seeds from 3 green
    cardamom pods,
    lightly crushed
10 whole toasted
    almonds or pistachios,
    coarsely crushed *or* 2
    tablespoons Mughal
    Ready Mix (page 25)
¼ teaspoon saffron
    threads, lightly toasted
    and crushed
3 tablespoons honey

The Kashmiris drink large quantities of this sweet, fragrant tea to keep warm, and it's just as welcome on a winter afternoon in my northern California home. Chilled, it also makes a refreshing drink for summer.

1. Combine the water, tea leaves, cinnamon, cloves, cardamom, and almonds in a medium saucepan. Cover and bring to a boil on medium heat. Simmer 1 to 2 minutes. Remove from the heat. Cover and let steep to a light brown color, another minute or two, then strain into a warmed teapot. Add the saffron and honey. Stir to mix. Serve in mugs.

# ROASTED GREEN MANGO THIRST QUENCHER
## (Pannah)

Serves 6 to 8
Preparation time:
35 minutes, plus
chilling time

2 large green mangoes
(see page 238), 10
ounces each
3 cups chilled water
4 tablespoons light
brown sugar or honey
Pinch of salt
Seeds from 4 green
cardamom pods,
ground
Mint sprigs, for garnish

This is one of my favorite drinks. It's very popular in southwestern India, but unless you have been there you probably haven't tasted anything like it. The mango can also be baked or cooked in water until soft, but grilling really gives it a distinctive taste. Roasting a couple of green mangoes in the dying embers of the fire was a daily affair in summer in my mother-in-law's house in Pune. The mango pulp may be stored in the refrigerator up to a week.

1. Grill the whole mangoes over a gas flame (or bake at 350°F) until the skin is brownish in color and the mangoes are soft inside, about 30 minutes. Let cool enough to handle. Cut off the blossom end of each mango, remove the peel, and stand the mango on the cut end. Using a sharp knife, slice the mango lengthwise on either side of the flattish pit into 2 pieces about ½ inch thick. Cut the remaining fruit from the pit in chunks and cut into small dice; there should be 1½ cups in all.

2. Combine the mango pulp, water, and sugar in a blender and whirl until smooth. Add more sugar if needed, according to the tartness of the mango. Pour into a pitcher. Chill for 3 to 4 hours if time permits.

3. Just before serving, season to taste with salt. Stir in the cardamom. Whirl a few seconds until frothy and serve in tall glasses, garnished with mint.

# MANGO NECTAR
## *(Amrut Khand)*

Serves 4 to 6
Preparation time:
  35 minutes, plus
  chilling time

1 green mango, about
  10 ounces
3½ tablespoons sugar
  or to taste
¼ teaspoon saffron
  threads, dissolved in 2
  tablespoons hot water
3 cups chilled low-fat or
  whole milk
Freshly ground nutmeg

Here's another drink based on roasted green mango pulp, this time with milk, sugar, and a delicate sprinkling of saffron and nutmeg. Serve it for holiday meals or get-togethers.

1. Roast, peel, and chop the mango as directed in the previous recipe; it should yield ¾ cup of pulp. Combine with the sugar, saffron, and milk in a blender and process until smooth and thoroughly blended. Pour into a pitcher and chill. Serve in demitasse cups with a sprinkle of nutmeg.

# YOGURT MANGO COOLER
## *(Aam Lassi)*

Serves 6
Preparation time:
  5 minutes

2 large ripe mangoes *or*
  1½ cups canned
Alphonso mango pulp
  (see page 238)
¼ cup sour cream
1 cup plain nonfat or
  low-fat yogurt
2 tablespoons sugar
¼ cup water
2 or 3 ice cubes
Freshly ground nutmeg

Serve this luscious cooler made from the king of tropical fruits at cocktail time or as a light dessert after a spicy meal. For a fancier touch, thread mango slices and maraschino cherries alternately onto long kabab sticks and place them in the glasses or pretty copper cups and serve for a fireside get-together.

1. Peel and cut up the mangoes as directed on page 238. Combine in a blender with the sour cream, yogurt, sugar, and water. Blend until smooth and until the sugar dissolves. Drop in the ice cubes and blend until the ice is crushed and the mixture is frothy. Serve in tall slender glasses with a sprinkling of nutmeg.

# SWEETENED BUTTERMILK SHAKE
## (Lassi)

Serves 4
Preparation time:
   2 minutes

2½ cups cultured low-fat
   buttermilk
½ cup water
3 tablespoons sugar,
   or to taste
⅛ teaspoon salt
Seeds from 3 green
   cardamom pods,
   ground
1 teaspoon rose water

On the Indian subcontinent, buttermilk is considered a health food similar to yogurt. It has fewer calories than low-fat yogurt. Because of its tangy-tart flavor and easy availability, it is enjoyed all over tropical India. One of the favorite ways to serve it is in a sweetened drink called lassi. It's very refreshing on a hot day, and a popular drink in restaurants.

1. Combine the ingredients in a blender and whirl until the sugar dissolves and the drink is frothy. Divide about a cup of crushed ice among four tall 10- to 12-ounce glasses and pour in the lassi.

# SPICY BUTTERMILK REFRESHER
## (Mattha)

Serves 2 to 4
Preparation time:
   8 minutes

1 fresh hot green chile,
   stemmed and minced
2 teaspoons fresh grated
   ginger
1 tablespoon minced
   fresh cilantro or mint
   leaves
⅓ teaspoon ground
   roasted cumin
2½ cups cultured low-fat
   buttermilk
½ cup water
1 tablespoon sugar
⅛ teaspoon salt

This is served in India at marriage banquets, where its spicy flavor is a nice balance to the numerous sweets that are served. Minced spices and herbs are left floating in the drink for a more rustic appeal and to stimulate digestion. In place of the buttermilk and water, you could use 2 cups plain yogurt and 1 cup water.

1. Combine all the ingredients in a blender and whirl until the sugar dissolves and the cilantro is minced. Pour into mugs or glasses and serve.

Variation: I like to serve this cooler like a Mexican margarita, in a glass with a salted rim. Moisten the rim of the chilled glass with lemon or lime juice, then dip it in margarita salt (or kosher salt, which is nearly identical and cheaper). It adds a pleasing tang to this refresher.

# FRESH MINT LEMONADE
## (Limbu Sharbat)

Serves 4
Preparation time:
    10 minutes, plus 20
    minutes steeping

½ cup boiling water
¼ cup sugar
2 (1x½-inch) strips lemon
    or lime peel
1 tablespoon bruised
    fresh mint *or* 1 tea-
    spoon crushed dried
    mint
4 tablespoons lemon
    juice
2 cups chilled sparkling
    mineral water
Lemon or lime slices
Mint sprigs

Whenever you see a good price on lemons, make the lemon-mint concentrate in large quantity and refrigerate it; then you can add chilled sparkling water and serve this refresher in minutes. Use lemons or limes or a combination, depending on the season; limes tend to be at their most plentiful and cheapest and lemons at their most expensive in summer, and the reverse in winter.

1. Combine the boiling water, sugar, and lime peel in a small pan. Cook on medium-high heat for 5 minutes, stirring occasionally. Combine the mint and lemon juice in a bowl. Pour in the hot syrup, cover, and let stand about 20 minutes for the flavors to infuse. Strain into a pitcher.

2. Add the chilled sparkling water. Pour into cocktail glasses. Thread each lemon slice with a sprig of mint and float on top.

# CRANBERRY COCKTAIL
## (Phal Sharbat)

Serves 6 to 8
Preparation time:
    3 minutes, plus
    chilling time

½ cup chopped fresh
    pineapple (or use
    canned pineapple
    chunks with juices)
1 cup cranberry juice
2 cups orange juice
1 cup strongly brewed
    Kashmir Spiced Tea
    (page 226), chilled
½ cup ginger ale
1 cup club soda
Fresh orange slices
Fresh lemon slices
Mint leaves

The delicate flavor of Kashmir Spiced Tea gives a subtle dimension to what is otherwise a simple mixed fruit punch. Pureed fresh pineapple lends body and acts as a natural sweetener. This punch is ideal for graduations or showers. Serve it with a tray of spicy hors d'oeuvre. You can substitute a can of jellied cranberry sauce for the juice; beat the sauce until smooth before stirring it into the other ingredients.

1. In a blender or food processor, process the pineapple to a smooth puree. Transfer to a 2-quart punch bowl. Add the cranberry and orange juice and tea and stir to blend. Cover and chill 2 to 4 hours.

2. Just before serving, carefully pour in the ginger ale and soda. Float orange and lemon slices and mint leaves in the punch. Let your guests ladle it into punch cups or wide-mouth glasses.

**Variation:** Add gin or vodka for those who favor it.

# MUGHAL MILKSHAKE ON SPARKLING ROCKS
## (Mughlai Doodh)

**Serves 6 to 8**
**Preparation time:**
  **5 minutes**

1 or 2 4-inch squares
  silver or gold leaf
  (*varak*)
2 cups whole or low-fat
  milk, chilled
2 medium-size ripe
  bananas, peeled and
  mashed
2 tablespoons khawa
  milk (page 238), crum-
  bled
1 cup chopped fresh
  mango or pineapple
4 tablespoons sugar or
  to taste

When I am entertaining, creative presentation is important to me. Sparkling ice cubes give extra visual appeal to this rich Mughal-style cooler, or to any fruit punch for that matter. You can make similar ice cubes with fresh mint leaves or rose petals.

1. *Several hours ahead of serving time,* fill an ice cube tray with water and place in the freezer. As the ice cubes are setting, cut the varak into 1-inch pieces and place them on individual ice cubes. Allow to freeze completely.

2. Combine the milk, banana, khawa milk, mango or pineapple, and sugar in a blender and process until smooth and thoroughly blended. Serve in goblets with one or two of the sparkling ice cubes in each glass.

# BOMBAY JUHU COOLER
## (Phal Aahaar)

**Serves 4**
**Preparation time:**
  **8 minutes, plus**
  **chilling time**

2 large ripe mangoes
  (or 1½ cups canned
  mango pulp, see page
  239)
½ cup plain nonfat or
  low-fat yogurt or fresh
  coconut milk (page
  236)
1 cup pineapple juice
1 cup orange juice
2 teaspoons lemon juice
Seeds from 5 green car-
  damom pods, ground
Fresh pineapple slices

My young sons always ask me to carry large flasks of this cooler (named after Bombay's famous Juhu beach) for their friends and coaches during their Little League baseball practices. For variety I freeze the cooler into a slush in an ice cream maker and serve it as a "slurpy."

1. Peel and cut up the mangoes (see page 238). Measure 2 cups of cubes. Set aside some of the prettiest ones for garnish.

2. Combine the remaining mango chunks with the yogurt, pineapple juice, orange juice, lemon juice, and cardamom in a blender and whirl until smooth. Pour into a pitcher or punch bowl and chill 4 to 6 hours. To serve, ladle the cooler into individual glasses or punch cups and garnish with mango chunks and pineapple slices.

# PAPAYA COOLER
## (Khatta Meetha Papita Lassi)

Serves 2
Preparation time:
    5 minutes

1 cup peeled, seeded,
    and chopped ripe
    papaya (about one 12-
    ounce papaya)
1 cup plain nonfat or
    low-fat yogurt
½ cup water
1 tablespoon fresh lime
    juice
¼ teaspoon salt
2 tablespoons sugar
    or honey
Seeds from 2 green car-
    damom pods, ground
2 ice cubes
Papaya slices and lime
    twists, for garnish

Papaya is referred to as a "poor man's fruit" in India since it is available all year in abundance. It is loaded with vitamins A and C, helps add bulk to the diet, and aids in digestion. This cooler makes a refreshing drink after morning workouts or games. You may also serve it on leisurely afternoon with snacks. For a spicy-hot flavor use freshly ground pepper in place of the cardamom.

1. Combine the papaya, yogurt, water, lime juice, salt, sugar, and cardamom in a blender and blend until smooth and the sugar is dissolved. Drop in the ice cubes and blend until the ice is crushed. Pour into two 10-ounce glasses and garnish with papaya slices and lime twists.

# PINEAPPLE PISTACHIO COOLER
## (Pista Thandai)

Serves 2 to 3
Preparation time:
    5 minutes

¼ cup shelled toasted
    pistachios
¼ cup sour cream
½ cup yogurt
2 tablespoons sugar
2 cups pineapple juice
    (fresh or canned)

As this is the last recipe in the book, it's a good time to thank my husband, who has provided critical commentary on all the recipes in this book as I have developed, tested, and modified them. He approved of this dynamic combination the very first time. Pistachios, pineapple, and a bit of sour cream add up to a rich-tasting, elegant, flavorful drink that is also quick and easy to prepare. Serve in attractive silver cups for holiday meals for family and friends. You can easily expand the recipe to a group of any size.

1. Grind the pistachios to a fine powder in a blender. Add the remaining ingredients and whirl until thoroughly mixed and frothy. Serve in old-fashioned glasses.

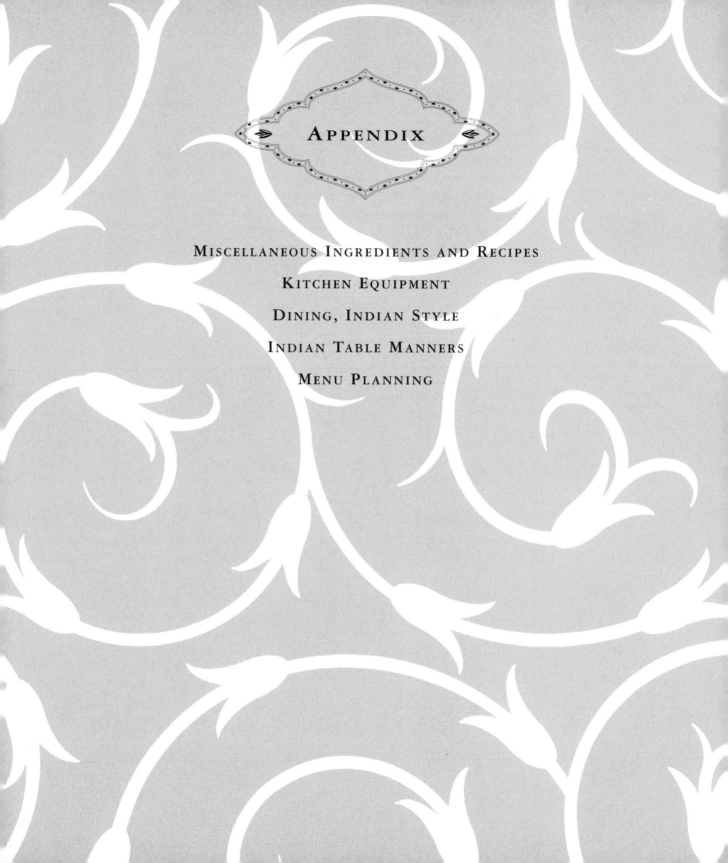

# APPENDIX

MISCELLANEOUS INGREDIENTS AND RECIPES

KITCHEN EQUIPMENT

DINING, INDIAN STYLE

INDIAN TABLE MANNERS

MENU PLANNING

# MISCELLANEOUS INGREDIENTS AND RECIPES

Included here are notes on some of the basic ingredients that recur in the recipes in this book. Some, like rice, legumes, and Indian cheese (paneer) are discussed in their respective chapters. For information on spices and herbs, see The Art of Seasoning, page 12.

## CLARIFIED BUTTER (*Desi Ghee*)

There is nothing like the wonderful aroma of a pot of desi ghee simmering on the stove. Since ancient times, Indian cooks have been turning the cream from their cows into butter. However, fresh butter would go rancid quickly in the tropical weather. Looking for ways to preserve it, someone discovered that when butter melted and separated, the pure butterfat would keep much longer if the water and milk solids were removed — and desi ghee was born. Not only does it keep better than fresh butter, but it has its own distinctive, sweetish-nutty flavor, which enhances stews, vegetables, rice dishes, and sweetmeats. Because of its relatively high smoking point (375°F), desi ghee can be used for sauteing and stir-frying.

Used by itself, *ghee* means clarified butter, but it has several other modified meanings. Three are basically synonymous: desi ghee, khare ghee, and usli ghee. *Desi* means pure from the country, *khare* is real in the Marathi language, and *usli* is Hindi for genuine. All three refer to real clarified butter, as opposed to *vanaspati ghee,* which is vegetable shortening.

The recipe given here starts with 1 pound of butter, but it is easily doubled or tripled. Desi ghee keeps well, so you might as well make it in a larger quantity.

## DESI GHEE

Makes 1⅔ cups
Preparation time: 30 minutes

1 pound butter (preferably unsalted)

1. Melt the butter in a large heavy saucepan over medium heat, stirring constantly. (Be sure to use a large pot, as the butter will spatter while simmering.) It will produce numerous bubbles initially, which gradually disappear. Simmer uncovered until the milk solids begin to settle to the bottom and turn lightly brown, about 25 minutes (longer if using a larger amount of butter). Turn off the heat while the desi ghee is still yellowish; it will continue to cook for 5 or 6 minutes from the retained heat. Cool completely. If by chance your desi ghee browns, you may still safely use it; the flavor will be more intense, with more of a burnt-caramel aroma.

2. Strain the desi ghee through a fine sieve or cheesecloth into a clean jar. (My sister saves the solids from the sieve and adds them to her chapati dough, making it especially soft and pliable.) Store at room temperature for up to 3 months in a cool dry place, or up to 6 months in the refrigerator, or freeze indefinitely.

**Microwave:** Place ½ pound (2 sticks) sweet butter in a 3-quart microwave-safe dish. Cover and cook at full power for 10 minutes. Remove from the oven, uncover, and set aside. It will continue to cook for few minutes from the retained heat, achieving a beautiful golden hue with the authentic nutty flavor. Strain and store as above.

# FLAVORED DESI GHEE

For added flavor, my mother adds various seasonings to the butter while it is clarifying: whole pods of star anise, or a sprig of kari leaves, or some drumstick leaves from the backyard (long skinny sticks that are cooked in curry sauce and then gnawed for their meaty bite), or betel leaves (this leaf is chewed after meals in India, and is available sporadically in Indian markets). Here are some other options, using familiar herbs and spices from the supermarket. Add one of these (or select your favorite spices or herbs) to 1 pound butter in the last 5 minutes of cooking for a delicate perfume. You can brush the flavored desi ghee on barbecued foods, toast, muffins, or bagels, or drizzle it on uppama, idli, dosa, rice, or flatbreads.

- ½ to 1 teaspoon black or white peppercorns, lightly crushed
- ½ to 1 teaspoon cumin seeds, lightly crushed
- 2-inch piece cinnamon stick
- ½ cup fresh basil leaves, bruised
- ½ cup fresh oregano, coarsely chopped
- 1½ tablespoons minced ginger
- 1 tablespoon minced garlic or shallots
- 2 fresh hot green chiles, stemmed and minced

# COCONUT AND COCONUT MILK

Coconut is one of the most important staples in southern India. Grated fresh coconut is used as a flavoring and garnish, and the rich milk extracted from the meat by grating it and boiling it with water is used in curry sauces and certain rice dishes. Both the meat and the milk are available in prepared form, but for an incomparable flavor and texture, you should try preparing them yourself from fresh coconuts.

Look for a coconut that is uncracked and without mold near the eyes. To open a coconut, first crack it in the center with a hammer. (Some instructions tell you to puncture one of the three spots near the stem end, but this is not done in India, because the coconut is identified with the head of Lord Shiva, and the pattern of the three spots suggests his eyes. Nor do I recommend another often-suggested technique for opening a coconut, baking it in the oven until it cracks; the meat will lose moisture and will have an oily, burnt odor.)

With a bowl underneath the coconut, drain the clear liquid out of the middle (this is not coconut milk) and smell and taste it; if it has a sweet flavor, the coconut is fresh, but if it tastes oily or rancid, discard the coconut and try another one. You can save the coconut water if you like to use in drinks, or for cooking rice or dals, or for making dough. Break the coconut in half. If you have an Indian, Southeast Asian, or Hawaiian style grater, you simply grate the meat out of the inside of each half. Otherwise, loosen the meat from the shell with a sharp paring knife (or freeze and defrost the halves, after which the meat pops out easily), peel off the brown skin, and grate the meat with a cheese grater or in a food processor. The meat is now ready to be used as grated coconut, or made into coconut milk (see recipe below).

For the times when it is not convenient to grate your own coconut or make your own coconut milk, the frozen grated coconut and canned coconut milk from Thailand make fine substitutes. For thick coconut milk, shake the can and use as is; for a thinner consistency, remove some of the cream or dilute with half as much water.

# COCONUT MILK *(Narial Doodh)*

Makes 2 cups
Preparation time: 20 minutes

2 cups water
4 cups freshly grated coconut (1 medium coconut)

Bring the water to a boil. Add the coconut and cook 2 minutes. Remove from the heat and let stand, covered, for 10 minutes. Blend in a food processor or blender until very thick. Strain through a fine strainer, squeezing the residue as much as possible to get out all the milk. Use the milk immediately or cover and store it in the refrigerator for up to 3 days; in the freezer coconut milk will keep indefinitely. Discard the residue.

**Note:** If you prefer a thinner coconut milk, add ¼ cup of boiling water to the coconut residue and squeeze it again. Use separately, or add to the regular coconut milk above.

## ESSENCE *(Ruh)*

Essences are concentrated liquid flavorings extracted from various plant products, including flowers, bark, and wood by steam distillation. Two in particular are commonly used in Indian cooking, as vanilla extract is in the West. Rose *(gulab)* essence is made from rose petals, and captures the familiar fragrance of the flower. Less familiar to Westerners, but very popular in India, is screwpine *(kewra)* essence, made from the long, leathery leaves of an Asian shrub with an intense sweet fragrance. Rose and kewra essences are sold in small bottles in Indian and Middle Eastern markets, and are used to aromatize pilafs, desserts, and beverages. They are also sold in more diluted form as rose water and kewra water. Either water or essence can be used in the recipes; use twice as much water as essence for the same intensity of flavor.

## FLOUR

In addition to wheat flours used in making breads (see page 78), two other flours have specialized uses in Indian cooking. Chick-pea flour *(besan)* is made by finely grinding yellow chick peas *(chana dal),* not the larger chick pea or garbanzo. Its distinctive nutty taste blends well into a wide range of Indian dishes. High in protein but low in gluten (the protein that gives wheat-flour doughs their elasticity), it is used in steamed breads, fritter batters, and sweets, and as a thickener in gravies. I have used chick-pea flour in moderation in my recipes; my grandmother warned me to use it sparingly, since it is relatively hard to digest. It keeps well in a cool place; for longer storage, refrigerate it in a tightly covered container.

Rice flour *(chawal ka atta),* sometimes called rice powder, is a pure white flour milled from long-grain rice. It is rich in starch but has no gluten. A small amount added to breads, crepes, fritters, and pastries makes them crisper. Rice flour is also used to thicken sauces. Available in gourmet and Indian markets. Chinese markets sell two types of rice flour, long-grain and glutinous; the former can be used in the recipes here, but not the latter.

## HOT CHILE OIL *(Theeka Tel)*

Aromatic and flavorful, this oil will add zing to fresh salads or chaats. You may also use it in place of other oils when making vinaigrettes, sauces, or marinades. This recipe produces a mildly flavored oil. If you prefer intense heat, add extra peppers. If you want a more subtle flavor, dilute with more oil.

**Makes ½ cup**
**Preparation time: 15 minutes, plus 1 hour resting time**

> ½ cup mild vegetable or peanut oil
> ½ teaspoon cumin seeds
> 6 dried red chiles, stemmed and broken

1. Heat the oil in a small saucepan over medium heat until moderately hot, about 5 minutes. Add the cumin seeds and chiles. Simmer for 6 to 8 minutes, stirring occasionally, until the chiles are fried crisp and darken. Turn off the heat, cover, and set aside for 1 hour.

2. Strain the oil into a small bottle with a narrow neck. (Minimizing the exposure to air will help keep the oil tasting fresh.) Store at cool room temperature away from direct light.

# INDIAN CONDENSED MILK (*Khawa*)

Khawa milk is used mainly in Indian desserts and some Mughal dishes. This fudge-like soft dough is made by cooking milk slowly until 85 percent of its water content evaporates. Although it is not traditional, I use half-and-half to make khawa milk; the yield is greater than with whole milk, and it takes less time. A deep, wide-mouthed pan (such as the popular woklike "stir-fry pans") is ideal for this recipe, but any large skillet or scrupulously clean wok will do.

Makes 1 cup
Preparation time: 40 minutes

   1 quart half-and-half

1. Bring the half-and-half to a boil in a large skillet or wok. Reduce the heat to medium-high and continue to cook, stirring and scraping the pan occasionally with a wide wooden spatula, for 20 minutes.

2. As the cream starts to thicken, reduce the heat to medium and stir constantly to prevent scorching. Cook until the khawa milk is thick and starts to pull away from the sides of pan, about 15 minutes. Remove the pan from the heat. As it cools the khawa milk will firm to a fudge-like consistency. If not using the khawa milk immediately, cover and refrigerate it for up to 1 month, or freeze it for up to 6 months.

# MANGOES (*Aam*)

India is a heaven for mangoes, and this tropical fruit is popular both green and ripe. Green mangoes, picked at an early stage so they are firm and tart rather than soft and sweet, are used in both savory dishes and drinks. Ripe mangoes give their incomparable flavor to beverages and desserts.

True green mangoes can be hard to find in North America. However, most of the "ripe" mangoes are picked at what greengrocers call the "green-ripe" stage, when they have matured enough that they will ripen to a yellow or red skin and sweet flesh. So when I call for a green mango in a recipe, I mean the greenest, least ripe in a batch of one of the common supermarket varieties. To select a green mango, choose the greenest fruit you can find; if they are all turning yellow, ask the grocer if there are some greener ones back in the storeroom. The flesh should be hard, and the fruit should feel heavy for its size. Use as soon as possible, or it will ripen within a few days.

For sweet dishes and beverages like mango lassi, you want to go to the other end of the spectrum for the sweetest, ripest mangoes you can find. Look for yellow skin with a reddish-orange blush at the blossom end. The flesh should still be firm, but should give slightly to gentle pressure. The aroma should be pleasant and sweet; a strong smell indicates over-ripeness. Don't buy those that are bruised, over-ripe or with soft spots. For the best flavor, let mangoes ripen a few more days at room temperature, away from direct sunlight. A fully ripe mango will keep wrapped in plastic for up to four days in the refrigerator.

To prepare a mango for use in recipes (or for eating reasonably elegantly), wash it well and dry it. Cut off the blossom end. Stand the unpeeled mango on the cut end, and using a sharp knife, slice the mango lengthwise, on either side of the flattish pit, into two pieces about ½ inch thick. Score the flesh of each half, making a fine crisscross pattern. Turn each half inside out and scoop or cut the flesh away from the skin. Peel the remaining skin from the pit and cut the flesh into chunks, avoiding the hairy fibers right around the pit. Alternately, the supermarket mango flesh can be first pureed and then strained to rid it of fibers.

Another alternative for many dishes is canned mango from India. Normally I prefer fresh produce over canned, but I have never tasted a fresh mango in this country that matches the nectarine-pineapple-rose flavor of the finest Indian variety, the brilliant orange-red, fiber-free Alphonso. Fresh Alphonso mangoes are not available in the West, but canned Alphonso mango pulp is imported. Ask for Ratna or Amrit brand names at Indian markets.

# OIL *(Tel)*

In addition to ghee, Indian cooking uses various vegetable oils. Some are distinctively flavored, and give a characteristic aroma and taste to the foods of a particular region: peanut in the west, sesame and coconut in the south, mustard in the east, and occasionally walnut and almond oils in the north. Otherwise, the preference is for mild-tasting oils such as sunflower and safflower. Unless a specific oil is mentioned in the recipes, use one of these milder oils. I generally use canola oil.

# PEANUTS, CRUSHED ROASTED *(Danyache Koot)*

This is a staple in my kitchen, as it is all over Maharashtra state in India. Crushed peanuts are used in stir-fry dishes, stuffed vegetables, raitas, and pearl tapioca pilaf. I make them regularly in small batches. Simply put 1 cup of roasted salted or unsalted peanuts in a mini-blender, blender, or food processor and pulse until coarsely crushed, about 15 to 20 seconds. Store in an airtight glass jar in a cool dry place for up to 2 months.

# SALT *(Namak)*

I have used regular table salt in testing the recipes. Feel free to use kosher salt or sea salt if you prefer. The only special salt I use is *kala namak* or black salt, and only for a specific dish (see *chaat masala*, page 21). Generally I use salt moderately in cooking, so adjust the proportions to taste.

# SILVER AND GOLD LEAVES *(Varak)*

Fragile and delicate as butterfly wings, these thin sheets of silver or gold foil are especially associated with Mughal cooking. Varak is made by placing minute silver pellets between sheets of tissue paper, which is then enclosed in a leather pouch and hammered to form feather-thin foil. Flavorless, odorless, and perfectly edible, it is used as a garnish, especially on sweets. Relatively inexpensive silver and moderately priced gold leaves are available at gourmet and Indian markets. It's a little tricky to use at first, but gets easier with practice. The leaves are sold in packages of a dozen, each between two tissue papers. Holding one of these sets in your open palm, peel off the top layer of paper to expose the varak, then invert your hand onto the food and carefully press the paper against the surface. The varak should stick to the food as you peel away the paper.

# SPROUTS (*Matki*)

Pea, bean, and lentil sprouts offer an attractive alternative to the dry legumes and are an important part of the diet in India. Sprouting transforms the dry legumes (also certain spices and grain seeds) into an edible form with a distinctive nutty flavor and crisp texture, and turns the starches into more digestible sugars. My aunt Kusum, in India, often tops fresh sprouts with finely chopped onion, tomato, cilantro, a drizzle of sesame oil and a sprinkle of *kala masala* (page 23) to serve as a side dish. Try them raw in salads, chaats, and vegetables. You can also stir them into soups for extra crunch or sprinkle them over pilafs. Mung beans, chick peas, lentils, fenugreek seeds, sunflower seeds, and whole wheat berries are all suited for sprouting. It is fairly easy to grow sprouts at home and economical too.

Makes 2 to 3 cups
Preparation time: 5 minutes, plus soaking and
    sprouting time

½ cup dried beans

1. Pick the beans clean. Wash in several changes of water. Add enough water to cover by at least 2 inches and soak 20 to 24 hours. Drain and rinse. Transfer into a colander or wicker basket lined with cheesecloth. Cover loosely with a damp muslin or cheesecloth. Place in a warm dark place.

2. Sprinkle some water on the cheesecloth once or twice a day, or as needed to keep the beans moist. The beans will start to sprout within 2 to 3 days (if the temperature is cool, it may take a little longer).

3. Sprouts are mature when the tails are ⅓ to ½ inch long. If you need longer sprouts keep for 1 more day. Discard any beans that have not sprouted. Store in a covered container up to 7 days in the refrigerator. In order to enjoy the maximum nutritional value, use within 2 days.

# TAMARIND (*Imli*)

Tamarind is the fruit of a tropical tree that grows in most parts of India, also known as Indian date. The fruit looks like a large legume seed pod, with a fragile, grayish-brown shell enclosing the seeds and a moist reddish-brown pulp. Although it contains sugar, the pulp is intensely sour and imparts piquancy to curries, chutneys, and relishes. Tamarind is used mainly in southern Indian cooking, and its cooling effect on the body makes it a perfect hot weather flavoring. It is available commercially peeled and pitted in compressed blocks of 1 pound or less, or as a liquid tamarind concentrate in gourmet and Indian markets. To use the compressed form, see page 39.

# YOGURT (*Dahi*)

Yogurt is one of the ingredients common to all regions of India, and its tangy flavor is savored by children and adults alike. This dairy product always accompanies an Indian meal in one form or another — mixed with vegetables and spices as a raita, in a hot or cold soup, or most commonly, just a little plain yogurt spooned over rice to soothe the palate and stomach at the end of a spicy meal. As youngsters, when my brother Sunil and I requested dessert, mother would quickly sprinkle some sugar and saffron threads on fresh yogurt and serve us the "glamorous" mousselike treat. Now, my sons are the beneficiaries of the same.

The recipes in this book will work with the plain nonfat or low-fat commercial yogurt sold in nearly every supermarket in America. Because American yogurt is less rich than Indian, I sometimes add some sour cream to my raitas to approximate the sweeter flavor and creamier texture of the latter. However, most commercial yogurt is still slightly sour to my taste, and contains thickeners like gelatin, pectin, or tapioca that may increase shelf life but disguise its natural delicate flavor. All in all, I prefer and recommend homemade yogurt, which I make twice a week.

The technique of making fresh yogurt is very simple, and it does not require any special utensils. All you need is fresh milk — whole, low-fat, or nonfat — and a starter of commercial plain yogurt (look for the words "live culture" on the label). The amount of fat determines not just the calorie content, but also the flavor and texture: whole milk makes firm, sweet yogurt, low-fat milk yields yogurt that is a little more liquid but still quite thick, and nonfat produces the most liquid consistency. For an especially rich flavor and solid consistency, use 1 part half-and-half to 3 parts whole milk. If you make your own yogurt regularly, save a little of each batch as a starter for the next.

Temperature control is the key to all stages of making yogurt. First the milk must be heated to the boiling point, then cooled to 110° to 115°F before the starter is added. If the milk is too hot, the bacteria will die; if it is too cold, the bacteria will take a longer time to multiply, and may not grow at all. After the starter is added, the yogurt needs to sit in a warm place without being disturbed. I usually use my oven, either cooled for about 15 minutes after I have finished baking cookies or cakes, or preheated for 10 minutes if it has not been on. A gas pilot light or the oven light bulb helps maintain a regular temperature while the yogurt sets, anywhere from 6 to 12 hours.

Ceramic bowls are good for setting yogurt, but any nonreactive container (heatproof glass like Pyrex or Corning Ware or even stainless steel) is a good choice. Smaller cups or jars can be used for convenience, for single servings (see variation). Cover with a dinner plate or a lid, but do not use airtight covers because the bacteria need to breathe.

# HOMEMADE YOGURT

Makes 5 cups
Cooking time: 12 minutes, plus setting time

　4 cups milk
　2 tablespoons plain yogurt, homemade or store-bought

1. Bring the milk to a boil on medium-high heat in a heavy medium saucepan. Remove from the heat and let the milk cool to 110° to 115°F. (A thin layer of clotted cream forms at the top. You may just leave it as is or remove it with a slotted spoon for another use.) Transfer the milk into a ceramic bowl or other nonreactive container.

2. Place the yogurt in a cup and add 2 or 3 tablespoons of the warmed milk. Stir to blend and pour back into the milk. Cover the container loosely and set in a warm place (70° to 100°F) until the texture resembles a flan or cheesecake, anywhere from 6 to 12 hours depending on the temperature and your starter.

3. When the yogurt has set and watery whey begins to collect at the top, cover and refrigerate. You can skim off the whey and use it in lassi or stir it into yogurt while serving. Homemade yogurt is best used within 4 days, although it keeps well for up to 7 days.

**Variation:** After mixing the milk and yogurt starter, pour the mixture into individual custard cups and place the cups in a deep pot or roasting pan. Pour very hot tap water into the pot to equal the level of the milk in the cups. Set the pan in a warm place. In small containers, the fermentation usually takes less time, 4 to 5 hours.

241

# KITCHEN EQUIPMENT

Indian cooking does not require an elaborate collection of equipment. Even the kitchen of an occasional cook is likely to contain the cookware to prepare all the dishes in this book.

## COOKWARE

In the traditional Indian kitchen, the most basic utensils are a round-bottomed pan called a *kadai,* a griddle *(tava),* and a rolling pin *(belan).* The *kadai* is similar to a Chinese wok, although it is deeper and smaller in diameter than a typical wok. It is used for frying, sauteing, braising, and just about all other forms of stove-top cooking. Like a wok, it is an ideal pan for deep-frying; its rounded bottom provides a large frying area with a relatively small amount of oil. A wok or a deep skillet makes a fine substitute.

The *tava* is a round, single-burner iron griddle used in toasting spices and flatbreads. It is smooth with a concave surface, so a little oil drizzled around the edges of a chapati will slowly drift down into the center. A cast iron griddle or a heavy skillet makes a good substitute.

Like other cast iron implements, a *kadai* or *tava* should be seasoned before use. To season, wash with a dishwashing liquid and wipe it dry. Rub the surface with a few drops of vegetable oil. Heat on medium heat until hot, about 6 minutes. Remove from the heat. Sprinkle with one tablespoon each salt and whole wheat flour. When the pan is cool enough to handle, wipe the salt mixture around the interior surface with a paper towel. Wash and dry thoroughly. Heat for five minutes over medium heat. Now the pan is ready to use.

Other utensils frequently mentioned in this book include heavy-bottomed saucepans, in small (1½ to 2 quarts capacity), medium (2 to 3 quarts), and large (5 quarts or more) sizes, and skillets in a couple of diameters, one small (6 to 8 inches) for toasting spices and heating small amounts of oil, another 10 to 12 inches for sauteing larger quantities. Copper-clad stainless steel (Revere, Farberware), nonstick and anodized surfaces like Magnalite and Circulon are all good choices, but whatever you use, look for pans with a heavy bottom, which helps in distributing the heat evenly.

## MICROWAVE COOKWARE

A 2½- to 3-quart microwave-safe casserole and plate will handle all the microwave cooking chores in this book. I use pieces specially designed for this use, but any microwave-safe glass, china, or ceramic cookware may be used.

## ROLLING PIN

The first time I came to America, I was carrying some unusual baggage on the airplane. In my suitcase, nestled among my dresses and sarees, were long-handled ladles, an old-fashioned wooden buttermilk churn, and a tapered rolling pin *(belan)* for making flatbreads. About a foot long, with a long taper from the center to each end, the belan is my favorite tool for rolling out doughs easily to the right thickness. Similar but larger "French" rolling pins are available in department stores and gourmet shops. However, any rolling pin that you are comfortable using will work for flatbreads.

## SPICE GRINDER

A peep into an old-time or modern Indian kitchen will reveal a wide variety of grinding stones. So important is the spice blend to Indian cookery that in some parts of the subcontinent, the bride ensures a solid foundation to the marriage by making her vows standing on a grinding stone. However, you can achieve all the rich and superb artistry of Indian cuisine using a coffee or spice grinder, either manual or electric. A blender may be used for large quantities, but for small measures a mortar and pestle made of stone, marble, or brass will do admirably well. Even a rolling pin is sufficient in certain instances for crushing a small amount of spices.

## SPICE BOX

No Indian kitchen is complete without a spice box, a beautiful and functional piece of equipment that is always within easy reach of the stove. The spice box provides the cook convenient, easy access to a whole variety of spices at once without having to open several little bottles. A typical version consists of a round, lidded stainless steel container about 7 inches in diameter, inside which are seven or more small bowls for individual spices. I have a larger one that I created myself to hold the spices I use most often — mustard, cumin, turmeric, salt, cayenne, *kala masala, urad dal* (which I often use as a seasoning), and cardamom. I predict that once you get used to having a spice box in your pantry, you will never want to be without one again. Indi-

an grocery stores carry a wide variety of spice boxes, some with glass tops; or you can create one of your own out of any round or rectangular metal box that will hold seven to nine identical small metal bowls. Arrange the bowls in a petal pattern or in rows, place one or two tiny spoons inside the box, and display it proudly in your kitchen.

## FOOD PROCESSOR AND BLENDER

Many of the repetitive tasks in Indian cooking — chopping, grating, mincing, and pureeing — can be accomplished easily in a food processor. Some jobs, particularly certain purees and the ground rice mixtures for idli and dosa batters, actually work better in a blender. I am most grateful for the food processor when making bread dough. I even toss in my leftovers (raw and cooked vegetables, dals, broths, raitas) in the work bowl, add whole wheat flour, and make tasty chapatis. If your model has a short plastic blade designed for kneading doughs, use it; otherwise, you can use the S-shaped metal blade.

# DINING, INDIAN STYLE

When I give cooking classes, I notice that the students are interested not only in the art of cooking but also in presentation, table manners for an Indian setting, eating with fingers, and the like, as well as how to combine dishes into menus for various occasions. I find these questions quite interesting and would like to pass along some useful hints.

## INDIAN TABLE MANNERS

### What is a typical setting at an Indian dining table?

In a traditional Indian home, meals are served on decorative floor mats, with the diners seated on the floor or on very low platforms *(mani)*. Today this style has mainly given way to dining tables, but floor mats are still used for auspicious occasions. Whether you dine at the table or on the floor, the same basic rules that have applied for centuries apply today. The dining room should be clean and pleasant. A light colored, delicate floral tablecloth and linen napkins add grace to the table. Placing sticks of incense in a corner creates a sweet fragrance that stimulates the appetite. A pleasant, joyous atmosphere goes a long way toward making food enjoyable. Conversations play an important role here. Indians like to chat, discuss and debate ideas and issues, and engage in humorous conversations at the dinner table with family and friends. Soft background music of the sitar or tabla is perfect.

### How is Indian food traditionally arranged?

Our ancestors served the whole meal all at once, from appetizer to dessert, and the tradition continues in many Indian families. This way, one can sample each dish in small portions, taking more of what is most appealing, much like today's Western-style buffet.

A typical place setting consists of a dinner plate and 2 or 3 small bowls, depending on the number of dishes served. These may be set directly on the table, or in individual round trays called *thali* (or, in my mother tongue, *tatte)*. Brass or stainless steel is used for everyday meals, and silver for memorable events. The dishes are served into the bowls in a systematic order around the plate. The thinnest, most liquid dish, which may be a curry or dal, is to the extreme right, where it is easiest (for right-handed people) to dunk or scoop a piece of bread into a bowl and then pop it into the mouth without spilling. Moving counterclockwise, thick dals and side-dish vegetables come next. Relishes such as raitas, chutneys, and pickles continue to the left of the vegetables, in that order, with a wedge of lime to finish. Rice or bread goes in the center of the plate; the two are rarely served at the same time except in restaurants. If crisp appetizers like pakora and papad are served, they are usually on the extreme left of the plate.

Design your place setting in such a way that it does not look too crowded or thinly distributed. You may eat with your fingers or use spoons and forks. You will rarely require additional silverware for vegetarian meals.

### What rules govern eating food with the fingers?

From an early age, when the mother feeds her infant, Indian children learn the pleasures and the skills of eating with the fingers. They quickly develop the dexterity to eat without spilling or making a mess around their plate. For adults as well as children, this typically Indian way of eating is part of the enjoyment of a meal; touching, feeling, sniffing, licking, and savoring the food with the fingers fulfills more than just hunger. On a visit to India, the Shah of Iran was so enamored with it that he quipped, "I understand now why Indians want to eat all this delicious food with their fingers. Anything else would be like making love through an interpreter!"

Before sitting at the table, washing both hands is mandatory. Eating is done with the right hand only; the left hand is used only for drinking beverages or to handle serving dishes and spoon portions onto one's plate. With a little practice, you can learn to tear off a piece of flatbread with one hand, grasping a section with the thumb and forefinger while pinning down the rest with the other fingers. It is considered improper to offer food from one's thali or plate to another.

### Are there any ground rules for mixing different types of foods?

Some foods are meant to be eaten together with others, but that does not mean that anything goes. Bread is used for dipping and dunking in various foods, from curries and dals to raitas and chutneys, but using bread to scoop up a mouthful of rice would strike an Indian as quite odd. Nor is it proper to dip bread in several bowls at once. Dunking or scooping is preferred to placing food onto a poori or chapati before popping it into one's mouth.

Rice is another food that is frequently combined with other dishes, and again there are some basic rules. Dal is poured on rice but not vice versa. Chutneys, raita, and even crumbled papads are also suitable as toppings for rice.

An Indian table usually offers several ways of seasoning and garnishing one's own serving to taste. In the southwest, powdered chutneys are sprinkled on other foods like salt and pepper. Various garnishes — chopped herbs, fresh grated or toasted coconut, fried julienned ginger, sauteed peppers, crisp fried garlic and onion slices, crunchy fried potato shreds, paneer, chopped bell peppers, raisins, nuts, the list goes on and on — can be sprinkled over dals and other relatively plain dishes to add color and texture as well as flavor. Pickles are tasted in small quantities, often just a little bit licked off a fingertip.

### Lastly, what do you do if you happen to bite down on a clove or other whole spice?

Since many dishes use whole spices such as cloves, cardamom pods, or cinnamon sticks, it's inevitable that a whole chunk will wind up in someone's mouth at some point. For the daring, biting on whole spices produces a welcome burst of flavor, but for others it may not be an amusing experience. To begin with, after serving myself I pick out any clearly visible whole spices before attacking the dish. But, if accidentally I happen to chew on one, I will politely take it out and place on the extreme left side of the plate (remember, drier foods are on the left side, and we hardly advance to the left). Of course, if they are peppercorns, which I like, I just bite down on them!

## MENU PLANNING

Indian cuisine offers a wide range of choices when it comes to combining dishes into a menu. Whether you are planning a simple family meal or a formal banquet, the principles are the same: each dish should complement the others, with pleasing flavor and color contrasts, and the overall selection should provide nutritional balance.

At our home in America, our typical daily dinner consists of a legume curry, one or two contrasting side dish vegetables (one of them being leafy greens), raita, chapatis, and plain rice, all served in small portions. Chutneys, papads, and pickles are not obligatory, though I make them ahead in quantity. Garnish is vital, and for everyday cooking it may be as simple as chopped fresh cilantro. I pass a pot of desi ghee at the side, to brush on chapatis and drizzle some on dal and hot rice. Additional plain yogurt is always at the table; my husband likes to spoon a tablespoon over the rice toward the end of the meal to cleanse the palate. Desserts are optional (although my young sons consider a meal incomplete without ice cream).

Many of the recipes in this book will fit nicely into Western menus; try a raita with your main course, or a hearty curry with any pasta dish. If you are making an all-Indian dinner for family, serve thali-style or in separate courses, whichever is more convenient and comfortable. Don't worry too much about the rules in Indian Table Manners above; if you like, you can place vegetables on flatbread, roll it up and eat like a Mexican burrito, and treat a curry or dal like soup.

When entertaining, despite a deep affection for traditional ways, I prefer to serve food to suit today's habits. The menus that follow can be your guide in selecting dishes for various occasions. Fortunately, most of the dishes in this book can be made ahead of time, and some even taste better the second day, a great advantage for the hostess. For a large crowd, you can save time by purchasing flatbreads from an Indian market.

Presentation is very vital to me, and I spend an equal amount of time in skillful garnishes and setting an attractive table. I like to make a centerpiece from seasonal vegetables and fruits like flowering kale, baby zucchini, berries, corn, or my very own handcrafted fabric flowers. A garnish of contrasting color or texture can transform a plain dish into a distinctive one. Dals and sambars can be topped with a wide assortment of colorful, crunchy bits of vegetables and herbs, and pilafs can be dressed up with toasted nuts and/or silver leaf. Raitas look best with fresh herb sprigs or a sprinkle of paprika and served on a bed of crisp greens. A few pomegranate seeds give a perfect finishing touch to chaats and pilafs.

Begin with appetizers in small plates with dips, which can be served away from the dining table if you like. Beverages such as lassis or sparkling wines may accompany the appetizers and these may be served before you sit at the dining table.

Buffet service is ideal for serving an Indian-style meal to a large crowd. There are no set rules for placement of serving dishes on a buffet table, but I suggest beginning with accompaniments at one end of the table, then following with a sequence of dry foods (bread and rice), then vegetable and dal dishes, and end with curries. Keep backups of the hot dishes on low heat in the kitchen, and of raita in the refrigerator. I like to stand at the end of the table with a pot of ghee, to spoon a little onto curries or sambar for those who desire; at the same time I make sure they have served themselves a bit of everything. Of course, I encourage them to come back for seconds, even thirds.

Wine or beer make good accompaniments for those who favor them, and the Beverages chapter offers a selection of nonalcoholic drinks for the abstainers. In any case, a glass of water should accompany each dinner plate. Dessert should come as a separate course at the end of the meal. Conclude with delicately spiced tea or coffee.

# All-Occasion Menus

### Light Salad-Rice Table
When the weather is warm and you do not want to fuss in the kitchen, turn to this low-calorie, make-ahead luncheon. If you prefer a milder flavor, substitute your favorite vinaigrette for the chili oil dressing on the asparagus.
- Fresh Cilantro Pilaf (page 134)
- Asparagus Chaat with Chile Oil (page 184)
- Light Yogurt Rice (page 133)
- Lentil Sprouts Salad with Tomatillo Dressing (page 181)
- Pickled Baby Carrots (page 207)
- Yogurt Mango Cooler (page 229)

### Sunday Morning Special
Make the *dosa* batter and cook the potatoes a day or two ahead of time, and you can create this healthful, filling menu in less than 45 minutes. Serve with freshly brewed coffee or cappuccino.
- Freshly squeezed orange juice
- Paper-Thin Rice Crepes Udupi Style (page 72)
- Seasoned Potatoes with Peas and Raisins (page 97)
- Flaked Coconut Chutney (page 194)

### Dinner for Two by the Fireside
This special meal, for Valentine's Day or some other romantic occasion, features delicate flavors of the tropics. You can prepare half recipes of the soup, pilaf, and curry, but any leftovers will keep well. A basketful of two or three varieties of griddle toasted flatbreads and a wine of your choice round out the menu.
- Aromatic Lentil Soup (page 46)
- Assorted flatbreads
- Roasted Paneer Cheese "Sandwich" in Fragrant Silky Sauce (page 169)
- Peas Pilaf with Almonds (page 132)
- Mangalore Pineapple Curry (page 113)
- Tomato and Cucumber Raita (page 174)
- Fragrant Fresh Coconut Bars (page 212)

### All Vegetarian Barbecue
Show off your outdoor cooking skills with this menu. Make the bread dough ahead and pack it in a cooler. At the picnic site, pinch off portions of the dough and pat them between your palms into ragged rounds, then toast them directly on a well-oiled barbecue grill. Use the same fire to roast the eggplant before combining it with the onion, tomato, salt, and spice blend. Bring along the pilaf, chaat, and mango drink to complete the meal.
- Tandoori Salad Chaat (page 180)
- Roasted Eggplant Smothered with Tomatoes (page 96)
- Rustic Kidney Bean Flatbread (page 81)
- Quick Savory Rice with Peas and Peanuts (page 135)
- Roasted Green Mango Thirst Quencher (page 228)

### Mughal Extravaganza
Try this Mughal-style dinner for holiday entertaining. If you like an additional appetizer, start with Paneer Cheese Walnut Kababs accompanied by an herb dipping sauce. Balloon breads can be made in advance and reheated. Send any leftover pilaf home with your guests.
- Yogurt Balloon Bread (page 90)
- Veggies and Fruits in Fragrant Korma Curry Sauce (page 112)
- Baked Yam Koftas in Green Gravy (page 125)
- Stewed Black-Eyed Peas with Cherry Tomatoes (page 153)
- Shahjahan Corn Pilaf (page 140)
- Rose-Scented Ricotta Patties in Cream (page 219)
- Mughal Milkshake on Sparkling Rocks (page 232)

### Salad and Soup Supper

With a little advance planning, you can come home from work, reheat a hearty soup made earlier in the week, and have this satisfying hot supper on the table in no more time than it takes to prepare something from a box. Finish with fruits and frozen yogurt.

* Vegetable Mulligatawny with Pink Lentils (page 50)
* Warm Cabbage Salad with Cracked Pepper (page 178)
* A platter of sliced fruits
* Vanilla frozen yogurt

### Afternoon Tea

Try something different for your afternoon tea, present steaming mugs of spiced Indian tea with wedges of fragrant cashew nan and an assortment of fruit chutneys. Crisp spiral crunchies offer a balance to the sweet flavors.

* Fragrant Cardamom Tea (page 226)
* Rose-Cashew Skillet Nan (page 86)
* Nectarine and Currant Chutney with Pecans (page 199)
* Garbanzo Bean Spiral Crunchies (page 40)

### Children's Birthday Party

Serve an array of snacks and cookies. Pass the sauce along with freshly sliced seasonal fruits and ice cream. Carrot halvah, the centerpiece of this menu, makes a nutritious cake.

* Candied Whole Cashews (page 29)
* Cream of Wheat Cakes with Petite Peas (page 67)
* Garbanzo Beans Spiral Crunchies (page 40)
* Baked Carrot Halvah (page 223)
* Milk or orange juice

### Maharaja Dinner

Celebrate a special family event with this elegant menu fit for the emperors. As a starter serve Sweet-spiced Royal Almonds with sparkling white wine. This menu will serve a crowd of six to ten.

* Calcutta Plain Flakybread (page 82)
* Braised Paneer Cheese in Rich Tomato Sauce (page 167)
* Vegetables and Fruits in Aromatic Korma Sauce (page 112)
* Royal Vegetable Basmati Rice (page 138)
* Chile Lima Beans with Fresh Dill (page 157)
* Cool Onion and Tomato Raita (page 174)
* Frozen Mango "Pie" (page 220)
* Pineapple Pistachio Cooler (page 233)

### Indian-Style Buffet for Twelve

To serve this size crowd, you will need to make double recipes of the potatoes, rice, cabbage, and pasta. Most of this can be prepared ahead of time so that you can relax and enjoy the time with your friends.

* Baked Cottage Cheese Pastries (page 32) with Sweet Date and Tamarind Chutney (page 193)
* Baked Bombay Potatoes (page 167)
* Gujarat Baked Cabbage (page 115)
* Fragrant Spinach Pilaf (page 142)
* Pasta Indian Style with Lentils (page 159)
* Nutty Rice with Shredded Mango (page 131)
* Kashmir Mixed Fruit Chaat (page 186)
* End-of-the-Garden Mixed Veggie Pickle (page 204)
* Chilled beer

### Afternoon Chaat Feast

Impress your new neighbors or friends with this exotic assortment of flavors. Garnish the salads to taste with hot and sweet chutneys and chaat masala. Offer a refreshing soup with crunchy lentil wafers.

* Hasty Lentil Wafer Platter (page 29)
* Zippy Cucumber and Mint Soup (page 53)
* Bombay Chowpatty Beach Chaat (page 185)
* Lucknow-Style Potato Chaat (page 189)
* Pearl Tapioca Pilaf (page 62)

# INDEX

Acorn Squash Wadas in Garlicky Peanut Oil, 126
Almond Fudge, 211
Almonds, Peas Pilaf with, 132
Almonds, Sweet-Spiced Royal, 28
Anaheim chiles, 15
    Smothered with Sesame Seeds, 100
    Potato-Stuffed, in Cream Sauce, 106
Appetizers, 26-41
Apple-Tamarind Dipping Sauce, 39
Apple-Tomato Sauce, 118
Apricot Chutney, Tangerine and, 200
Aromatic Lentil Soup, 46
Aromatic Spice Powder, 24
Art of Seasoning, The, 13-25
asafetida, 14
Asparagus Chaat with Chile Oil, 184

Baked Goodies, 221-223
baked vegetables, 94, 114-121
Balloon Bread, Yogurt, 90
Bangalore Pancakes with Green Pepper and Cabbage, 74
Bangalore Spongy Cake Platter, 69
Bars
    Easy Fudge, 210
    Fragrant Cream of Wheat, with Yogurt, 221
    Fragrant Fresh Coconut, 212
Basil-Coconut Vegetable Casserole, 121
basmati rice, 129
    Microwave, 131
    Plain, 130
    Pudding, 217
bay leaves, 14
bean curd, 164
Bell Peppers, Garlicky Smothered, 98
Beverages, 224-233, 246
biryani, 129, 138
black-eyed peas, 149
    Stewed, with Cherry Tomatoes, 153
blender, 243
Bombay Chowpatty Beach Chaat, 185
Bombay Juhu Cooler, 232
Bombay Potatoes, Baked, 116
Braised Bread Morning Special, 60
Braised Leeks with Split Peas, 161

Braised Paneer in Rich Tomato Sauce, 167
Breads, 76-91
Breakfast & Brunch, 55-75
Butter, Clarified, 235
Buttermilk Refresher, Spicy, 230
Buttermilk Shake, Sweetened, 230

Cabbage
    Bangalore Pancakes with Green Pepper and, 74
    Flatbread, Shredded Green, 81
    Gujarat-Style Baked, 115
    Packets in Saffron Sauce, Royal, 117
    Salad, Warm, with Cracked Pepper, 178
Calcutta Plain Flakybread, 82
Candied Whole Cashews, 29
Caramelized Onion and Garlic Shreds, 141
cardamom, 14
    Tea, Fragrant, 226
carrot(s)
    Fragrant Spinach Pilaf with Baby, 142
    Halvah, Baked, 223
    Pickled Baby, 207
carum seeds, 14
cashew(s)
    and Dates, Morels with, 111
    Candied Whole, 29
    Fresh Cilantro Chutney with, 192
    Skillet Nan, Rose-, 86
Casserole, Basil-Coconut Vegetable, 121
cassia, 14, 17
Cauliflower and Pepper Stir-Fry, 101
chaats, 173, 184-189
    Asparagus, with Hot Chile Oil, 184
    Bombay Chowpatty Beach, 185
    Kashmir Mixed Fruit, 186
    Lucknow-Style Potato, 189
    Tandoori Salad, 188
    with Pistachios, Mughal, 184
Chaat Masala, 21
chana dal, 148
Channa, 164
chanterelles, 110
chapati, 77, 79

chapati flour, 78
Chard Rolls, Baked Swiss, 118
chatni, 191
Chayote Curry with Peanuts, 109
Chayote Halvah, 212
Cheese
    Fresh Homemade, 165
    Homemade Soft Curd, 164
    Paneer Walnut Kababs, 36
    Tandoori, 36
Cherry Tomatoes, Stewed Black-Eyed Peas with, 153
chick peas, 148
    (see also garbanzo beans)
chick peas, yellow, 148
    Soup with Dill Oil Seasoning, 48
Chick-Pea Broth, Soothing Spicy Tamarind and, 52
chick-pea flour, 148, 237
Chile Lima Beans with Fresh Dill, 157
Chile Oil, Asparagus Chaat with Hot, 184
Chile Oil, Hot, 237
chiles, 15
    Anaheim, Smothered with Sesame Seeds, 100
    Potato-Stuffed Anaheim, in Cream Sauce, 106
Chinese parsley, 15
Chowpatty Beach Chaat, Bombay, 185
chutneys, 190-201
    Cilantro-Onion, 193
    Dry Coconut, 201
    Flaked Coconut, 194
    Fresh Cilantro, with Cashews, 192
    Fresh Ginger, 196
    Fresh Mint, 192
    Nectarine and Currant, with Pecans, 199
    Powdered Peanut, 201
    Quick Tomato-Cinnamon, 198
    Sweet Date and Tamarind, 193
    Tangerine and Apricot, 200
    Tropical Pineapple, 198
cilantro, 15
    Chutney with Cashews, 192
    -Onion Chutney, 193
    Pilaf, Fresh, 134

cinnamon, 17
Clarified Butter, 235
cloves, 17
Cocktail, Cranberry, 231
coconut, 236
    Bars, Fragrant Fresh, 212
    Chutney, Dry, 201
    Chutney, Flaked, 194
    milk, 236
    Rice, Malabar, 138
    -Stuffed Mini-Crescents, 222
    Vegetable Casserole, Basil-, 121
coffee, 225
Condensed Milk, Indian, 238
cookware, 242
Coolers
    Bombay Juhu, 232
    Papaya, 233
    Pineapple Pistachio, 233
    Yogurt Mango, 229
coriander, fresh, 15
coriander seeds, 17
Corn
    and Potato Flatbread,
        Grandmother's, 84
    and Yellow Mung Bean Soup,
        Creamy, 54
    Pilaf, Shahjahan, 140
    Raita, Whole-Kernel, 175
Cottage Cheese Pastries, Baked, 32
Cranberry Cocktail, 231
Cream of Rice Cakes, Kancheepur, 70
cream of wheat
    Bars, Fragrant, with Yogurt, 221
    Cakes with Petite Peas, 67
    Pilaf, Warm, 59
    with Veggies and Nuts, 58
Crepes, Mysore Lace, with Cracked
        Pepper, 75
Crepes, Rice, Paper-Thin Udupi Style,
    72
Croquettes, Baked Popcorn, 35
croutons, 51
Cucumber
    and Mint Soup, Zippy, 53
    Boats, Scrambled Paneer in, 170
    Flatbread, Peasant, 81
    Light Yogurt Rice with, 133
    Raita, Tomato and, 174
cumin, 17

Currant Chutney, Nectarine and,
        with Pecans, 199
Curried Mixed Sprouts with Potatoes,
    158
Curried Mung Beans, Garlicky, 156
curry, 94
    leaves, 18
    powder, 17, 22
    Sauce, Veggies and Fruits in
        Fragrant Korma, 112
    Mangalore Pineapple, 113

Daikon Salad with Aromatic Oil,
    188
dal, 147
Date and Tamarind Chutney, Sweet,
    193
Dates, Morel Mushrooms with
        Cashews and, 111
Dates, Spicy-Sweet Pickled, 206
Deep-frying tips, 41
Desi Ghee, 235, 236
Desserts and Baked Goodies, 208-223
Dill
    Oil Seasoning, Yellow Chick-Pea
Soup with, 48
    Chile Lima Beans with Fresh, 157
    Fragrant Baby, with Garlic and
        Mung Beans, 152
Dipping Sauce, Tamarind-Apple, 39
dosa, 57, 63, 72, 75
Dry Coconut Chutney, 201

Eggplant
    Raita, Smoky , 179
    Roasted, Smothered with Tomatoes,
        96
    with Sesame and Walnuts, Sauteed,
        102
    with Shallots, Stuffed, 105
End-of-the-Garden Mixed Veggie
        Pickles, 204
essences, 237

fennel, 17
fenugreek, 18
Flakybread, Calcutta Plain, 82
Flatbreads, 77-86
    Grandmother's Village-Style Corn
        and Potato, 84

Green Mango, 81
    Mung Bean and Spinach, 83
    Peasant Cucumber, 81
    Rustic Kidney Bean, 81
    Shredded Green Cabbage, 81
    Spicy Sesame, 80
    Tomato-Spinach, 81
    Whole Wheat, 79
Flavored Paneer Cheese, 164
flours, 78, 237
food processor, 78, 243
fresh cheese, homemade, 165
fried breads, 77
Frozen Mango "Pie," 220
Fruits in Fragrant Korma Curry Sauce,
        Veggies and, 112
Fudge Balls in Rose-Perfumed Syrup,
        216
Fudge Bars, Easy, 210
Fudge, Almond, 211

Garam Masala, 21
garbanzo beans, 148 (see also chick
        peas)
    in Tangy Tomato Sauce, 160
    -Milk Confection, Glazed, 218
    Pilaf, 144
    Spiral Crunchies, 40
Garlic
    and Mung Beans, Fragrant Baby Dill
        with, 152
    and Onion Shreds, Caramelized, 141
    Croutons, 51
    Relish, Fiery Pepper-, 195
Garlicky Curried Mung Beans, 156
Garlicky Peanut Oil, Acorn Squash
        Wadas in, 126
Garlicky Rice, Tanjore Tamarind, 145
Garlicky Smothered Bell Peppers, 98
ghee, 235
ginger, 18
    Chutney, Fresh, with Cinnamon and
        Pistachios, 196
Glazed Garbanzo-Milk Confection, 218
gold leaf, 210, 239
Green Gravy, Baked Yam Koftas in,
    125
green mango, 238
    Flatbread, 81
    Pickles, 206

Thirst Quencher, Roasted, 228
Green Papaya Roast, Tropical, 114
Green Pepper and Cabbage, Bangalore
    Pancakes with, 74
green peppercorns, 19
Green Tomato Spread with Peanuts, 34
grinding stone, 63
Gujarat-Style Baked Cabbage, 115
Gumbo, Vegetarian, with Roasted Kari
    Leaves, 44

halvah, 209
    Baked Carrot, 223
    Chayote, 212
Homemade Cheese, Fresh, 165
Homemade Soft Curd Cheese, 164
Homemade Yogurt, 241
Hot Chile Oil, 237
Hyderabad Stuffed Zucchini, 107

idli, 57, 63, 64
    stand, 64
    Uppama, 66
Indian Condensed Milk, 238
Indian Table Manners, 244
Indore Spinach Puffy Bread, 89

Jahangir Pilaf with Yellow Mung
    Beans, 144

kachumber, 173
kadai, 94
Kancheepur Cream of Rice Cakes, 70
kari, 17, 22, 94
kari leaves, 18
    Roasted, Hot Yogurt Soup with, 55
    Roasted, Vegetarian Gumbo with,
    44
kari pudi, 17, 22
Kashmir Mixed Fruit Chaat, 186
Kashmir Spiced Tea, 226
kewra, 210, 237
khawa, 210, 238
Kidney Bean Flatbread, Rustic, 81
Kitchen Equipment, 242-243
koftas, 95, 122-127
    in Rustic Swiss Chard Sauce,
        Pumpkin, 124
    in Velvety Cream Sauce, Vegetable,
        122

korma, 94
    Curry Sauce, Veggies and Fruits in
        Fragrant, 112
    Sauce, Spinach Wadas in Aromatic,
        127

Lace Crepes with Cracked Pepper,
    Mysore, 75
lassi, 225, 230
Leeks with Split Peas, Braised, 161
Legume Puree
    Conventional Stove-Top Method,
        151
    Pressure Cooker Method, 150
Legumes, 146-161
    basic cooking, 149
    cleaning, 149
    pressure cooking, 150
    shopping for, 148
    soaking, 149
    storing, 148
    stove-top cooking, 151
Lemon-Sesame Rice Crowned with
    Vegetables, 136
Lemonade, Fresh Mint, 231
lentil(s)
    brown, 148
    Pasta Indian Style with, 159
    pink, 148
        Vegetable Mulligatawny with, 50
    Soup, Aromatic, 46
    Soup, Fragrant Yellow, 49
    Sprouts Salad with Tomatillo
        Dressing, 181
    Stew, Classic Madras, 154
    Wafer Platter, Hasty, 29
    wafers, toasting, 30
    yellow, 148
        Light Yogurt Rice with
            Cucumber, 133
Lima Beans, Chile, with Fresh Dill, 157
Lime Pickles, No-Cook Spicy, 203
Lime Pickles, Sweet, in Peppercorn
    Syrup, 202
Lucknow-Style Potato Chaat, 189

mace, 19
Madras Lentil Stew, Classic, 154
Madras Spongy Cakes, 64
    Spiced, 66

Malabar Coconut Rice, 138
Mangalore Pineapple Curry, 113
mango, 238
    canned, 239
    Cooler, Yogurt, 229
    Flatbread, Green, 81
    Mist, Melon-, 54
    Nectar, 229
    Pickles, Green, 206
    "Pie," Frozen, 220
    powder, 19
    Roasted Green, Thirst Quencher,
        228
    Shredded, Nutty Rice with, 131
Masala Chah, 226
Matar Paneer, 171
Melon-Mango Mist, 54
"Melt-In-Your-Mouth" Pan Bread, 120
menus and menu planning, -248, 245
metric conversion chart, 255
Microwave Basmati Rice, 131
microwave cookware, 242
Milk, Indian Condensed, 238
Milkshake, Mughal, on Sparkling
    Rocks, 232
Mini-Crescents, Coconut-Stuffed, 222
Mint Chutney, Fresh, 192
Mint Lemonade, Fresh, 231
Miscellaneous Ingredients and Recipes,
    235
Mixed Fruit Chaat, Kashmir, 186
Mixed Greens Soup, Classic, 51
morel mushrooms, 110
    with Cashews and Dates, 111
Mughal Chaat with Pistachios, 184
Mughal Milkshake on Sparkling Rocks,
    232
Mughal Ready Mix, 25
Mulligatawny with Pink Lentils, 50
mung beans, 148
    and Spinach Flatbread, 83
    Fragrant Baby Dill with Garlic and,
        152
    Garlicky Curried, 156
    yellow, 149
        Jahangir Pilaf with, 144
        Salad with Walnuts, 182
mung dal, 149
Mushrooms Braised in Mustard Greens,
    110

Mushrooms, Morel, with Cashews and Dates, 111
mustard greens, 51
  Mushrooms Braised in, 110
mustard seeds, 19
My Mother's 25-Ingredient Spice Blend, 23
Mysore Lace Crepes with Cracked Pepper, 75

nan, 77
  Rose-Cashew Skillet, 86
Nectar, Mango, 229
Nectarine and Currant Chutney with Pecans, 199
No-Cook Spicy Lime Pickles, 203
nutmeg, 19
Nuts, Sauteed Potatoes with Crushed, 104
nuts, spiced, 28, 29
Nutty Rice with Shredded Mango, 131

oil, 239
  Hot Chile, 237
  seasoning, 13, 147, 149, 173
Okra Raita, Crisp, 176
Okra with Crushed Peanuts, 102
oligosaccharides, 147
Onion
  and Garlic Shreds, Caramelized, 141
  Chutney, Cilantro-, 193
  Salad, Sweet, in Tomato Baskets, 182
  -Sesame Puffy Bread, 91

Pan Bread, "Melt-In-Your-Mouth", 120
Pancakes, Bangalore, with Green Pepper and Cabbage, 74
paneer cheese, 162-171
  Braised, in Rich Tomato Sauce, 167
  Flavored, 164
  homemade, recipe, 165
  in Creamy Spinach Sauce, 166
  "Sandwich," Roasted, in Silky Chard Sauce, 169
  Scrambled, in Cucumber Boats, 170
  Simmered with Aromatic Peas, 171
  Walnut Kababs, 36
  Tandoori, 36
papad, 29, 30

Papaya
  Cooler, 233
  Roast, Tropical Green, 114
  Salad with Walnuts, 183
Paper-Thin Rice Crepes Udupi Style, 72
pappadams, 29, 30
paprika, 19
paratha, 77, 82
Pasta Indian Style with Lentils, 159
Pastries, Baked Cottage Cheese, 32
Peanut(s)
  Chutney, Powdered, 201
  crushed roasted, 239
  Crisp Okra with Crushed, 102
  Quick Savory Rice with Peas and, 135
Pearl Tapioca Pilaf, 62
Peas
  and Peanuts, Quick Savory Rice with, 135
  and Raisins, Seasoned Potatoes with, 97
  Cream of Wheat Cakes with, 67
  Paneer Cheese Simmered with Aromatic, 171
  Pilaf with Almonds, 132
Peasant Cucumber Flatbread, 81
Pepper Stir-Fry, Cauliflower and, 101
Pepper-Garlic Relish, Fiery, 195
peppercorns, 19
Peppers, Garlicky Smothered Bell, 98
Pickled Baby Carrots, 207
Pickled Dates, Spicy-Sweet, 206
Pickles, 202-207
  End-of-the-Garden Mixed Veggie, 204
  Green Mango, 206
  No-Cook Spicy Lime, 203
  Sweet Lime, in Peppercorn Syrup, 202
pilaf, 129
  Fragrant Spinach, with Baby Carrots, 142
  Garbanzos, 144
  Pearl Tapioca, 62
  Shahjahan Corn, 140
  Sun-Dried Tomato, 143
  Tomato, with Yellow Split Peas, 143
  Warm Cream of Wheat, 59

  with Almonds, Peas, 132
  with Yellow Mung Beans, Jahangir, 144
Pineapple Chutney, Tropical, 198
Pineapple Curry, Mangalore, 113
Pineapple Pistachio Cooler, 233
pink lentils, 148
  Vegetable Mulligatawny with, 50
Pistachio(s)
  Candies, 210
  Cooler, Pineapple, 233
  Mughal Chaat with, 184
  Roasted Honey, 28
Pizza, Spongy Cake, 71
Poha, 61
pooris, 77, 87-91
Popcorn Croquettes, Baked, 35
Potato(es)
  Baked, Raita with Walnuts, 178
  Baked Bombay, 116
  Chaat, Lucknow-Style, 189
  Curried Mixed Sprouts with, 158
  Flatbread, Grandmother's Village-Style Corn and, 84
  Savory Beaten Rice with, 61
  -Stuffed Anaheim Chiles in Cream Sauce, 106
  with Crushed Nuts, Sauteed, 104
  with Peas and Raisins, Seasoned, 97
Powdered Peanut Chutney, 201
Pressure Cooker Method for Legume Puree, 150
protein, 147
puffy bread, 77
  Indore Spinach, 89
  Onion-Sesame, 91
  Whole Wheat, 87
Pumpkin Chews, 213
Pumpkin Koftas in Rustic Swiss Chard Sauce, 124

Quick Ricotta Paneer, 164
Quick Savory Rice with Peas and Peanuts, 135
Quick Spinach Bites, 38
Quick Tomato-Cinnamon Chutney, 198

Raisins, Seasoned Potatoes with Peas and, 97
raitas, 173, 174-179

Baked Potato with Walnuts, 178
Crisp Okra, 176
Smoky Eggplant, 179
Spinach, with Sesame Oil Seasoning, 176
Tomato and Cucumber, 174
Whole-Kernel Corn, 175
Raw Papaya Salad with Walnuts, 183
religious festivals, 143, 209
Relish, Fiery Pepper-Garlic, 195
Relish, Warm Tomato, 194
rice, 128-145
    with Shredded Mango, Nutty, 131
    basmati, 129
    beaten (pohe), 61
    Crepes, Paper-Thin Udupi Style, 72
    flour, 237
    Fragrant Spinach Pilaf with Baby Carrots, 142
    Fresh Cilantro Pilaf, 134
    Jahangir Pilaf with Yellow Mung Beans, 144
    jasmine, 129
    Lemon-Sesame, Crowned with Vegetables, 136
    Light Yogurt with Cucumber, 133
    Malabar Coconut, 138
    Microwave Basmati, 131
    Peas Pilaf with Almonds, 132
    Plain Basmati, 130
    Pudding, Basmati, 217
    Quick Savory, with Peas and Peanuts, 135
    Royal Vegetable Basmati, 138
    Shahjahan Corn Pilaf, 140
    Tanjore Tamarind Garlicky, 145
    Tomato Pilaf with Yellow Split Peas, 143
    varieties of, 129
    wild, 134
ricotta, 164
    Patties, Rose-Scented, in Cream, 219
Roasted Eggplant Smothered with Tomatoes, 96
Roasted Green Mango Thirst Quencher, 228
Roasted Honey Pistachios, 28
Roasted Paneer "Sandwich" in Silky Chard Sauce, 169
rolling pin, 242

rose
    essence, 210, 237
    Cashew Skillet Nan, 86
    Perfumed Syrup, Fudge Balls in, 216
    -Scented Ricotta Patties in Cream, 219
Saag, 51
saffron, 19
    Sauce, Royal Cabbage Packets in, 117
    Yogurt, Creamy, with Almonds, 215
Salads, 172-189
    Daikon, with Aromatic Oil, 188
    Lentil Sprouts, with Tomatillo Dressing, 181
    Raw Papaya, with Walnuts, 183
    Sweet Onion, in Tomato Baskets, 182
    Warm Cabbage, with Cracked Pepper, 178
    Yellow Mung Bean, with Walnuts, 182
salt, 21, 239
Sambar, 154
Sambar Powder, 24
Samosa, 32
sauteed and stir-fried vegetables, 94, 101-104
Savory Beaten Rice with Potatoes, 61
Scrambled Paneer in Cucumber Boats, 170
screwpine, 237
Seasoned Potatoes with Peas and Raisins, 97
Sesame
    and Walnuts, Sauteed Eggplant with, 102
    Flatbread, Spicy, 80
    Oil Seasoning, Spinach Raita with, 176
    Puffy Bread, Onion-, 91
    Rice, Lemon-, Crowned with Vegetables, 136
    Seeds, Anaheim Chiles Smothered with, 100
Shahjahan Corn Pilaf, 140
Shallots, Stuffed Eggplant with, 105
silver leaf, 210, 239
Soft Curd Cheese, Homemade, 164

Soups, 42-55
    Aromatic Lentil, 46
    Classic Mixed Greens, 51
    Creamy Corn and Yellow Mung Bean, 54
    Fragrant Yellow Lentil, 49
    Hearty Vegetable, 45
    Hot Yogurt, with Roasted Kari Leaves, 55
    Melon-Mango Mist, 54
    Soothing Spicy Tamarind and Yellow Chick-Pea Broth, 52
    Vegetable Mulligatawny with Pink Lentils, 50
    Yellow Chick-Pea, with Dill Oil Seasoning, 48
    Zippy Cucumber and Mint, 53
    Vegetarian Gumbo with Roasted Kari Leaves, 44
spice blends, 20-25
spice box, 243
Spiced Madras Cakes, 66
Spiced Tea, Kashmir, 226
spices, 13-14
    grinding, 20, 242
    storing, 14, 20
    toasting, 20
    whole, 14, 245
Spinach
    and Split Pea Spread, 34
    Bites, Quick, 38
    Flatbread, Mung Bean and, 83
    Flatbread, Tomato-, 81
    Pilaf with Baby Carrots, Fragrant, 142
    Puffy Bread, Indore, 89
    Raita with Sesame Oil Seasoning, 176
    Wadas in Korma Sauce, 127
Spiral Crunchies, Garbanzo Bean, 40
split peas, 148
    Braised Leeks with, 161
    Spread, Festive Spinach and, 34
    Tomato Pilaf with Yellow, 143
    Yellow, Tomato Pilaf with, 143
Spongy Cake Casserole Drenched in Cream Sauce, 66
Spongy Cake Pizza, Indian Style, 71
Spongy Cake Platter, Bangalore, 69
Spongy Cakes, Madras, 64

Spread, Green Tomato, with Peanuts, 34

sprouts, 240
    Curried Mixed, with Potatoes, 158
    Lentil, Salad with Tomatillo Dressing, 181

Squash Wadas, Acorn, in Garlicky Peanut Oil, 126

star anise, 20

Stewed Black-Eyed Peas with Cherry Tomatoes, 153

stewed vegetables, 94, 109-113

Stir-Fry, Cauliflower and Pepper, 101

stir-frying, 94

Stove-Top Roasting, 95

stuffed breads, 77, 84

stuffed vegetables, 94, 105-107

Sun-Dried Tomato Pilaf, 143

Sweetened Buttermilk Shake, 230

Swiss Chard Rolls with Apple-Tomato Sauce, Baked, 118

tableware, 244

tamarind, 39, 240
    and Yellow Chick-Pea Broth, Soothing Spicy, 52
    Chutney, Sweet Date and, 193
    Garlicky Rice, Tanjore, 145
    -Apple Dipping Sauce, 39

Tandoori Cheese, 36

Tandoori Salad Chaat, 188

Tangerine and Apricot Chutney, 200

Tanjore Tamarind Garlicky Rice, 145

Tapioca Pilaf, Pearl, 62

tea, 225
    Fragrant Cardamom, 226
    Kashmir Spiced, 226

Toasted Lentil Wafers, 30

tofu, 164

Tomatillo Dressing, Lentil Sprouts Salad with, 181

Tomato(es)
    and Cucumber Raita, 174

Baskets, Sweet Onion Salad in, 182

-Cinnamon Chutney, Quick, 198

Pilaf with Yellow Split Peas, 143

Relish, Warm, 194

Roasted Eggplant Smothered with, 96

Sauce, Rich, Braised Paneer in, 167

Sauce, Tangy, Garbanzo Beans in, 160

Spread with Peanuts, Green, 34

-Spinach Flatbread, 81

Stewed Black-Eyed Peas with, 153

Tropical Green Papaya Roast, 114

Tropical Pineapple Chutney, 198

turmeric, 20

Umbelliferae, 14

Uppama, 58, 60

Uppama Idli, 66

*urad dal*, 149

*varak*, 210, 239

vegetable dishes, 92-127
    baked, 94, 114-121
    curried, 109-113
    dumplings, 122-127
    oil-seasoned, 96-100
    sauteed and stir-fried, 101, 102, 104
    stuffed, 94, 105-107

Vegetable(s)
    Basmati Rice, Royal, 138
    Casserole, Basil-Coconut, 121
    Koftas in Velvety Cream Sauce, 122
    Lemon-Sesame Rice Crowned with, 136
    Mulligatawny with Pink Lentils, 50
    roasting, 95
    Soup, Hearty, 45

Vegetarian Gumbo with Roasted Kari Leaves, 44

Veggies and Fruits in Fragrant Korma Curry Sauce, 112

*wadas*, 95
    Acorn Squash, in Garlicky Peanut Oil, 126
    Spinach, in Aromatic Korma Sauce, 127

Walnuts
    Baked Potato Raita with, 178
    Raw Papaya Salad with, 183
    Sauteed Eggplant with Sesame and, 102
    Yellow Mung Bean Salad with, 182

wet masala, 167

white gram beans, 149

Whole Wheat Flatbread, 79

Whole Wheat Puffy Bread, 87

Whole-Kernel Corn Raita, 175

Wild Rice with Cilantro, 134

Yam Koftas in Green Gravy, Baked, 125

yellow chick peas, 148
    Broth, Soothing Spicy Tamarind and, 52
    Soup with Dill Oil Seasoning, 48

yellow lentils, 148
    Soup, Fragrant, 49

yellow mung beans, 149
    Jahangir Pilaf with, 144
    Salad with Walnuts, 182
    Soup, Creamy Corn and, 54

yogurt, 173, 240
    Balloon Bread, 90
    Creamy Saffron, with Almonds, 215
    Homemade, 241
    Mango Cooler, 229
    Rice with Cucumber, Light, 133
    Soup with Roasted Kari Leaves, 55

Zesty Croutons, 51

Zippy Cucumber and Mint Soup, 53

Zucchini, Hyderabad Stuffed, 107

## About the Author

Food writer, cooking teacher, and artist Laxmi Hiremath is a lifelong vegetarian. Born and raised in India, she moved to the U.S. with her husband in her twenties. First in Columbus, Ohio, and later in the San Francisco Bay Area, she learned to tailor the cooking traditions of India to the fresh vegetables, fruits, and other ingredients available in this country. Her recipes and articles on Indian cooking have appeared in numerous newspapers and magazines, including *Bon Appetit, Better Homes & Gardens, Sunset,* the *San Francisco Chronicle* and *Examiner,* the *Columbus Dispatch,* and *India Currents.*

## Metric Conversion Table

Follow this chart to convert the measurements in this book to their approximate metric equivalents. The metric amounts have been rounded; the slight variations in the conversion rate will not significantly change the recipes.

| Liquid and Dry Volume | Metric Equivalent |
| --- | --- |
| 1 teaspoon | 5 ml |
| 1 tablespoon (3 teaspoons) | 15 ml |
| ¼ cup | 60 ml |
| ⅓ cup | 80 ml |
| ½ cup | 125 ml |
| 1 cup | 250 ml |

| Weight | |
| --- | --- |
| 1 ounce | 28 grams |
| ¼ pound | 113 grams |
| ½ pound | 225 grams |
| 1 pound | 450 grams |

| Linear | |
| --- | --- |
| 1 inch | 2.5 cm |

| Temperature | |
| --- | --- |
| °Fahrenheit | °Celsius |
| 155 | 70 |
| 165 | 75 |
| 185 | 85 |
| 200 | 95 |
| 275 | 135 |
| 300 | 150 |
| 325 | 160 |
| 350 | 175 |
| 375 | 190 |
| 400 | 205 |
| 450 | 230 |

**Other Helpful Conversion Factors**

| Sugar, Rice, Flour | 1 teaspoon = 10 grams |
| --- | --- |
| | 1 cup = 220 grams |
| Cornstarch, Salt | 1 teaspoon = 5 grams |
| | 1 tablespoon = 15 grams |

# OTHER COOKBOOKS AVAILABLE FROM HARLOW & RATNER

## CONTEMPORARY ITALIAN: FAVORITE RECIPES FROM KULETO'S ITALIAN RESTAURANT
*by Robert Helstrom*

Exuberant Italian cooking with a uniquely American accent, from the chef of one of San Francisco's most popular restaurants. Hardcover, 176 pages, more than 80 color photographs by John Vaughan.

## CONTEMPORARY SOUTHWEST: THE CAFÉ TERRA COTTA COOKBOOK
*by Donna Nordin*

Nordin's exceptionally flavorful southwestern food has repeatedly landed Tucson's Café Terra Cotta on America's best-restaurant lists. Hardcover, 85 recipes, 168 pages, with more than 40 pages of color photos and graphics.

## MORE VEGETABLES, PLEASE: DELICIOUS VEGETABLE SIDE DISHES FOR EVERYDAY MEALS
*by Janet Fletcher*

All the home cook needs to know to serve a tasty, nutritious vegetable as part of dinner every day. Includes 34 easy-to-cook vegetables and more than 200 ways to serve them. Quality paperback, 228 pages including 32 full-page color photos.

## THE COOKING OF SINGAPORE
*by Chris Yeo and Joyce Jue*

A cook's guide to the vibrant cuisine of Singapore—a unique blend of Chinese, Malaysian, Indonesian, and Indian traditions. Hardcover, 176 pages including 35 pages of color photos.

## NOW YOU'RE COOKING: EVERYTHING A BEGINNER NEEDS TO KNOW TO START COOKING TODAY
*by Elaine Corn*

An upbeat, encouraging, information-packed guide for beginners of all ages, with 150 recipes that are simple to cook and impressive to serve. Hardcover, illustrated, two-color throughout, 320 pages. Winner of the 1995 Julia Child Cookbook Award and James Beard Book Award.

## ONCE UPON A BAGEL
*by Jay Harlow*

What will you eat on your bagel today? Harlow provides nearly 100 tasty possibilities. Quality paperback, illustrated, 2-color, 120 pages.

## JAY HARLOW'S BEER CUISINE: A COOKBOOK FOR BEER LOVERS

Much of the world's best food goes very, very well with beer. This lively collection offers 78 recipes ranging from snacks to elegant dinners for company. Quality paperback, 132 pages, including 30 full-page color photos.

## EVERYBODY'S WOKKING *and* THE WELL-SEASONED WOK
*by Martin Yan*

Companion books to the ever-popular public television series "Yan Can Cook." Both quality paperbacks with stunning color photos.